TURNING

D0196351

Sophie Haroutunian-Gordon

TURNING THE SOUL

Teaching through Conversation in the High School

THE UNIVERSITY
OF CHICAGO PRESS
Chicago & London

THE UNIVERSITY OF CHICAGO PRESS, CHICAGO 60637
THE UNIVERSITY OF CHICAGO PRESS, LTD., LONDON
© 1991 by The University of Chicago
All rights reserved. Published 1991
Printed in the United States of America
00 99 98 97 96 95 94   5 4 3 2

Library of Congress Cataloging-in-Publication Data

Haroutunian-Gordon, Sophie.
   Turning the soul : teaching through conversation in the high
school / Sophie Haroutunian-Gordon.
      p.   cm.
   Includes bibliographical references (p.) and index.
   ISBN 0-226-31675-0 (cloth).—ISBN 0-226-31676-9 (pbk.).
   1. Teaching.   2. Discussion—Study and teaching.   I. Title.
LB1027.H339   1991
373.13'7—dc20   90-43533
                                                                        CIP

♾ The paper used in this publication meets the minimum requirements of the American
National Standard for Information Sciences—Permanence of Paper for Printed Library
Materials, ANSI Z39.48-1984.

For Bob, Rachel, and Ben

CONTENTS

ACKNOWLEDGMENTS

As one might guess, this book is the outcome of many conversations that took place over many years. The large number of these exchanges cannot be acknowledged here, as the particular participants and their specific remarks have merged into more general memory. Yet, unrecorded as they are, these discussions—with students, colleagues, other teachers, family members, and friends, which occurred in classrooms, hallways, conference rooms, hotels, restaurants, living rooms, gardens, on the street, and on the telephone—are at least as significant as those I am about to mention in shaping the form and the content of the present volume.

Let me begin with the institutions that have made the work possible. First, there is the University of Chicago, which has provided financial, secretarial, intellectual and emotional support, and whose ideals (at least some of them) helped to inspire the substance of the volume. That the University of Chicago Press wished to publish the work is especially gratifying, as I had all along believed I was writing a "University of Chicago book." The Benton Center for Curriculum and Instruction at Chicago supported preliminary research from 1986 through 1988 and provided me with my valuable transcriber, Nancy Cook. Finally, the Spencer Foundation awarded me a research grant for 1988–89, during which time it continued support services and allowed me to devote the year to writing the manuscript. I am deeply indebted to all of these institutions, each of which has played an indispensable role in the project.

In addition, there are others whose assistance was crucial. In the book, I refer to the Belden and Chalmers schools, fictitious names for real places that were enormously cooperative. They allowed me into their classrooms and gave me permission to record discussions that took place there. Many teachers in these and other schools conversed with me about their experiences, as did principals and others indicated in the endnotes. I wish particularly to thank Robert D. Brazil, principal of Sullivan High School in Chicago and the coordinator of the Paideia Program there, Kathy Ruffalo, for their cooperation over a number of months. Sullivan was neither Belden nor Chalmers in disguise; but its role in the project was highly significant.

There were, of course, many individuals who worked with me in various ways on the research and writing of *Turning the Soul: Teaching through Conversation in the High School*. The two teachers I present in the book, Mrs. Prince and Mrs. Spring, again fictitiously named, were indeed real and remarkable educators from whom I learned a great deal. Not only did they allow me into their classrooms, but they conversed with me extensively about the students and their own experiences. Perhaps what made them most striking was their great concern and affection for the students, along with their willingness to listen and learn from them. While I long to acknowledge these schools and teachers, concealing their identities—as I promised them I would do—has the advantage of allowing the reader to focus upon the educational issues without the distraction that such knowledge invites.

There were several people who read much if not all of the several drafts of the manuscript, and my debt to them is indeed great, for their criticisms were invaluable. They are René V. Arcilla, Ethan Feinsilver, Ilene B. Harris, Julie W. Johnson, Darlene Z. McCampbell, and Dan Sofaer.

In addition, the following persons read some of the conversations and again offered helpful criticism, frequently at crucial moments: Charles E. Bidwell, Kenneth D. Benne, Laura Bornholdt, Martha K. McClintock, David T. Hansen, Frederick F. Lighthall, Martin E. Marty, Peggy J. Miller, Ted Newman, William D. Pattison, D. C. Phillips, Robert J. Richards, A. G. Rud, Jr., Nathan A. Scott, Jr., Jonas F. Soltis, Harvey Siegel, Anne P. Wheeler, and Stanton E. Wortham.

Finally, I have been enormously lucky in two ways which I wish to mention. First, the University of Chicago Press has helped me to improve the volume in various ways. The outside reviews solicited were excellent and guided me toward constructive revision. I am indeed grateful for the great care that the many departments of the Press have given to the project. Second, my family has given me unfaltering encouragement and support through all phases of the project. My husband, Robert P. Gordon, read every version of every chapter and offered cogent criticism time and time again. Indeed, he did all he could to make *Turning the Soul: Teaching through Conversation in the High School* a readable book. If, in fact, I have achieved success in that respect, much of the credit belongs to him.

My hope is that this book about conversation, which is so very much the product of conversation, will inspire the reader to enter the dialogue and to ponder the place of a particular kind of conversation in the school.

INTRODUCTION

Teaching through Conversation

> Education is not in reality what some people proclaim it to be in their professions. What they aver is that they can put true knowledge into a soul that does not possess it, as if they were inserting vision into blind eyes. . . . But our present argument indicates that the true analogy for this indwelling power in the soul and the instrument whereby each of us apprehends is that of an eye that could not be converted to the light from the darkness except by turning the whole body. Even so, this organ of knowledge must be turned around . . . together with the entire soul, like the scene-shifting periactus in the theatre, until the soul is able to endure the contemplation of the essence and the brightest region of being.
>
> Socrates, in Plato *Republic* 518B–D

While the metaphysics of Plato are no longer fashionable, his vision of education remains a powerful one; for there is much appeal in the idea that understanding is derived from turning the soul—from shifting one's view so that the nature of situations may be seen and contemplated. Yet we in America are painfully aware that the educational experiences of many students in our elementary and secondary schools tend to dim the view of life rather than shifting and illuminating it.[1]

As we struggle to determine how best to provide educative experience for students, we must ask ourselves: What does society need from its schools? What must be the outcome of this educative experience with respect to society? Peterson argues, persuasively, that since the mid-nineteenth century, business and political interests have played a central part in American school reform.[2] One answer to the question, then, is that society needs the schools to provide competent workers, people who can help to sustain its economic

1

prosperity. But surely, such a response seems limited. John Dewey's idea is more comprehensive:

> An undesirable society . . . is one which internally and externally sets up barriers to free intercourse and communication of experience. [In so far as] society . . . makes provision for participation in its good [by] all members on equal terms and . . . secures flexible readjustment of its institutions through interaction of the different forms of associated life, [it is] democratic. Such a society must have a type of education which gives individuals a personal interest in social relationships and control, and the habits of mind which secure social changes without introducing disorder.[3]

American society has traditionally professed the ideals that Dewey speaks of here, that is, free communication of experience (including but not limited to freedom of the press), access to its goods by all of its members, and the willingness and ability to adjust its institutions as needed. While one might argue that these goals have not been realized—that for some, freedom of experience is limited, that many persons do not have access to opportunities and goods that others enjoy, that institutions such as the schools have not responded to meet needs as they should—these failings do not invalidate Dewey's statement of social ideals. Consequently, Dewey's description of the aims of education is appropriate for Americans to consider. He claims that educational experience should interest people in relating to one another effectively, in learning how to act so that interpersonal situations are managed satisfactorily and social change can be orderly.

What then should be the characteristics of an educated person, given the needs of society?

> He would not be an individual if there were not something incommensurable about him. . . . Whatever distinctive quality is developed, distinction of personality results, and with it greater promise of social service which goes beyond the supply in quantity of material commodities. For how can there be a society really worth saving unless it is constituted of individuals of significant personal qualities?[4]

According to Dewey, then, what American society needs is individuals whose unique qualities have been developed so that they may contribute productively to the welfare of all. This involves more than contributing to the economy. In addition, it means having the ability to communicate effectively with others so that institutional change is effected, social barriers are eliminated, and change is orderly. People who can contribute to society in the way that Dewey describes have developed their unique talents, talents that enable them to make their own special contributions to social concerns.

Some have argued that society could not tolerate the education of talented, thinking citizens that Dewey envisioned,[5] and that for this reason, we find the schools encouraging conformity[6] and mindlessness,[7] in teachers[8] as well as students. The main problem, these critics declare, is that American society is capitalistic rather than democratic. As a consequence, they argue, society needs to encourage mindlessness, conformity, and social stratification so that citizens will accept their places and leave the power to those few who have it already.

Unless we are willing to embark upon social revolution, such arguments invite us to let our schools remain pretty much as they are. Why should we struggle to make them more democratic—to make them meet the needs described above—if society will defeat such efforts from the start? Some of the critics propose radical approaches to school reform, such as de-schooling society and abandoning the traditional curriculum for the study of present and relevant concerns.[9] Must we choose either radical overhaul of our schools and society or educational practices that have proved unsatisfactory for so many?

The aim of *Turning the Soul* is to lay open for consideration an educational activity I shall call *interpretive discussion,* an activity that may be of use in the quest for effective schooling through orderly change. There are teachers at all levels of elementary, secondary, college, and postgraduate schooling who have held interpretive discussions in their classes for many years.[10] But by and large, the approach has not been seriously entertained for use in many settings, particularly in our impoverished urban schools.[11]

Why is this so? For one thing, it is not a "quick fix" solution from which teachers see immediate results. Furthermore, since it may be difficult for students and teachers initially, it is easy to give up and revert to old practices. Perhaps most important, the approach rejects a view of learning that runs contrary to the one Socrates advocates above—a view most Americans know and accept without question. Consequently, relatively few have participated in interpretive discussions in school. However, teaching through such discussion may hold promise for many educational situations,[12] a promise which, if fulfilled, could more than compensate for the effort required. The pages that follow explore its features, potential, and feasibility.

WHAT IS INTERPRETIVE DISCUSSION?

Picture a classroom in which fifteen to eighteen chairs (with armrests) are arranged in a circle.[13] The teacher, like the students, sits in one of the chairs, and each person in the group holds a copy of *Romeo and Juliet*. The students have been assigned to read act II, scene iv (or perhaps they have just finished reading it aloud), and the teacher asks, "Why does the nurse decide to help Romeo and Juliet to marry, even though the woman knows it may bring them harm?" The question can be answered in several ways, given what Shakespeare tells us. As a consequence, the teacher lacks certainty about the resolution of the question. Her aim in asking it is to explore students' thoughts about the answer and in so doing draw out their ideas about the meaning of the play. As people speak, she and the others question them about their beliefs. Interpretations of particular passages emerge, only to evolve as new ideas about them enter the conversation. The question with which the group began may be modified or give way to another. The teacher summarizes ideas from time to time, but she is not pushing the group to reach consensus. Consensus may emerge, however.[14]

The high school class portrayed in this scene is studying literature. Indeed, *Turning the Soul* focuses entirely on the use of interpretive discussion in literature classes. However, text interpretation might well have a central place in the study of other subjects such as history, science, and mathematics.[15] Teaching through interpretive discussion is appropriate for any subject area that offers "discussable" texts for the students to reflect upon and interpret.[16] Furthermore, the "texts" may be films, art works, primary source documents, artifacts—anything whose meaning is sufficiently ambiguous to permit interpretation.

The scene above stands in striking contrast to ones frequently witnessed in American elementary and high schools, especially in the impoverished urban schools. Indeed, there are still classrooms where the students sit in rows, their seats bolted to the floor. The teacher, instead of sitting with the students, is likely to be in the front of the room, lecturing to them—telling them what to think and do—rather than eliciting their ideas. The text under discussion is likely to be a textbook rather than a work of literature, art, or a primary source. The teacher's questions are generally ones for which she has answers in mind, answers that either she or the students will give. The aim of the class, then, is to arrive at those answers. Tomorrow, if there is no time today, the students will be asked to show that they know what the answers are, probably on a written test. The teacher comes to class as the "authority," rather than one seeking help with a question whose resolution is uncertain.[17]

The skeptical reader is no doubt beginning to squirm: Is interpretive discussion a practical approach to education in today's schools? While it might benefit students who come from child-centered homes full of privilege, what may be gained by those who can barely read, whose dialogues with others may often be utilitarian rather than reflective, and whose ideas may have never been explored, let alone valued? Even if evidence suggests that it might be useful with such students, there are still further questions of practicality, such as: Can a teacher be both a teacher and a discussion leader? After all, who is going to believe that the teacher *really* gives up authority and brings a genuine uncertainty to the group? And won't students become unruly with this sort of situation, especially if the teacher relinquishes authority? Then, too, how should interpretive discussion be used in conjunction with other educational activities, such as giving lectures and tests, or does it eschew such things? Does it ignore the "facts" that students must know in order to be well-versed in a discipline? Furthermore, under what conditions is discussion likely to succeed, and can these be arranged in schools? Finally, where are the discussion leaders to come from, and how shall they be prepared?

These are important questions to which we shall return in the course of the conversations that follow and again in the conclusion. In order to begin to address them however, one needs a deeper feel for the interpretive discussion itself. Toward that end, let us consider its basic assumptions about how people learn. As shall be seen, these differ dramatically from those which undergird traditional instructional approaches.

Assumptions about Learning

As indicated initially, teaching through interpretive discussion is consistent with a conception of teaching and learning that is suggested by Plato in the *Republic*. Elsewhere in the passage previously quoted, he says: "On the assumption that [the soul] possesses vision but does not rightly direct it and does not look where it should, [the art of teaching] is the art of bringing this about" (*Republic* 518D).

There are many assumptions undergirding Plato's statement that we find problematic today. For example, we blanch at the mention of a "soul" and shudder at his claim that the soul is immortal. Also unpopular these days is his belief that knowledge—which only the soul may see—exists, predefined, in some reified "Form."[18] I am not subscribing to these Platonic assertions. But the fundamental insight in the above quotation is, I believe, profound and worth contemplating. Teaching, Plato says, is *turning the soul,* which I take to mean directing the students toward objects that draw out the vision or understanding they already possess, thanks to their experience in the world. The teacher, then, is there to help the students "look where they should."[19] Plato does not imagine the learner to be some sort of empty container into which vision or understanding must be poured. On the contrary, he assumes that the students have understanding that may be drawn out and directed. This assumption is so fundamental and so unlike our common view of the student that we should not turn away from it too quickly.[20]

When Plato says that learners already possess vision or understanding, I take him to mean that they already have a basis for making sense out of—for interpreting—objects and ideas to which their attention is directed. Today, we might say that the "basis" is the students' understanding of language and culture, together with the experiences comprised in their personal histories. The task of the teacher is to guide the students' focus toward objects that will draw out the understanding they have, understanding that, once expressed, will enrich the meaning of their experiences in significant ways. The teacher, does not, however, tell students what to find in the objects.

And what are those objects to which the students should look? Ideally, they are works of literature, art, music, science, social science, mathematics, theater, and film,[21] which, when one ponders them, draw out powerful ideas about oneself, other persons, and the events in life.

Let us consider again the high school students who participate in the discussion of *Romeo and Juliet* described above. When the teacher asks why the nurse agreed to help Romeo and Juliet marry even though she knew it might bring them harm, the students say such things as: "The nurse loved Juliet and wanted to make her happy"; "The nurse was busy thinking about herself instead of the danger that the couple might face"; "The nurse felt sorry for Juliet, because her father was forcing her to marry someone she didn't love, and so she helped Romeo and Juliet get together."

To answer the teacher's question, the students must connect the facts in the play with some aspect of their own experience so as to interpret or explain the facts. The teacher's question, then, draws out the students' understandings of human feelings and motives. The discussants imagine why the nurse acts as she does by knowing her relation to Juliet and by using ideas they have about human motivation to explain the woman's actions. By drawing upon their own experiences in this way, the students arrive at new ideas about the meaning of the play. Furthermore, their ideas about the play become a basis for understanding their own lives in new ways. For example, the student who comes to see the effects of long-term bitterness and hatred through a study of *Romeo and Juliet* may begin to view personal estrangements very differently.

Teaching through the discussion of texts is based on a view of human experience that is really quite commonsensical. The idea is that as people live in the world, events befall them, evoking responses of one sort or another: a grandmother dies and they weep over her loss, recalling what she has meant in their lives; a child is born and they shout for joy, anticipating the warmth and companionship ahead. Each response that one has to situations is the consequence of relating it to present understanding—understanding that is, in turn, the consequence of relating events to prior understanding. The meaning events acquire depends on that aspect of one's understanding to which they are related. Teaching through the discussion of such works focuses the students' attention on objects—texts—that have the potential to draw deep and powerful ideas from them. The teacher's questions serve as catalyst. As they address the questions, the students form ideas about the meaning of the texts, which they may then draw upon as they live their lives and interpret the happenings of the day.[22]

While a great many educational theorists, including Rousseau, Pestalozzi, Comenius, Montessori, Dewey, as well as contemporaries such as Ivan Illich, Paolo Freire, John Holt, Herbert Kohl, Jonathan Kozol, and even Jean Piaget, have espoused the idea that teaching is drawing out understanding from the learner,[23] by and large, education both in America and abroad has assumed that teaching is showing or telling students what to think and do.[24] To see that this is the case, pick a classroom in this country or most any other—elementary, secondary, or collegiate—and stop in for a few minutes. Chances are you will see the teacher lecturing or demonstrating to the students rather than probing their ideas through questions. Even if you do observe the teacher questioning, chances are the aim is to determine whether the students have acquired some predefined competence or understanding rather than to conduct an open-ended exploration of their thoughts.

Now, when the teacher presents students with information and ideas that they are to master and recall on tests, she is doing what Aristotle calls teaching. To teach, says Aristotle, is not to draw out of students what they know and understand but rather to *demonstrate* things to them.[25] In the demonstration, the teacher assumes some preexistent knowledge, things she and the students agree upon and take as given. From these starting points or assumptions, the teacher shows or "demonstrates" the truths that follow. And the students learn the deductions or inductions that the teacher presents.[26] According to

Aristotle, mathematics, logic, rhetoric, and other subjects can be demonstrated, that is, they can be taught by one person to another.[27]

Aristotle is careful to argue that not everything can be taught, since not everything can be learned through such demonstration. Art, he says, is learned through creating things; and moral virtues—courage, self-control, generosity—are acquired by acting virtuously, that is, by acting the right way under the right circumstances for the right reasons.[28] Practical wisdom comes over time through living a virtuous life,[29] theoretical wisdom develops through contemplative study,[30] and "intelligence"—the ability to intuit first principles—seems to be embedded in man's nature.[31]

If one accepts Aristotle's narrow definition of teaching as demonstration, one is led quite naturally to the position that the teacher is the dispenser of knowledge, not only the one who demonstrates the truths that follow from given premises but the giver of the premises as well. After all, teaching cannot begin until some starting points have been agreed upon; and if the student is unaware of the starting points, then the teacher must identify these. The student, on the other hand, is the receiver, the more or less empty container into which the information is poured[32] by means of demonstration. Teaching, then, is showing and telling; and learning is receiving that which is shown and told.

Perhaps few teachers believe that all teaching is demonstration. But many devote large numbers of hours to "demonstrating" things to their students. Furthermore, America is not the only country where the practice prevails. On the contrary, virtually every nation in Europe, not to mention the Far East, emphasizes teacher demonstration. What effects has this concept of teaching had upon educational practices in the United States?

Lawrence Cremin, in his remarkable history of American education, reminds us that many towns in mid-eighteenth-century America could boast of a church-affiliated Sunday school before they had a public school, and that when the latter came into being, it was often an extension of the former.[33] Various European traditions of schooling had influenced the American Sunday school and thereby many of the practices in our public schools. As we shall see, a central feature of the American Sunday school was the view of teacher as demonstrator.

In 1872, when John Heyl Vincent established his International Sunday School Union, he also set up a Union Sunday School Institute, which Cremin describes as follows:

> [It was a] regional, interdenominational convention at which Sunday school teachers . . . [came] to hear lectures by authorities on

the Bible, on pedagogy, and on the practical side of Sunday school work. . . . [Vincent] decided that a rationally ordered curriculum was needed, so he set out to construct one, with the Bible as the textbook. Each Sunday school class each week would have a particular passage from Scripture called the Golden Text, along with a topical outline, readings to be done at home . . . graded questions, and illustrations and notes. . . . The lessons, appropriately organized, became a system of instruction.[34]

The Union Sunday School Institute was characterized by features that have become hallmarks of American education: the assumption that people come to school to learn about things through lecture or some form of demonstration; the belief that there should be a fixed, predetermined "curriculum"; that what people study and what they gain from that study should be defined by someone other than students; that what students learn should be uniformly specified and "rationally" organized, i.e., ordered according to the curriculum writer's rationale; that students should be "tested" to see whether they have learned the specified, predetermined content; that study of the material should take place at home as well as in the school.[35]

These assumptions about learning and schooling have not gone unquestioned. Cremin reminds us that there were renegades even within the religious education tradition. In 1910 a number of groups brought together under the auspices of the Sunday School Council of Evangelical Denominations objected to the idea of uniform lessons on the grounds that they ignored individual differences among learners. Other voices raised objections as well.[36] Perhaps the most influential of these voices belonged to John Dewey.

JOHN DEWEY: AMERICAN EDUCATIONAL REFORMER

Dewey and his fellow progressives took some of their inspiration from Plato and Jean-Jacques Rousseau.[37] Building an educational program around the needs and interests of the student was an idea championed by the latter. Consider what Rousseau has to say about the subject of geometry, commonly taught in the American high school and in grades below:

I have said that geometry is not within the reach of children. But it is our fault. We are not aware that their method is not ours, and that what becomes for us the art of reasoning, for them ought to be only the art of seeing. Instead of giving them our method, we would do better to take theirs. For our way of learning geometry is an affair just as much of imagination as of reasoning. When the proposition is stated, it is necessary to imagine its demonstration—that is to say, to find of which proposition already known this one must be a consequence and, out of all the consequences that can be drawn from that same proposition, to choose precisely the one required.

In this way the most exact reasoner, if he is not inventive, has to stop short. So what is the result of this? Instead of our being made to find the demonstrations, they are dictated to us. Instead of teaching us to reason, the master reasons for us and exercises only our memory.

Make exact figures, combine them, place them on one another, examine their relations. You will find the whole of elementary geometry in moving from observation to observation, without there being any question of definitions or problems or any form of demonstration other than simple superimposition. As for me, I do not intend to teach geometry to Emile [the pupil]; it is he who will teach it to me; I will seek relations, and he will find them.[38]

In this passage, Rousseau discusses children's thinking and argues that it is not like that of adults. Interestingly enough, he directly opposes the use of demonstration in teaching geometry, a branch of mathematics. Why? Because children cannot grasp demonstrable truths of geometry in the same way adults can. The result is that if teachers demonstrate geometry, the thinking of children in such situations can only amount to remembering what the teacher said. On the other hand, children are quite capable of observing geometric figures and identifying relations among them. Their powers of observation and inference based on observation should provide the basis and means of instruction.

Rousseau's classic work *Emile* stresses the nature, needs, and interests of children, using these to design educational experiences for the pupil, Emile. While Rousseau's emphasis is on the ideal student rather than individual differences among actual children, he nevertheless takes a crucial step toward child-centered education—one which forms the starting point for Dewey's contributions. In *Democracy and Education* Dewey wrote:

An educational aim must be founded upon the intrinsic activities and needs (including original instincts and acquired habits) of the given individual to be educated. . . . By an interest, we . . . mean the point at which the object touches or engages a man; the point where it influences him. . . . Interest represents the moving force of objects—whether perceived or presented in imagination—in any experience having a purpose. . . . The value of

recognizing the dynamic place of interest in an educative development is that it leads to considering individual children in their
specific capabilities, needs, and preferences. . . . Too frequently
mind is set over the world of things and facts to be known; it is
regarded as something existing in isolation, with mental states and
operations that exist independently. Knowledge is then regarded
as an external application of purely mental existences to the things
to be known, or else as a result of the impressions which this outside subject matter makes on mind, or as a combination of the
two. Subject matter is then regarded as something complete in itself; it is just something to be learned or known, either by the
voluntary application of mind to it or through the impressions it
makes on mind.

The facts of interest show that these conceptions are mythical.
Mind appears in experience as ability to respond to present stimuli
on the basis of anticipation of future possible consequences, and
with a view to controlling the kind of consequences that are to
take place. The things, the subject matter known, consist of whatever is recognized as having a bearing upon the anticipated course
of events, whether assisting or retarding it.[39]

Dewey's notion of interest differs from that of "readiness" that educational
psychologists sometimes speak of. An interest is not simply capability or a set
of skills that the student brings to the situation. Rather, it is a combination of
need, skill, and preference that places the child in contact with other things
and other people. It inclines the child toward a meaningful connection with
the situations in which he or she is located.[40]

By locating the student's interest at the center of his educational vision,
Dewey posed a radical alternative to the idea of teaching as demonstration. If
the curriculum is based upon the student's individual interests, then it cannot
be defined in the abstract, apart from the knowledge of the individual children
and their concerns. Indeed, one would have to identify and respond to their
needs and interests, which means understanding the features of children's
thinking—as distinguished from that of adults—as well as the individual preoccupations that each child brings to school. Instruction, then, would have to
draw upon students' interests and abilities, using them as a basis for enabling
the child to touch the subject matter.[41]

The mind, as Dewey saw it, is not an abstract entity which "grasps" the subject matter outside it. Rather, it is an activity—the activity of connecting
objects or ideas to one's interests. To illustrate his point about the mind, Dewey describes the typist who suddenly has difficulty with the machine. All at

once her attention shifts from the manuscript she is typing to the mechanical aspects of the typewriter itself—the ribbon, the keys, the roller, perhaps. She comes to discover new features of the machine that she was unaware of before—the holes in the ribbon, the gnarled keys, the stickiness on the roller. She then relates these observed "facts" to the difficulties she has found with her typed copy. Her attention to the typewriter is directed toward only those features that have bearing on the manuscript. The color of the machine, for example, goes unnoticed. The typist is "intelligent" in so far as she is able to relate the features of the machine to the problem she has encountered. It is the relating of observations to present problems in terms of possible consequences that constitutes the activity of "mind."[42]

The modus operandi of the classroom that Dewey envisions is "learning by doing" as opposed to "learning by being shown and told." Here, the student is active rather than passive. To "learn by doing" is to act and to learn from the experience. As Dewey says: "[It is] to make a backward and forward connection between what we do to things and what we enjoy or suffer from things in consequence. Under such conditions, doing becomes a trying; an experiment with the world to find out what it is like; the undergoing becomes the instruction—discovery of the connection of things."[43]

Plato, Dewey, and Interpretive Discussion

There are two questions one ought to consider at this point. First, what is the relation between Plato's vision of learning and Dewey's? Second, can one say that participation in interpretive discussions is "learning by doing"?

To begin with the first question, it might appear that Dewey and Plato do not really share a concept of teaching and learning. After all, Plato says that teaching is turning the soul so that it focuses upon objects that draw out the understanding that it has but does not realize it has, while Dewey's views about learning through doing seem to focus on developing understanding that was not there to begin with. Are the views in genuine conflict here?

It seems that in fact they are not and that in a profound sense learning by doing amounts to turning the soul—the vision—of the student so that he or she sees what is otherwise obscured. The important thing about learning by doing is, as Dewey says, that the student discovers connections between things. Those connections, which lie hidden at first, are revealed as objects and are acted upon, and one observes the consequences of these actions. By changing the typewriter ribbon, the typist discovers that the typed copy is no longer besmeared. There existed, then, a relation between the old ribbon and the page, which she did not see until she made the change. The discovery of that relation constitutes the "new understanding" that Dewey seems to have in mind. At the same time, the "new understanding" is the consequence of focusing upon the right object, the ribbon, which, when changed, drew out of the typist a recognition of the precise problem. So, the typist was capable of understanding the relation, given her previous experience with typing, type-writers, and so on, but her vision remained obscured until she changed the ribbon.

Let us turn now to the second question: In what sense is interpretive discussion a case of learning by doing? After all, it involves no physical action on objects, so how can the learning come from doing? The "doing" in this instance is a kind of imagining, and the learning comes from reflecting upon that which one imagines. One is reminded again of Rousseau, who maintained that young children under the age of twelve or so should be given no books, as these excite the imagination in unproductive ways.[44] At the right age, however, about twelve, *Robinson Crusoe* is the recommended reading. Why? Because at this age, the child's imagination can be used to advantage, that is, used to uncover relations that exist between things. Rousseau writes.

> I want it [*Robinson Crusoe*] to make [the pupil] dizzy; I want him constantly to be busy with his mansion, his goats, his plantations; I want him to learn in detail, not from books but from things, all that must be known in such a situation; I want him to think he is Robinson himself, to see himself dressed in skins, wearing a large cap, carrying a large saber and all the rest of the character's grotesque equipment, with the exception of the parasol, which he will not need. I want him to worry about the measures to take if this or that were lacking him; to examine his hero's conduct; to investigate whether he omitted anything, whether there was nothing to do better; to note Robinson's failings attentively; and to profit from them so as not to fall into them himself in such a situation.[45]

Would Dewey subscribe to Rousseau's use of *Robinson Crusoe?* I think so. Why? Because even though the action on things is imaginary, it is nevertheless focused on personally observing the consequences of treating things in various ways. The child who pictures himself or herself as Robinson and hence worries about what to do under like circumstances, noting the advantages and limitations of various courses of actions, is doing precisely what Dewey recommends.

Indeed, the fact that the actions are imaginary allows the child to encounter many more situations than if constrained by actual physical circumstances.

When the child becomes capable of sustained, systematic reflection, Rousseau would urge, and I think Dewey would agree, that such imaginative reflecting can be enormously educative. So we come to the subject of the interpretive discussion.

Group discussion of the sort we shall observe in the conversations of this volume is, in effect, an acting out of Rousseau's mandate. In trying to interpret the meaning of the text, students are required to think about why characters act as they do, why things happen as they do, and what would have occurred had people behaved differently. In short, the discussants must reflect upon the meaning and consequences of action. As students participate in the discussion, ideas about the relations between action and circumstances come to mind. By listening to others' ideas, the group members become engaged in the fantasy situation in a way that opens them up to new possibilities. They come to connect their own experiences with a circumstance they might never actually experience. By exploring and interpreting that situation, their lives acquire new meaning; they uncover relations between things that they had not seen before.

Now, I am not recommending that all concrete, physical activities be replaced by an interpretive discussion of reading assignments.[46] Indeed, there are many instances where reading cannot draw out of the student an understanding of situations. Sometimes there is no substitute for concrete action upon objects and reflection upon the consequences. Certainly, the typist in Dewey's example could not have solved her problem without some overt trials. My only claim is that the experience of interpretive discussion is one sort of "learning by doing," for it involves thinking about a text using ideas that arise in the discussion, thereby uncovering relations that exist in the text and in life. Since interpretive discussion is "learning by doing," it is therefore educative.

AMERICAN EDUCATION TODAY AND JOHN DEWEY

Let us think again about the American educational tradition and John Dewey. Dewey has been intensely criticized.[47] The criticisms of Dewey and the progressive tradition surface particularly when the "accomplishments" of American students are compared with students in other countries. How can we enjoy the "leisure" of learning by doing when our students score far behind the Russians and Japanese on mathematics and science tests?[48] And how can we be concerned with developing students' individual interests when many of them turn out to be functionally illiterate?[49]

The response to such pressure is always the same: We fall back on the idea that teaching is telling and demonstrating. We assume that American students do less well because they haven't been stuffed with enough facts.[50] Recently, some have become so distressed about the "facts" that students do not know (e.g., D. Ravitch and C. Finn, *What Do Our Seventeen-Year-Olds Know? A Report on the National Assessment of History and Literature*) that we find attempts to catalogue the knowledge essential for every educated American (e.g., E. D. Hirsch, Jr., *Cultural Literacy: What Every Educated American Needs to Know*).

When the focus is upon the facts that the students do not know, the tendency is to bemoan their ignorance. How, we ask, can we get them to "know more"? Perhaps the teachers are insufficiently prepared, we say, and so we propose longer teacher preparation programs that stress the study of academic disciplines (e.g., The Holmes Group, *Tomorrow's Teachers: A Report of the Holmes Group*, 1986). Perhaps we need to enforce "higher standards" and refuse to pass those students who fail to meet them (e.g., W. J. Bennett *James Madison High School: A Curriculum for American Students*, 1987).

The problem with this line of response is that it inclines us not to draw out, explore, and ground instruction in—nay, even notice—that which the students do know. As Dewey rightly maintained, the students' present and personal understanding provides the only basis on which they can "learn more." The plea in this book is that we turn our focus toward the resources that students bring naturally into the classroom. By so doing, we resuscitate the hope of connecting school experience with effective learning.

The claim is not that there is no place for lecture and demonstration in the school curriculum. On the contrary, there are moments when students need precisely that. But the moments when students *need* a lecture occur only when a place for that information has been created, when the interests and ideas students bring to the classroom have been drawn out enough so that the material the teacher demonstrates has meaning and significance. At those moments, the students come as the hungry to the table.

How does the teacher create such hunger in students? There are many ways. One option is interpretive discussion. While the purpose of the discussion is not to prepare students to receive lectures, there is no question that participation in discussion may open students to ideas that might otherwise mean little to them. A well-positioned demonstration or lecture may then prove truly educative.

Happily, there are schools where teaching through interpretive discussion goes on. For example, in January of 1988 I was asked by an English teacher in a Chicago private high school to observe a class of juniors and seniors discussing Plato's *Meno*. Instead of lecturing to these students about the meaning of this text, instead of telling them about its truths, the teacher asked the students questions that drew out and scrutinized their ideas about its meaning. Day after day I watched as she did no "teaching" in the sense of telling but instead posed only questions and asked the students to interpret the text. While she probed their responses for clarification and applauded their efforts to contribute, I heard few if any verbal judgments of right or wrong greeting their comments. The students needed no such evaluation by the teacher, for the soundness of the ideas became evident by their usefulness in explaining the text.[51]

Sounds good, right? But what about the so-called "less privileged" students in the impoverished, inner-city schools? We don't often see discussions of this sort there. Is it because these students are unable to engage in such discussions with much success? Would the teachers of these students, most of whom may be unfamiliar with the approach, find it too time consuming and frustrating? Are the books that justify such discussion too difficult for the students to read? Suppose they reach high school having never participated in discussion before. Can they adjust to and benefit from the new approach?

TURNING THE SOUL: TEACHING THROUGH CONVERSATION

To address these questions, I spent three months doing two things. First, I continued my observations in the private high school, which I call Chalmers, but shifted to a class of sophomores discussing *Romeo and Juliet*. At the same time, I was leading discussions of *Romeo and Juliet* with a group of "less privileged," black students, fourteen to sixteen years of age, in a Chicago public high school, which I refer to as Belden. I was able to tape-record the sessions in both schools.

The students in the Belden classroom were "special education" students. They had been placed in that class because they exhibited learning difficulties, often reading problems; but I was told that their scores on intelligence tests were average or above. The teacher, whom I call Mrs. Prince, indicated that the students had had little experience with interpretive discussion and that they had not read Shakespeare with her. She wanted them to read and learn to enjoy the bard and had chosen the play. While I am not a Shakespeare scholar and had never led discussions of *Romeo and Juliet*, I have more than twenty years of discussion-leading experience with students of all ages. Hence, I was invited into Mrs. Prince's classroom, and together we led the discussions.

Now, it may seem to the reader that these Belden students were in no position to appreciate Shakespeare. How could they possibly deal with what, for

all intents and purposes, is a foreign language to them? And from what resources would they get the patience and discipline needed? Most high school
students, even those in the elite private schools, have difficulty reading Shakespeare, especially at first. How, then, could these students be expected to
succeed with such a task? Mrs. Prince requested that no gimmicks—no
movies, simplified versions, teaching aids—be introduced into the discussion.
The students were simply asked to read the text aloud in class and interpret it.
I left a recording of the play with them, to which they sometimes listened in my
absence. To my knowledge, the students did not read the play at home, nor did
they write essays about it.[52]

The conversations in this volume suggest that those in the Belden class had
significant resources to bring to a discussion of *Romeo and Juliet*. The tale of
the two young lovers explores universal themes that, in many cases, these students knew all too well. For example, in preparing them for Shakespeare's
tragedy, I followed my Chalmers counterpart's example and asked the students to tell about a time when they had taken revenge on someone. As readers
will see in Conversation 1, one girl spoke of the day she had called the police
on her brother because he was drunk and had knocked her to the ground and
kicked her. When the police came, the girl cried because she didn't want them
to take her brother away—which they did anyway. "Sometimes it's not nice to
take revenge," she said. Was this student ready to appreciate *Romeo and
Juliet*? There is no question that her own experience could allow her access to
Shakespeare's world. And once there, she would have the opportunity to explore life's powerful themes—revenge, love, death—in ways that were bound
to alter her own daily experience.

Turning the Soul takes the reader back and forth between the Belden and
Chalmers classrooms. One observes, then, a series of conversations, discussions that the students have about the play. I provide short summaries and
the passages from the text that the students are considering so that the reader
may form an interpretation of the material as well as of the classroom
exchanges.

To reflect on the potential of interpretive discussion, it helps to understand
the issues with which the teacher grapples in pursuing it. As will become apparent, some of the same issues confront the teachers in both schools. At
times, the tension over these issues threatens to defeat the teachers, and the
approach, entirely. The reader may find it slow and painful to watch as I grope
in the unfamiliar setting, at times most pathetically. I include these faulty per-
formances because neither the issues nor the struggles I faced were unique. If
interpretive discussion is to be effective, teachers need to understand the

obstacles to successful conversations that they are likely to encounter so as to be able to cope with them.

As a step toward such understanding, the conversations in this book, with the exception of Conversations 1 and 8, have two parts. In the first part one of the two groups of students discusses passages from *Romeo and Juliet*. These conversations are prepared from transcripts of actual classroom discussions.[53] In the second part the teacher and the observer (in the case of Chalmers) or the two teachers (in the case of Belden) talk about the class that has just occurred. Each dialogue with the teacher focuses upon one or two significant topics and pursues the complexities of these in depth.[54] The two parts are unified by a common focus: the issue of how one teaches through interpretive discussion. To explore at length and in an organized manner the issues that arise in such teaching, I do not present the "teacher dialogues" as they actually took place. They are, however, faithful to the spirit of many of the actual conversations I had with the teachers.

As the book progresses, the reader watches as students and teachers alike come to respond differently to the discussion situation, that is, as they come to respond differently to one another in certain, visible ways. Furthermore, some find meaning in the play *Romeo and Juliet* that they did not find at first and, at moments, new meaning in their personal views and experiences. This is not to say that the journey for either students or teachers is an easy one. On the contrary, many experience enormous frustration, anger, and boredom at moments. There are days when the teachers in both the private and the inner city school are ready to throw in the towel.

However, the reader also sees miracles occur: The boy who refuses to speak for days becomes an active participant; the "gross misinterpretation" turns out to have merit; some students work to understand what others are saying; Shakespeare begins to throw life's experiences into relief; and students begin to care about getting Shakespeare right. The reader watches as the conversations move the students and teachers toward more effective action and understanding.

Furthermore, the reader sees that as the students participate in discussions, they acquire analytic habits and skills that allow them to direct their vision— to relate ideas in books to life's events—thereby giving those events new meaning. These are the very habits and skills that allow them to read with understanding, to evaluate ideas for themselves, to persevere with difficult and sometimes frustrating problems, to arrive at formulations of ideas, and to defend those ideas with relevant evidence. One also sees both students and teachers learning to listen to others, looking for and exploring options that did not occur to them initially, and so, moving beyond their initial perspectives.

In short, the discussion brings everyone together, including the teachers, as equals before the great mysteries of life that Shakespeare's play addresses. It quickly becomes clear that no one, not even the teacher, has a monopoly on all the good ideas. Interpretive discussion utilizes the contributions of all, and it thrives on attention to the common task. Most of all, it teaches the great pleasure that comes from contributing one's own ideas to a common concern.

It appears, then, that students can learn to interpret texts for themselves, given appropriate questioning. The evidence herein for this claim comes not from a parade of replicated success stories but from a close look at the kind of progress that occurred in two high school classrooms. The book is meant to be suggestive, to inspire readers to explore the potential of interpretive discussion in settings where they would not have imagined trying it out. Perhaps they will discover that it can improve some learning experiences in some settings at some times.

In the first conversation, we watch a student discussion in each of the two schools, Chalmers and Belden. As one might expect, the contrast between the two classrooms is striking. The Belden students, it turns out, have at least one significant advantage over their Chalmers counterparts.

PART ONE

Interpretive Discussion in the School

CONVERSATION 1

An Introduction to Chalmers and Belden Schools

In this first conversation, the reader is introduced to the two high school classes I came to know well. The students in each were about the same age, fourteen to sixteen; and as I have indicated, both groups were discussing Shakespeare's *Romeo and Juliet*. In what we are about to see, the two groups were responding to the same assignment, designed to orient them to the play. These excerpts show some important features of the interpretive discussion in each setting, including patterns in the conversations and the role each teacher plays. As one might expect, there are striking differences between the two groups, the most dramatic being the use that students make of their personal experiences.

The reader may recall that *Romeo and Juliet* is about two star-crossed young lovers who marry, despite the fact that tensions between their two families, the Montagues and Capulets, forbid it. A central theme in the play is that of revenge: Juliet's cousin Tybalt kills Romeo's friend Mercutio, and Romeo responds by slaying Tybalt. The play, then, explores the consequences of Romeo's act.

THE CHALMERS CLASSROOM

Let us first enter a sophomore English class in Chalmers, a private, racially integrated school located in metropolitan Chicago. The school is one where the gray stone walls of the building may sometimes be detected amidst the sprawling ivy that likewise encases the leaded glass windows and carved oak portals. The students in the class, like the building itself, are accustomed to careful attention, as can be seen in the following exchange with their teacher, Mrs. Madeline Spring (MS):

MS: I thought we'd begin today by taking a few minutes, maybe ten or so, to let you write a few lines about a time when somebody hurt you in some way and you took revenge, or thought about doing so. Very briefly tell us about the situation, how you reacted, and looking back, are you glad you did what you did?

STUDENT 1: So we are supposed to describe when a friend hurt
us? And how?
STUDENT 2: Any situation with any person we know?
MS: That's right, and it can be physical hurt or emotional.
STUDENT 2: But anybody hurts you and how you felt about it?
MS: Yes, and how you reacted. Not just how you felt.
STUDENT 3: Do you have to put in whether you forgave
somebody or not?
MS: Just tell how you responded to the situation and then tell
how you feel about that response looking back on it. Real briefly.
This will be just jotting down for five or ten minutes.

The questions seem a little bit pesky. Why don't the students just write as
directed instead of seeking so much clarification? After all, it is only a short,
in-class assignment, not a term paper. They seem very concerned, perhaps
overly so, about following the teacher's instructions and pleasing her. The
teacher, for her part, responds with additional direction, suggesting that she
has something rather specific in mind for them to write about, much as they
seem to sense.

As the questions dwindle and the students turn toward the assigned task, we
notice something odd about the configuration of chairs in this room. While
the desks were apparently prearranged to form a square, the entire row of students directly facing the teacher have somehow moved their chairs some six
feet backwards. Chairbacks rest precariously against the wall as the occupants
teeter on one or two of the four legs. How has a whole row of students, perhaps eight or ten of them, managed this grand migration? We hadn't noticed
anyone moving!

As we ponder the matter, we suddenly become aware of a sound in the room
which had heretofore escaped our attention—or has it only just begun? Our
focus on the back wall has alerted us to the fact that there is rather loud rock
music to be heard by those who position themselves in that location, music
that is apparently a part of the curriculum next door. Can Mrs. Spring hear
this? we wonder. The students have caught on, it seems, for all that bobbing
and teetering appears to be in vague sync with the neighboring vibrations. We
return our attention to the front of the room, where the discussion is about to
begin.[1]

MS: Would you read what you have been jotting down? Larry.
LARRY: It seems to me that the reaction of revenge has to do with
two factors: the frame of mind that you are in at the time and also

maturity or age. When I was a little kid, I would have a very different reaction than I do today.

MS: That's a very interesting comment, Larry. Brian?

BRIAN: I think that when you get hurt, it's not necessarily a situation where you feel anger, but you just don't feel satisfied with being hurt. The other person doesn't know what you are thinking. So what comes out like revenge is really a need to establish communication.

MS: Edna.

EDNA: I agree with Brian, but I think that when you get hurt or you are sad or something, that you look at them and are like, how come they don't know that would make me sad? You feel bad and you want revenge because you want to show them that they were like so stupid not to realize that what they did would obviously hurt you.

BRIAN: It's like when you feel like something unjust has been done to you. You feel like the only way to make the other person feel that same thing is to do another something that's unjust.

ABE: This sort of goes along with what Larry, Brian, and Edna just said. In a way it's sort of pride. In a sense, you feel that you have certain rights. And when people hurt you, they violate the rights and you want to sort of make them feel that it was wrong.

Although the students are not discussing a text here, it is clear that they have had a lot of experience with interpretive discussion. How can we tell? First, they are eager to talk about the topic assigned. From the start of the conversation, the teacher has had several hands waving in front of her, begging for the opportunity to speak. The students know what the teacher expects from them and they are ready to comply.

Second, their comments are not at all random and disconnected from others' comments. For example, Edna begins her remarks by agreeing with Brian. While it is not exactly clear what she is agreeing with, she enters the conversation by joining her comment with his through the form "I agree with." She knows that she cannot speak unless she can build, in some way, upon what has already been said. Likewise, Brian first enters the discussion by addressing the topic set by the teacher, remarking that one sometimes takes revenge in order to communicate. He, like Larry before him, and Edna have learned about the conditions under which one may enter interpretive discussion. And these conditions are governed by rules, which is why the comments are not random.

The students have learned to play what Wittgenstein has called a "language game."[2]

By following the rules for discussion—playing the language game—these students are gradually being drawn into a conversation that has a real focus.[3] For an issue is gradually emerging, namely: For what reasons do people take revenge? Is it to communicate the feeling of pain to another? To make another recognize that it was wrong to violate one's rights? As Brian first enters by stating why he thinks people take revenge—i.e., to communicate to one another the impact of an act—Edna sees that she can enter by agreeing or disagreeing with the reason he has offered. Her doing so offers Brian the opportunity to clarify his position, and Abe then enters by amending them all. As they agree and disagree with each other, they add further ideas about why people take revenge.

There is something striking about the conversation so far. Although asked to write and speak about their personal experiences, no one has mentioned a specific personal experience. Instead, each speaker has moved immediately to abstract generalizing about the topic. This is not to say that the students did not write of specific instances on their papers; they may well have done so. But so far, they have not shared these with the class. Larry, for example, begins by saying that one's response to opportunities for revenge depend upon one's age and maturity. Brian adds that what looks like attempts to gain revenge may be instead efforts to communicate. The conversation thus far is abstract and theoretical. How do the students respond when Mrs. Spring asks them to be more specific?

————

MS: Now, thinking about your own particular examples, for those of you who took revenge or wanted to, what did it make you feel like when you took revenge? What was your reaction? Edna.

EDNA: Well, in my case, I wasn't feeling . . . I was half satisfied. I wanted more. Like, I was a little kid. My parents quickly came in and reacted. I don't think I got to fully revenge myself. But it was a good feeling knowing that I did get him back.

MS: Abe.

ABE: I didn't take revenge in mine, but I think that when you do, you feel good at the time, doing it. You feel yeah, this is great, I'm getting her back. But in your mind, you are saying to yourself, "This is just as wrong as what they did to me." So you are never really satisfied.

MS: Edna.

> EDNA: That's what I was going to say. Once you take your
> revenge, you feel, "I'm just as immature, as childish as them."
> MS: Janeen.
> JANEEN: I didn't act mine out. Just thinking about it made me
> feel really good. I knew I wasn't going to act it out, but just
> thinking about, yeah, I can do this. But then, when it comes the
> time to do it, you just say, "No, come on." It's not worth it, really,
> to feel that bad. I think I would feel too bad after I acted it out.
> MS: That is fascinating. You are talking about imagining it,
> giving you much delight. But you think you would feel bad if you
> actually did it. That goes back to what Abe was saying. Betty.
> BETTY: I agree with Abe. Many times I've sat down and I've been
> really conscious as to what I am going to do. I've planned it out,
> the most wonderful revenge. But then I stop and I'm like, "Are
> you serious?" I realize that it is just not going to pay off, meaning
> that I will hurt the other person as much as I was hurt. It'll just
> continue—go on and on.
> MS: Very interesting what you just said, that it will just continue.

Here, Edna begins to tell about an actual experience, a time when she began
to take revenge on someone as her parents entered the room. But she does not
describe the time, place, or nature of the situation. Abe returns to abstract
generalizing: "So you are never really satisfied [when you take revenge]"; and
Edna then follows with more: "Once you take revenge, you feel, 'I am just as
immature, as childish as them.' " Janeen and Betty likewise omit personal examples, making instead the general comment that one is discouraged from
taking revenge when the consequences are anticipated.

The problem with the discussion so far is that it lacks substance. Without
reference to their personal examples, the students make general statements
that seem rather empty. As we shall see, while the ability to generalize from
particular experiences is crucial if one is to gain insight into them, generaliza-
tion in the absence of particulars often lacks illumination. The discussion
continues.

> MS: But if taking revenge causes problems, why is it so difficult to
> give up the idea, to forgive the other person and put the incident
> behind you? Brian.
> BRIAN: I think that the only person that can really hurt you is
> someone that you care enough about that it does affect you. If
> you feel hurt by them, you sort of wonder, "How could they do

this to me?" You sort of feel like, "Don't they know that they would hurt me by doing that?"

EDNA: If you get hurt by someone that you really care about, at first it's so exaggerated. At first you are like, "Oh! I hate them so much! How could they do that?" But while you think about it you realize how much they mean to you and that they aren't trying to hurt you. That's why revenge is such an immature thing. You know, because you have to realize that this person isn't just all bad and trying to hurt you. So, in order to forgive someone you have to just let it sink in and talk about it with the person, let them know that you don't feel like what they did was a nice thing to do.

MS: So you are implying that to forgive you have to get out of your own point of view and also understand what the other person intended. Janeen.

JANEEN: Sometimes you don't take revenge because you're trying to make an impression of being mature. And like people said, it's not the kind of hurt that really, really hurts, so it's worth it to look more mature. Also, it can be an even sweeter revenge if you ignore the person and act like, "You didn't hurt me; you didn't do anything."

MS: Very interesting. Elizabeth.

ELIZABETH: I think that's what I did. The person hurt me and I ignored it. Inside, I was very upset. But the other person couldn't figure out what was going on. That was like, so great. They were really upset. I guess that shows immaturity on their part, because they really had no idea what was going on.

Here, we see the students beginning to draw upon their personal experiences. In response to the teacher's question as to why it is so difficult to give up the idea of revenge, Brian and Edna focus upon the pain that one feels in being hurt by someone you care about. The implication is that the intensity of the pain makes it difficult to abandon the thought of revenge. Here, one has the impression that the students are speaking from real experience: "At first you are like, 'Oh! I hate them so much! How could they do that,'" says Edna. While still at a general level, the teacher's question seems to require examination of emotional response.

In the course of answering the teacher's question, Edna explains what must be done in order to avoid taking revenge, which is, she says, "so immature." Janeen then offers an alternative account of why one might refrain: You might want it to appear that you had not been hurt, which would make the other suffer. Elizabeth offers an example of Janeen's general point and in so doing comes very close to presenting a personal experience. True, it is decontextualized; we are told nothing about the specifics of the case. But we are led to believe that the moment Elizabeth describes did occur, somewhere, someplace. So personal experience is allowed to enter the conversation in the form of abstracted example.

It is interesting that without pressing the students for specific cases or rejecting any of their general comments, the teacher had almost managed to draw specific examples out of the students. Reed and Abby give us other instances in the exchange that follows.

MS: What associations do you have with fighting? Abby.

ABBY: A lot of people fight to get attention.

REED: Well, sometimes you have to stand your ground. Regardless. That has happened once or twice to me. The person wants to fight and you say, "No, look, OK, I know you can kill me." And they won't back off. You have to defend your honor and pride.

MS: That's interesting, Reed. Jarvis.

JARVIS (seated along the back of the room, rocking violently back and forth on his chair; he calls out so that he can hear himself over the rock music behind him, which thumps on): I think that physical fighting is the kind of thing you do with somebody who is not really a close friend. With your good friend, you don't want to take revenge. No, no, forget that. You *do* want to take revenge on a good friend. You don't want to take revenge on somebody you don't care about.

REED: Well, it goes both ways! It totally depends on the person.

JARVIS (leaning forward on his chair, thereby returning its four feet to the floor) Well, if you don't really care about the person, then you can get into a physical fight with them. But if you care about the person, and you want to make them understand you, then you don't get into a physical fight. You get into a different kind of fight.

MS: Are you responding to Jarvis, Abby?

ABBY: In different cases, not fighting is also like caring. Like my sister. Sometimes I will be really mean to her. Then, I will look at her. And she will have a sad look on her face and then I will have to stop because I can't deal with it. I know that I am hurting her. There is, like, a lot of care.

Reed, like Elizabeth previously, refers to a decontextualized example in making a point about why people fight. He mentions an instance, with no specific time or place, when he fought with someone in order to defend his pride. Jarvis works out the idea that if you care about the person you wish to get revenge on, then you avoid a physical fight. Abby then exemplifies Jarvis's point with the most personal and powerful statement of the discussion. While still not a specific case, we can imagine the moment when she looks at her sister and, feeling both guilt and pain, ceases her attack. Here it seems that Jarvis's statement has drawn out of Abby a comment that makes a more direct use of her personal experience.

Let us note an interesting point about this Chalmers conversation. Jarvis, who seems to have made possible a powerful moment in the discussion, began the class teetering on his chair in the back of the room, apparently lost to the strains of rock music. He eventually reentered the conversation. Why? I saw no signs of the teacher coercing him, and indeed, she never seemed to notice the music or the fact that the students had moved. Perhaps Jarvis became interested in the issue of why people fight and had a view different from Reed's. Furthermore, the level of analysis was perfectly safe. He need not reveal a personal incident that might cause him shame and embarrassment.[4] Once he entered with the comment that one only wants to take revenge on one's friends, he contributed repeatedly until the end of that class. At one point, I realized that he, and the others who had lodged themselves against the back wall, had inched their chairs back up to the desks, the rock music seemingly forgotten.

In general, then, the students in the Chalmers classroom appear to be experienced discussants. They respond spontaneously to the comments of others and in so doing draw out their own ideas; they use the discussion as an opportunity to think further about topics; their remarks are far from random and conform to rules for discussion. Indeed, we have seen participants enter the conversation by agreeing and disagreeing, clarifying, exemplifying, amending others' remarks, or answering questions posed. All of these are acceptable routes of entry.[5] Another sign of their experience is the tendency to discuss topics at an abstract level rather than focusing on particular experiences directly. Abstract analysis has become habitual for these students. Why? Because they have participated in many interpretive discussions, and such discussions ask one to move toward understanding—a description with perspective—of particular events. As students become used to analysis, they often choose it over a focus on particular instances, as it is much safer than

sharing personal history and feelings. Over time, discussants tend to veer toward abstract analysis for this reason.

The teacher, Mrs. Spring, is an experienced and concerned teacher. Her ability to recall what students have said and skillfully relate remarks to one another comes only from practice and genuine care for what the students think. Is she aware that the group has a tendency to theorize at the cost of ignoring particular experiences? As we shall see in subsequent conversations, she struggles with this inclination.

The Belden Classroom

Let us now shift location to Belden, an urban public school located in Chicago's black ghetto. In this school the unwindowed, heavy metal doors swing knobless from large, rusted hinges. Each window is distinguished by its unique design of fractured glass, plywood boarding, wire mesh, or ruptured black shade, and the crumbling gray stone walls are splashed with profane graffiti. Here, I myself become a character in the drama.

One of the few white faces in the building, I gingerly make my way to the third floor and begin searching for room 308, where I have been invited to teach Shakespeare's *Romeo and Juliet* to a group of students. The door now open, the classroom teacher, Mrs. Margaret Prince (MP) can be seen seated on one side of two blond rectangular tables that have been pushed together, while the students, perhaps twelve of them,[6] are spread around the other sides. It is a little hard to hear what is being said, for the loud rumbling of passing trains drowns out all but a few isolated words. The teacher soon beckons me to join the group at the table. After introducing each student, she says:

> MP: This is Mrs. Gordon. She will be coming to read *Romeo and Juliet* with us.

Seating myself next to a large boy of about fifteen dressed entirely in prewashed blue denim, I begin to make out more of the teacher's words. I can now tell that they are discussing the topic I had asked each student to write about in preparation for our study of the tragedy.

> MP: Very interesting. Yes, Colette, why don't you read yours?
> This is about the time you took revenge upon somebody, right?
> COLETTE: Naw, I don't want to read it!
> MP: Would you like me to read it for you?
> COLETTE: No. . . . (Reading her essay:)
>   Well, my brother Clark is so bad that in front of my friends

he dragged me on the ground and kicked me in my face. I was
really hurt and I was embarrassed. I called the police to have
him arrested because he . . . because he was drunk. Therefore, I am not his child . . . his sister anymore.

SHG: So you are saying that you took revenge in that case?

COLETTE: Called the police.

SHG: Called the police. I see. How do you feel about that today?
Do you feel it was the right thing to do?

COLETTE: Yeah.

SHG: So revenge seemed like a good resolution in that case, right?
Do you have anything to do with your brother today?

COLETTE: No.

SHG: When did this happen?

COLETTE: I don't know. It happened this year, though.

———

I am not prepared for Colette's story, not for the dramatic nature of its contents nor for the intensity of the feeling she brings to her narrative. Perhaps it is
the contrast between the discussion among Chalmers students, who have
shared no personal experience directly, and the episode described by the first
Belden student to speak. I am stunned by the power of this vignette and by the
willingness of the student to share it with others in the class. My response to
her is fumbling: "So you are saying that you took revenge in this case?" Even
after a few exchanges, I am unable to deal effectively with the extraordinary
material she has presented. Indeed, I am even unable to ask how she feels
about having nothing to do with her brother anymore. The discussion
continues.

———

MP: Now Sylvia, can I read your paper?

SYLVIA: No.

MP: I don't know why you are getting so shy with this. I can't
stop you from talking most of the time. Let me read this.

I have been hurt in many different ways. One of the ways was
my mother. It is the ways she acts towards me and my sister. I
don't think she should have her picks and chooses between
us. You might think that I am jealous of her, but I am not. But
that is one of the ways I have been hurt. Although I did not
get revenge, I do think of hurting myself at times. What did I
do? I went for a long walk one day and I planned not to come
back. Why? So I wouldn't say anything I would regret later. I
am glad I took this walk because if I hadn't we would have
been fighting.

———

Here, too, is more than I had bargained for. To begin with, the students seem unprepared for the fact that their papers are going to be shared with a stranger. I worry that my presence is inhibiting them, and I am anxious to reassure them. I also fear that the situation will cause tension between them and Mrs. Prince, who seems somewhat impatient with them at the moment. I am also once again stunned by the content of the writer's paper, the fact that her anger and pain had been so great that she has thought of hurting herself at times. And what about the foresight and self-control that the story reveals, her decision to take a walk? It may be that the intensity of her daily personal experience has already opened her eyes to the dangers of retaliation. The discussion continues:

> SHG: That is a very good paper, Sylvia. Can you tell us why you decided not to have the fight?
> SYLVIA: Because she was pregnant.
> SHG: She was pregnant and you didn't want to hurt her?
> SYLVIA: Uh-huh.
> SHG: Well, that is very interesting. How would some of the rest of you respond to that? Is there anyone who would have done something different in that situation?
> MICHAEL: I would have just packed my clothes and left.
> MP: Why would you do that?
> MICHAEL: If my momma had her picks and chooses, I would just have left.
> SHG: So you're saying you would have just left, Michael? Would you have left so as to hurt your mother, or, Sylvia mentioned in her story something about hurting herself. Would you have gone off to hurt who?
> MICHAEL: My mother would probably hurt me before I hurt her.
> SHG: So you would go off to protect yourself, because you think that if you fought with her you would have been the loser?
> MICHAEL: Yeah.

I continue to grope. I find myself wondering what "having picks and chooses" means, and I should ask but do not. Perhaps, I, too, am somewhat intimidated. I would then have to acknowledge how much of an outsider I really am. So I rely on the rules for discussion that I know: "Would you have left for the same reason that Sylvia did?" Perhaps by comparing the ideas that each had, we would become clearer about the two views. I push forward:

> SHG: Marcy, what would you have done in this situation?
> MARCY: I never thought about it.

SHG: You never thought about it? Well, just hearing it this time, do you have any response to it?

MARCY: I would be in my room and I would start crying.

MICHAEL: Yeah! Marcy is a crier!

SHG: Why do you think this situation would have made you cry, Marcy?

MARCY: That my mom treat me like that. When she do something like that, I just go to my room and cry and write in my diary about her.

SHG: You would write in your diary. That is very interesting. What do you say about that, Colette? Would you do that, too?

COLETTE: Yeah.

SHG: Why do you think people write in their diaries at times like that?

COLETTE: To make them feel better.

SYLVIA: When you die and they find it, they would have found out how you felt throughout the year.

Never in twenty years of leading discussions with people of all ages had I heard an experienced discussant hesitate to answer a question by saying "I never thought about it." For most, the reaction is something like "I'm not sure, but I think I would. . . ." In the instance above, Marcy does not take my question as an invitation to muse out loud, and I have to coax her forward. Furthermore, the students do not volunteer to compare their responses with one another, as did the students in the Chalmers class. These facts suggest that they have had very little experience with interpretive discussion.

Once again, however, I am struck by the intensity of students' responses to my questions. Michael says he would leave home under the circumstances described, while Marcy would go to her room and cry. What does this undisguised, unmitigated gut reaction portend about their response to Shakespeare? Will it remain intact as they become more practiced discussants? The discussion continues.

MP: Can I read yours, James?

JAMES: Yes.

MP (reading):

> I have been hurt a hundred times by many people. Sometimes it makes me feel good, but most of the time it hurts and I refuse to stand for someone taking a cheap shot at me. Sometimes I am forced to do what I don't want to do to get revenge. It is hard to keep cool. I try not to let anyone blow my top. They think I won't do anything, but I will get them

back. I have decided not to be hurt anymore. For in my lifetime I have been hurt too many times. I am going to try to
make it better.
That is a good paper, too. It explains something about James and
the way he treats me. I feel better about that. I am glad I read this.
SYLVIA: Well, maybe sometimes you treat him wrong and you
wait for a while. That's maybe why he gets mad at you real fast
and talks back to you.
MP: And he is really afraid of someone taking a cheap shot at
him, right? But I need to ask a question, James. What is a cheap
shot?
JAMES: Something that's not expected. You're probably expecting
something from that person but you're not expecting a low blow
from them. It's coming but you don't think it's going to come
that way. You sit there and you be shocked and you be hurt. Then
you want to get them. So you just come back another day,
another time, another place.
MP: So I said something bad—you thought I would never say
anything like that to you. But it sounds like when you want to get
back at somebody, James, it's to protect yourself. It's not so much
to harm the person but to prevent this from happening in the
future.
JAMES: Right.

Again, I found my tongue tied. What encounter between student and teacher lay behind this exchange? Did the extraordinary forthrightness of these
students stem to some extent from that relationship? And what about the
analysis of relationships that I was witnessing—the ready ability to define a
"cheap shot," the commentary volunteered by Sylvia to enlighten the teacher,
or the obvious enthusiasm that the teacher had for this spontaneous scrutiniz-
ing? Between the intensity of daily experience and the ability and willingness
to analyze personal feelings and relationships, it seemed that these students
would bring extraordinary resources to the discussion of literature. The conversation continues:

COLETTE: Sometimes it's not nice.
MP: What is that you are saying, Colette?
COLETTE: Sometimes it's not nice to take revenge.
SYLVIA: In my house, you had better!
SHG: What are you saying, Colette? Why is it sometimes not
nice?
COLETTE: It's not smart because if you take revenge you could get

> hurt if you go back. Just like on my paper as I read when I called
> the police on my brother. And then my father told me and they
> handcuffed him and all this, and I was about to cry because they
> were taking him away. I felt sorry that I had called the police on
> him. But again, I look at it that he shouldn't have jumped on me.
> He jumped on me—I didn't do something wrong. When I called
> the police I was crying. I didn't want him to go to jail. But they
> took him anyway. When he got out, I thought he was going to
> jump on me again. But instead, he told me I did the right thing to
> call the police.

The classroom conversation has seemingly moved Colette to think again about the time she called the police to report her brother. At the beginning of the discussion, she said that she did not regret calling the police, as her brother should not have behaved as he did. Now, however, she points out how sad she was when they took him away and how she feared his subsequent retaliation. So "sometimes it's not nice to take revenge," she says. The conviction in her voice signals that her claim has arisen from reflection on personal experience; she does not seem to be repeating a platitude that she may have heard elsewhere. Her claim is a general, analytic statement, precisely the sort of statement that interpretive discussion moves the discussants toward.

We see in Colette an example of one kind of alteration that can occur in interpretive discussions. Sometimes, there are fundamental changes in response to the discussion situation, changes the actor is unaware of but that completely modify subsequent experience in ways visible to an observer. Sometimes there occur fundamental changes in perspective of which the actor is aware; he or she may have a kind of "aha!" experience that yields an entirely new view of seemingly diverse matters. Both sorts of alteration could involve a transformation, so that a discussant is not responding to the discussion situation as previously.[7] And sometimes the alteration is not so radical. Perhaps there is a shift in perspective on the topic under discussion that, in turn, brings about a modified vision of the claims that the actor has already made. Colette's alteration seems to be of the latter variety. She now asserts that taking revenge can have some negative consequences, a claim she did not make initially. Her change in perspective may have arisen because she was willing to discuss and reflect on a private, painful event. Change or transformation need not always spring from thought about such moments, but often they do. Why? Because the pain motivates us to search for new ideas about the consequences of our actions and the nature of our relationships. And those new ideas may be powerful ones if the incident is one we really wish to understand.

What seems clear, then, is precisely what Dewey said—that learning does not automatically and necessarily come from doing things. Indeed, Colette appears to come to new insight about the incident with her brother through her discussion of it. Her reflection may have been advanced by listening to the stories and observations of others, nor merely by speaking herself. Recall that early in the conversation she had agreed with Sylvia's decision not to strike her pregnant mother, so that even at that moment, Colette may have begun to think about the negative consequences of taking revenge. The exchange between James and Mrs. Prince, which had reference to a difficult moment in their own relationship, may have touched her as well.

The students in the Belden classroom do not manifest the habits of mature, interpretive discussants. Sometimes they react to each other's comments, thereby drawing out their own ideas, but they do not often do so. Sometimes they use the discussion to think aloud about things they do not yet understand, but such moments are infrequent. Sometimes they spontaneously follow rules of conversation that allow them to push their thinking further, rules that involve comparing, agreeing and disagreeing, exemplifying, amending, clarifying the statements on the floor. But once again, they do not engage in such moves with frequency.[8]

At the same time, these students seem to bring extraordinary resources to the discussion situation. They have intense personal relationships to draw upon; their daily experiences are powerful and thus potentially instructive; they are willing to share these experiences; they are not inclined to replace a report of concrete experience with abstract theorizing. Indeed, it may well be that they have an advantage over the Chalmers students in this respect, as it is easy to miss the rich resources of the specific instance if it is abandoned too quickly for analysis at a general level.

Over the course of this volume, we will see each group move toward more meaningful conversation. The Chalmers students come to draw upon personal experience with more regularity, while the Belden students begin to relate particular incidents in their lives to abstract ideas. As for Mrs. Prince and myself, we, like Mrs. Spring, are groping for ways to open the students to the practices and pleasures of classroom discussion. The powerful relation that seems to exist between this experienced Belden teacher and her charges signals that she cares about their ideas and is eager to help them. I, too, wish to be helpful, but as an outsider, I have much to learn about how to reach the goal. Indeed, I will make many mistakes as I venture forward.

In the next conversation, we watch one of my first fumbling attempts to engage the students of the Belden School in discussion of *Romeo and Juliet*. We see that for all my good intentions and years of discussion-leading experience, I do much to discourage the students from using their most powerful resource for understanding the play, their personal experience. How could such a thing happen when I was so clearly committed to doing otherwise?

CONVERSATION 2

Why Do Teachers Fail to Draw upon Students' Experiences in Discussion?

The following conversation is my fourth with the Belden students. The question before the reader is: How does one go about helping these students, who bring powerful personal experiences to classroom discussion, to infuse those experiences into a conversation about texts? In theory, it would seem an easy matter. As the students comment about the play, simply ask them to elaborate upon the events of their lives that they mention, their ideas about these events, and the values and interests to which they allude. However, it turns out that there are powerful constraints that deter me—and, I think, many teachers. I parade these constraints before the reader for one reason: Only when we recognize the constraints under which we labor can we hope to manage them and begin to draw upon student experience in powerful ways.

The class has now reached act I, scene iii, where we see Juliet's nurse, her confidante and lifelong companion, makes the focal speech about the girl's weaning. The students take parts and read aloud. Where they hesitate over unfamiliar words, I assist them.

*

JULIET: How now? Who calls?

NURSE: Your mother.

JULIET: Madam, I am here. What is your will?

LADY CAPULET: This is the matter—Nurse, give leave awhile;
We must talk in secret. Nurse, come back again.
I have—

SHG: "Rememb'red me"—I have remembered myself; I was mistaken in asking you to leave.

LADY CAPULET: —rememb'red me; thou's hear our—

SHG: "Counsel"—our conversation.

LADY CAPULET: —counsel.
Thou knowest my daughter's of a pretty age.

NURSE: Faith, I can tell her age unto an hour.

39

LADY CAPULET: She's not fourteen.
NURSE: I'll lay fourteen of my teeth—
And to my teen [sorrow][1] be it spoken, I have but four—
She's not fourteen. How long is it now
To—
_____
SHG: "Lammastide"—August 1 the note says.
_____

NURSE: Lammastide.
LADY CAPULET: A fortnight and odd days.
NURSE: Even or odd, or all days in the year,
Come Lammas Eve at night shall she be fourteen.
Susan and she (God rest all Christian souls!)
Were of an age. Well, Susan is with God;
She was too good for me. But, as I said,
On Lammas Eve at night shall she be fourteen;
That shall she, marry; I remember it well—
_____
SHG: "Tis"—it is.
_____

NURSE: 'Tis since the earthquake now eleven years;
And she was weaned (I never shall forget it),
Of all the days of the year, upon that day;
For I had then laid—
_____
SHG: "Wormwood."
_____

NURSE: —wormwood to my dug,
Sitting in the sun under the dovehouse wall.
My lord and you were then at—
_____
SHG: "Mantua"—a town in Italy.
_____

NURSE: Mantua.
Nay, I do bear a brain. But as I said,
When it did taste the wormwood on the nipple
Of my dug and felt it bitter, pretty fool,
To see it—
_____
SHG: "Tetchy."
_____

NURSE: —tetchy and fall out with the dug!
Shake, quoth the—
_____

SHG: "Dovehouse."

NURSE: —dovehouse—

SHG: " 'T'was"—there was.

NURSE: T'was no need, I—

SHG: "Trow."

NURSE: —trow.
To bid me trudge.
And since that time it is eleven years,
For then she could stand high-lone; nay, by the rood,
She could have run and waddled all about;
For even the day before, she broke her brow;
And then my husband (God be with his soul!
'A was a merry man) took up the child.
"Yea,"—

SHG: "Quoth"—said he.

NURSE: —quoth he, "dost thou fall upon thy face?
Thou wilt fall backward when thou hast more wit;
Wilt thou not, Jule?" and, by my—

SHG: "Holidam."

NURSE: —holidam.
The pretty wretch left crying and said, "Ay."
To see now how a jest shall come about!
I warrant, and I should live a thousand years,
I never should forget it. "Wilt thou not, Jule?" quoth he,
And pretty fool, it stinted and said, "Ay."
LADY CAPULET: Enough of this. I pray thee hold thy peace.

*

As is evident, these students have some difficulty reading the play aloud. The language is foreign to them, and even where they manage to decode the words, their tone of voice suggests they do not understand all of what they read. I worry that they will lose interest if, in fact, they are not following the action. So the question for me becomes: How much of the text have they grasped? I try to find out.

> SHG: OK, let's stop here. Now, what do you think about this
> nurse? What's the first thing that comes to your mind?
> COLETTE: She talks a lot!
> SHG: What was the question that the nurse answered? Yes,
> Colette.
> COLETTE: How old the child is.
> SHG: And what did the nurse say?
> COLETTE: The nurse said she was nine years old.

Now, at this point, one might ask Colette: Where does the nurse say that
Juliet is nine years old? In theory, that is the right question to ask. Why? Because to answer it requires the student to peruse the text, locating the passage
that has given her the idea and either explain why it supports her idea or withdraw the idea. In so doing, she will see her error for herself. But I do not ask the
question, fearing that if confronted with her error, Colette may refrain from
further participation. Perhaps I am right, but my fear has robbed the student
of the opportunity to pursue her own idea. I let the erroneous comment pass
and pose an interpretive question, one to which textual evidence suggests
more than one answer.

> SHG: Do you think the nurse really knows the girl's age when she
> answers?
> COLETTE: She really don't remember.
> SHG: She doesn't know? She is just talking? She does talk an
> awful lot, doesn't she? But do you feel like she remembers when
> the girl's birthday is? Marcy?
> MARCY: I think she knows.
> SHG: You think she knows? How come?
> MARCY: She has taken care of the child for all her life.
> SYLVIA: I think her mother should be beaten for not knowing
> how old she is!

Why didn't Colette think that the nurse knew the girl's age, given the de-
tailed account of the birthdate? I worry that she has not understood the nurse's
speech, and so I question her with a tone that belies my concern. Marcy, perhaps sensing that I find Colette in error, takes the opposing position, but her
reason for believing the nurse knows the girl's age ignores the details in the
nurse's speech. Have neither of these speakers understood the nurse?

My worry about comprehension has distracted me from Sylvia's tantalizing
comment! Why does she believe that Lady Capulet did not know her
daughter's age? Why does she condemn the mother for this failing? To ques-

tion Sylvia about her remark might draw out of her ideas about the relations between mothers and children as well as her understanding of the text. But do I question Sylvia? No, I am too concerned with discovering how much of the text everyone understands.[2]

When I begin to doubt that discussants have grasped the factual level of the text, I sometimes ask a nonfactual question. In responding to the question, students often mention information that they did not realize they had gleaned. Asking the fact question in direct form, e.g., "How old is Juliet?" is likely to stop the thinking, as either students feel they don't know the answer or they respond immediately without having to think. So I proceed as follows:

SHG: Who is Susan? Do you have any idea who she might be? Marcy?

MARCY: It might be a nickname.

SHG: A nickname for Juliet? The nurse says, "Well Susan is with God . . ." What does that mean when someone says—

COLETTE: Dead. So that probably means she had another child who died.

SHG: Do you mean that Juliet had a sister who died? Why does the nurse say, "she was too good for me"? Did the nurse do anything wrong?

COLETTE: Maybe the nurse had a child of her own named Susan.

SHG: Yes, she could have had a child of her own. After all, she is a woman, right?

COLETTE: Yeah. But she got too old. She sounds old on the record.

SHG: Well, what do we know about Susan and Juliet? See where it says, "Susan and she were of an age"? What does that mean? Look at the note. Yes Colette?

COLETTE: It says they are the same age. So that means Susan is Juliet's twin.

SHG: That is possible. Not a bad idea.

MARCY: But it could be that the nurse had a daughter the same age as Juliet.

SHG: Possible. That would explain something that comes later in the speech.

This exchange gives me hope. In spite of the halting and hesitant style with which they had read aloud, the students are able to make reasonable guesses about who Susan is, based on the evidence in the text. That she is either Juliet's twin or the nurse's own daughter are possibilities, although the evidence favors the latter. I want desperately to show the students that while Shakespeare didn't solve the puzzle definitively, he provided clues they can find through careful scrutiny of the lines. I want them to see that they can find the evidence themselves, that they do not need to have us tell them what the answer is. And so I proceed to question them about the meaning of the word "weaned," thinking that if they do not know it, they will work through the text and uncover the clues about its meaning and Susan's identity.

SHG: What does "weaned" mean? Yes, Colette.

COLETTE: I don't know. Dead?

MP: No. Think! She "weaned" the baby. Colette, you have an idea now?

COLETTE: Spanked? Slapped?

MP: No.

COLETTE: You tell us! You're the teacher!

SHG: Wait! Let's try to figure it out. Have you never heard that before? She weaned the baby?

SYLVIA: She had an abortion? A miscarriage?

MP: No.

SHG: Now we know this nurse has these two girls who are about the same age, right? Where are you going, Colette?

COLETTE: I'm going to the dictionary because I don't know.

SHG: Wait a minute. Come back here. Read it one more time.

COLETTE: "Now eleven years; and she was weaned." It means she was pregnant.

SHG: Now this nurse is taking care of two babies, right? And what would a nurse be likely to do? If the nurse had a child of her own and is also taking care of Juliet, which was one of our ideas, what could she do for Juliet? Yes, Colette?

COLETTE: Take care of them. Breastfeed them.

SHG: Right, exactly. Breastfeed them. If she had a child of her own, she would have milk and be able to breastfeed them. So the word "weaned" is related to breastfeeding. What happens next?

SYLVIA: She weans her daughter.

MARCY: Susan doesn't actually have to be her daughter. The nurse is taking care of Juliet and Juliet is not her daughter.

SHG: Is that what you think, Marcy? Yes, Colette.

COLETTE: The whole thing wouldn't matter if Juliet was dead instead of Susan.

Colette's last comment is again provocative. What "whole thing" would not matter? Would the nurse not have had the story to tell if Juliet had died? Would there be no play? Would we not be having this conversation?? I do not question Colette about her last remark. Why? Her comment falls over me like a wet blanket. I feel she is saying she finds the discussion tiresome. Perhaps the problem is that she and the others know that we teachers know the definition of "weaning"—or that if we do not the dictionary does. Why, then, work so hard to figure it out? This seems like a valid question, but my hope is still that by using what they do know, and what Shakespeare tells them, they will figure out what "weaning" means, thus becoming more self-sufficient. So I press on with the same line of discussion:

SHG: Let's go on reading. Look at line 25 where it says, "Of all the days of the year, upon that day;/For I had then laid wormwood to my dug." Any idea what is going on there? Myrna?

MYRNA: She's sitting in front of a fireplace.

SHG: OK, it could be a fireplace or a type of wall. Now, the word "dug" means nipple of the breast, or teat.

MYRNA: Dove?

SHG: No, "dug." And "wormwood" is a kind of medicine that comes from a plant. So that when she says, "I had laid wormwood to my dug," what do you think the nurse means? What is she trying to make happen as far as her breasts are concerned? James?

JAMES: She is trying to make the baby healthy.

MP (A good bit of snickering is heard around the table at this point but no telling words are distinguishable): By doing what? Come on, now, this is our bodies! We should be able to talk about this.

SYLVIA: She's putting medicine on her breast.

SHG: And why is she doing that, Sylvia?

SYLVIA: To make it feel bigger!

I become concerned that all but three of the students have remained silent thus far, so I question two who have not yet spoken, Myrna and James. It seems to me that they are responding with random guessing: Where did Myrna get the idea that the nurse is sitting in front of a fireplace? And what makes James say that the nurse put wormwood on her nipple to make the baby healthy? I give them definitions for "dug" and "wormwood," for I do not believe they should try to figure out every word they do not know. Indeed, I hope to give them enough information so that they can figure out the nurse's story, thereby discovering the meaning of "weaned" and the evidence Shakespeare has given about Susan's identity. I press forward, wishing to persevere until they feel the reward for their efforts.

SHG: Well, that is a possibility. Let's read a few more lines.
Remember now, she is talking about weaning and we haven't
quite figured out what that word means yet. We know that she
says, at line 30—see that?—

> But as I said,
> When it did taste the wormwood on the nipple
> Of my dug and felt it bitter, pretty fool,
> To see it tetchy and fall out with the dug!
> Shake, quoth the dovehouse!

Now James, what do you think happened there?
JAMES: She felt angry.
SHG: Who did?
JAMES: The woman.
SHG: The woman felt angry? What happened? Why did she feel
angry?
JAMES: The baby was sucking on her breast.
SHG: OK, that is possible. Marvin, did you think that was
happening? That the woman got angry?
MARVIN: I don't know.

Why did James say that nurse felt angry because the baby was sucking on
her breast? This remark puzzled me, as I saw no evidence of the nurse's anger.
It appeared that James's comment was simply off the wall, totally random. I
turned away from the opportunity to question James, not because I feared dis-
couraging him, as had been the case with Colette earlier, but because I had
grown impatient with comments that did not seem to advance our discussion
of "weaning."

However, Marvin's is the most demoralizing of all responses: "I don't
know." It feels as if he is not only saying "I don't have the answer," but "Leave
me alone. I'm not interested in talking about this." Now, it may well be that a
discussion of weaning with adolescent girls and two women is difficult for
Marvin and James. But this possibility does not compel me at the moment.
Instead, I cringe with discomfort.[3] Here I am, doing all I can think of to help
them read and understand Shakespeare for themselves, and the response is:
I'm not interested. But I cannot accept defeat.

SHG: Look at the lines there. Who is the woman speaking?
Colette?
COLETTE: The nurse.
SHG: Do you see where we are, Marvin? Page 57, line 29? OK.
Then she says, "But as I said, / When it did taste the wormwood

on the nipple / Of my dug and felt it bitter, pretty fool," Marvin?
"To see it tetchy and fall out with the dug." What do you think
happened there? We have got this nurse and she is nursing this
baby, right? She puts this medicine on her nipple, and what
happens?
MARVIN: The baby drank.
SHG: Yes, and then the baby did what? If the word "tetchy"
means "fussy" or "irritable," then what did the baby do? Yes,
Colette.
COLETTE: When the baby started nursing off her dug, the milk
was bitter. What was that stuff she put on?
SHG: The wormwood.
COLETTE: Yeah, the wormwood was bitter. Then the baby
stopped.
SHG: Stopped or started?
COLETTE: She stopped nursing.
SHG: Is that what happened, Myrna?
MYRNA: Yeah.
SHG: Yes, Colette.
COLETTE: Why did the baby stop sucking?
SHG: Yes, Myrna.
MYRNA: Because it was bitter.
COLETTE: It didn't taste right?
MYRNA: Uh-huh.
SHG: OK, now what do you think "weaning" means?
CHORUS: Breastfeeding!

I can hardly believe my ears! After all this discussion, they are still telling me
that the word "weaning" means breastfeeding. Not only that, but Colette has,
just a moment earlier, given the correct definition of the term. Yet, having
done so, she immediately asks why the baby stopped sucking. Did she not
understand her own explanation? Did she get it after Myrna repeated it back
to her? Maybe they all understand but are putting me on with their last response. I have to try once more.

SHG: Now what has happened here? The woman has put this
stuff on her breast, the baby tastes it, it's bitter, and the baby spits
it out, doesn't want to suck anymore.
MARCY: Well, it wasn't her mom.
MP: That doesn't matter! We are trying to find out what "wean"
means. And "wean" *does not mean breastfeed!* "Weaning" is
what is taking place right here! This is why the nurse remembers

the day Juliet was weaned. What happens is the baby sucks, it
tastes awful, so the baby doesn't want to suck anymore, right?
CHORUS: Right.
MP: And that is what "weaning" is. The baby stops sucking. We
hear that word a lot. We don't hear so much about weaning from
the nipple anymore. But people say weaning from the what?
CHORUS: Breast.
MP: No, no. What do babies use these days? Colette.
COLETTE: Pacifiers.
MP: Pacifiers or bottles, right? When you are trying to cut the
baby off from this, you call it what?
CHORUS: Weaning!
MP: That is it. You call it "weaning." Colette.
COLETTE: When the baby doesn't suck anymore, she can have a
pacifier or a bottle.
MP: No, they want her to drink out of a cup.
COLETTE: Oh.
SHG: Now you see how we started out by seeing what some of the
other lines were telling us? Once we understand the story about
the nurse putting the medicine in her nipple, then we could figure
out what "weaning" might involve.
MARCY: She put that stuff on her nipple?
SHG: *Yes!* Remember the wormwood? She put that medicine on
her nipple.
MARCY: Oh.
SHG: OK, now, lets move on. Who wants to read? Colette? Do
you want to read Juliet? What about you, James?"
JAMES: I don't want to be nothing.
SHG: Why not?
JAMES: Nope. Nothing doing.

At this point, everyone, including Mrs. Prince, has lost patience. Why, I
wonder, did I persevere in having the students figure out the meaning of
"wean" instead of telling them the definition or letting them look it up? I have
spent nearly the whole class on the project, and it is not clear what has been
grasped from Shakespeare's text as a consequence. I have ignored many opportunities to ask the students about their experiences and views and to relate
these to the play. The participation has not been enthusiastic, with the exception of Colette. James's refusal to read at the end signals that the conversation
has alienated him, at least temporarily. So why have I persisted in the face of
this failure?

The answer suggested by the foregoing commentary is clear. My own convictions about teaching and learning had fixed me upon a certain course of action that made sense to me at the time. I believe that students have resources—understanding, past experience, interests, abilities—for discovering things they think they do not understand. Therefore, my task as teacher is to direct the search: to help them look in the right places, or better, to find the right places to look so that they discover what they *do* understand. Consequently, I defined my role as one of helping these students to realize that by looking at what Shakespeare said, they could discover what they thought they didn't know, namely, the meaning of the word "wean." Once they had figured out what the nurse had done, they could identify a meaning that fit the activities she described, like finding out which piece is needed for a particular place in a jigsaw puzzle by putting the other pieces together and letting the shape reveal itself.[4]

My plan of action was sustained by the students' responses. Since they had offered what seemed to me to be groundless ideas, they aroused my fear that they were guessing randomly because they did not comprehend the factual level of the text. I did not want to discourage their efforts by indicating their ideas were "wrong." Hence, I posed questions I thought they could answer— and ones which, if answered correctly, would allow them to comprehend what the nurse was saying. So, my beliefs, fears, and convictions about what the students can and should do to unlock the secrets of the text distracted me from exploring their personal experiences and views.

Despite my good intentions, then, this discussion had been painfully frustrating. What had caused it to differ so from the first one we had had on revenge? This was the topic of the following conversation with Mrs. Prince:

> SHG: The fact is that the students did not seem very interested in
> our discussion. I felt this was like pulling teeth. In fact, James
> refused to read at the end. Even Colette, who seemed more eager
> to participate, did a lot of wild guessing.
> MP: What are you thinking of?
> SHG: Colette began by saying that the nurse thought Juliet was
> nine years old. Then she said the nurse didn't really remember
> how old the girl was. I couldn't believe that comment! And then
> what about all that guessing she did when I asked what
> "weaned" meant. She was the one who said it meant "dead,"
> didn't she? That was just a wild guess. And then she said it meant
> "spanked" and "slapped."
> MP: The thing I noticed was that as soon as you asked what

"weaned" meant, Colette put up her hand and when called on said, "I don't know." Then right away she said "dead," almost as if wild guessing was better than saying nothing at all. But *why* was she so eager to talk, even if she had nothing to say?

SHG: But does she have nothing to say? I am beginning to wonder whether she might not have had a lot to say but found that this conversation was a hard one to say it in. I know that sounds strange, but I can't help but think of the contrast between this discussion and the one we had with them on the topic of revenge. Do you remember how much they had to say about that? Maybe they didn't think they had anything to say today. I mean they didn't think they knew the meaning of the word.

MP: You're right. Remember how at one point Colette asked me to tell them what "weaned" meant? It's possible that she believed she had nothing to say *until* we told her the definition.

SHG: If that's the case, then her belief about the conditions under which she could talk and mine were in opposition. I believed she could, by talking about the right things, figure out the definition, and she believed that she had nothing to say *until* she knew what the word meant.

MP: Aha! This conversation is giving me another idea about why the discussion was so difficult.

SHG: Yes?

MP: We were really asking them to do something different than I usually ask of them. I mean most of the time they do look up words they don't know, or they ask me and I tell them. Or they tell me what they think about something—like the answers they have to math problems—and I tell them whether they are right. But this asking them to figure out things they think they don't know—and are not expected to know until the moment arises— is not something they have had too much experience with. Maybe they just didn't know what to make of it all.[5]

SHG: This seems to me quite possible.

MP: Remember when Colette said that the whole thing wouldn't mater if Juliet were dead instead of Susan?

SHG: How could I forget? What a wet blanket!

MP: Well, as I recall, she said that after someone else said that Susan didn't have to be her daughter. I had the feeling that at that point, these comments were kind of floating, like nobody knew what the purpose of the conversation was.

SHG: But hadn't I made clear that the purpose was to figure out the definition of "weaned"?

MP: Yes, but perhaps the students felt that that wasn't the *real* purpose. Since they could look up the word in the dictionary and they had little idea of how to use the play to figure out its meaning, they may not have shared the purpose that you had declared. In other words, they may have been trying to go along with you but doing so without a real sense of the reason why.

SHG: Actually, the original purpose was to figure out who Susan was, but we never really got back to that. I guess I lost sight of the issue with all the discussion of weaning. No wonder they were confused. And I suppose that the procedure we followed for figuring out what "weaning" meant was difficult for them too. Shakespeare is hard if you aren't used to the language.

There seem to be several things that distinguish this conversation from the one these students had had on the topic of revenge. For one thing, I had had no objective on that occasion but to hear and understand their personal thoughts and experiences. So there were no blinding convictions about learning to contend with, as I was not worried about their learning something from the discussion. I was free to ask students for clarification because I had no predetermined end in mind, no question that I wanted them to answer. Without these constraints, I could allow the students to direct their focus over a wider range of topics and issues. The only restriction was that they had to focus on a personal experience that involved revenge. In the present conversation, the students were given less latitude. They had to define a word by looking at what the nurse says in her speech rather than by looking it up in the dictionary. And, as Mrs. Prince suggests, the Belden students were not used to that sort of task, nor were they used to Shakespeare.

It is not possible to explore every idea that students offer in a discussion, so one must always make choices. But the fact that I did not explore more of the personal ideas and feelings they offered me had at least one negative consequence: The group never arrived at a shared focus, a question it really wanted to resolve. Lacking such a focus, the discussion seemed to "float," that is, the comments were tied to no issue the students cared about. Since they did not seem to share my interest in defining the term "wean," they seemed not to experience any sense of progress as they worked out a definition. Lacking a meaningful issue, it is not surprising that the students failed to find the discussion of interest.

Teachers often have objectives and beliefs that distract them from questioning students about the meaning and implications of their remarks. While they may work to become more sensitive and open—less myopic—the tendency to focus on their own concerns is there. Indeed, if it were not there, the interpretive discussion, not to mention all sorts of other classroom activities, could quickly become chaotic. So what hope is there that such a discussion, directed by a teacher with her own concerns and convictions, can engage the students in a deep and genuine way?

In the next conversation, we explore this issue by considering the criteria for a good interpretive discussion and asking: What needs to happen in the conversation such that the students' personal experiences and interests are brought to bear upon the text in a way that is meaningful to them?

CONVERSATION 3

What Does a Good Interpretive Discussion Look Like?

What is a "good" interpretive discussion? What criteria should it meet? One can well imagine discussions that do not benefit students, much as one can imagine such lectures or demonstrations. Indeed, the one we have just observed in the Belden School might seem to some readers to be just such an example. The one thing that seems certain is that the students' interests need to be engaged, and their personal experience should be brought to bear upon the text. Under what conditions do these things occur?

To address these issues, let us return to the Chalmers school,[1] where Mrs. Spring is leading a discussion of act I, scene v, of *Romeo and Juliet,* the scene where Romeo crashes Lord Capulet's party and first lays eyes on Juliet. Tybalt, who is Juliet's cousin, identifies the invader in this first segment that the students read.

*

ROMEO: [To a Servingman] What lady's that which doth enrich the hand
Of yonder knight?
SERVINGMAN: I know not, sir.
ROMEO: O, she doth teach the torches to burn bright!
It seems she hangs upon the cheek of night
As a rival jewel in Ethiop's ear—
Beauty too rich for use, for earth too dear!
So shows a snowy dove trooping with crows
As yonder lady o're her fellows shows.
The measure done, I'll watch her place of stand
And, touching hers, make blessed my rude hand.
Did my heart love till now? Forswear it, sight!
For I ne'er saw true beauty till this night.
TYBALT: This, by his voice, should be a Montague.
Fetch me my rapier, boy. What! Dares the slave
Come hither, covered with an antic face,
To leer and scorn at our solemnity?

Now, by the stock and honor of my kin,
To strike him dead I hold it not a sin

MRS. SPRING: All right, let's stop here. What can you tell about
Tybalt's character just from these lines? Abe.

ABE: It seems that in a way, Tybalt is playing God. He is deciding,
"Well, this is a sin and this isn't." His authority is coming from
the family. Because he is a Montague he has some right to say,
"This is right and this is wrong."

MS: Capulet, you mean. Brian.

BRIAN: This kind of adds to what Abe was saying. It was like
Shakespeare was trying to say that most people are so selfish that
if they can justify their sins by putting a value on them then they
think it's OK—they're not wrong. And this guy is saying that
since I am doing it for the good of my family, then it's not
considered a sin so I'm not going to have to pay for it. God will
realize I'm doing it to save my family. But that's wrong because
he's the only one to say that his family is right or wrong in the
first place.

MS: That's very lovely. Jarvis.

JARVIS: I thought this speech was showing the stupidity of the
fight in general. It's just because of honor and so forth. Not for
any good reason, but just to make it look like he, Tybalt, has the
right to put a value on one life over another. This judging of a
person's life doesn't show any real thinking, of letting the honor
of your family rule your actions. But maybe his kin is fighting for
something that doesn't retain anything. You know, he just has to
keep killing and showing his power and all, which just shows the
stupidity of it all.

MS: Very interesting, Jarvis. I think you can get some more
evidence that will help you build up your case.

As we observed in Conversation 1, these are experienced discussants. The
verbal exchange among the students and teacher is governed by clear conversational rules that define the conditions under which remarks of given kinds
are appropriate. Everyone knows what the conditions are, and the remarks of
both teacher and students conform to them. The discussion begins with the
teacher asking an interpretive question, a question for which there is more
than one answer, given the textual evidence. Here, the question is: "What can
you tell about Tybalt's character from these lines?" The students respond as
they should in that circumstance, given the constraints of the discussion. For

example, Abe, when recognized, addresses the question directly. Had his comment been, "I think Romeo is a fool," he would have been out of order. For in a discussion, anyone who speaks after a question is posed will address it, except under certain circumstances.[2] Brian then enters by saying that he is adding to what Abe said, and Jarvis enters by speaking to the initial question, presenting what he seems to think is a somewhat modified position—both acceptable moves. After Brian and Jarvis comment, the teacher says "lovely" or "interesting." The teacher need not follow the student comments with a positive response, but the practice is fairly common in these conversations.[3]

The first criterion that an effective interpretive discussion must meet, then, is that all participants must observe the constraints under which remarks of given sorts are acceptable. That is to say, they must know and follow the rules for responding to one another that the "game" of interpretive discussion specifies. Why is such rule-following necessary? Perhaps the most important reason is that following the rules allows people to build on the ideas of others. As we shall see, it is out of this construction that a genuine issue—a question the group really wants to answer—emerges. If discussants do not follow the rules, then the question does not arise and the discussion lacks focus, precisely as we saw happen in the Belden classroom. The comments often feel scattered, as they are not tied to a genuine group concern; and the group is likely to feel a lack of progress in resolving issues.

However, a word of caution is in order. It may appear that students are sometimes following rules when, in fact, they are not. For instance, Abe begins by saying that Tybalt was playing God, and Brian says he was "adding" to what Abe said. But Brian's point seems to be that Tybalt believed that God would forgive him, not that Tybalt was playing God. As for Jarvis, it is not clear that he is addressing the teacher's question when he says that the passage shows the "stupidity" of the fight in general. How does that remark relate to Tybalt's character? Jarvis does mention that Tybalt does not seem to be thinking of letting family honor "rule" him. But these comments about Tybalt's character, if one can call them such, are not the main focus of Jarvis's remarks. Indeed, he ends the way he began by saying that Shakespeare is trying to show the stupidity of the feud between the families. Upon closer examination, then, it appears that the students actually may not be following the discussion rules they seem to be observing.

Next, we see the students discussing the word "stock." That word is mentioned in the text when Tybalt says, "Now by stock and honor of my kin, To strike him dead I hold it not a sin."

MS: Larry.

LARRY: I was going to say something about the "stock." That stock, was, I thought, material that makes up something, like the stock of a store or something. It sort of makes it. Like with Tybalt, honor is one part of him; it is part of what makes him up.

MS: OK, nice. Edna?

EDNA: I was going to say that it sounds like Tybalt believes that he should give up this man's life for his honor and the [reputation] of his family and all this. But maybe he doesn't feel so strongly about all this. Maybe he just wants to humiliate Romeo.

MS: Now, that's really lovely—what you said about Romeo and Tybalt's motivations here. Jonathan.

JONATHAN: Well, what I was going to say is that Tybalt here reminds me of that fight scene at the beginning of the play.

MS: Why is that?

JONATHAN: Well, he is saying that these two families are just things. They are not individuals. It is just, you know, the Montagues and the Capulets. And when he says, "And by the stock and honor of my kin," first of all, this doesn't have anything to do with his own honor. It has to do with the Capulet family overall, the big thing.

MS: Very nice. OK, Martin.

MARTIN: I just thought of "stock" as in stock market. With sort of like a lot of potential gain. His family could be potentially very rich, sort of.

MS: Well even though they didn't have a stock market in Italy at this time, your association could work because this is a hard financial connection here.

JARVIS: Here! I looked up "stock," and it says, "the first of the line."

MS: The line of what?

JARVIS: Of the family—

MS: Which goes back to some of the things Jonathan was saying—the fight is over family honor, not individual honor.

Notice that Jarvis does not ask permission to look up the word, and the teacher does not try to stop the activity. Spontaneously, the students associate ideas to the word "stock"—precisely what Mrs. Prince and I were asking the Belden students to do with "wean." Free association is sometimes appropriate in an interpretive discussion.

However, the reader may wonder: Is free association always beneficial? In this instance, it seems not to encourage students to listen to and build upon others' remarks, since they are simply reporting what the word "stock" brings to mind. And does free association encourage thoughtful response? For example, what does the stock market have to do with this situation? Why think about the beginning of the play before the present context has been thoroughly explored? Why bring in a dictionary definition when it merely repeats an idea that is already on the floor, that the concern is with family rather than individual honor?

While free association is not always productive, it has one powerful advantage: It allows the speaker to draw directly upon personal experience in order to find meaning in the text. Here, it allows participants to uncover additional features of Tybalt's character, and hence contribute new ideas to the conversation. Larry begins by saying that honor was "part of him [Tybalt]." Edna counters that perhaps Tybalt wants to humiliate Romeo rather than protect his own honor. Jonathan maintains that as was true at the start of the play, Tybalt is concerned with the honor of his family, not his personal honor. Martin ventures that he may be concerned with financial prowess. Perhaps, then, the free association has drawn out ideas about Tybalt that the students would not otherwise have come to—much as Plato and Dewey might hope would happen in the discussion.

We have so far considered two criteria for a good discussion. First, the students and teacher need to follow rules of conversation, as these allow people to build on each others' comments in creating and pursuing textual issues. A second criterion is that the conversation should generate new ideas about the topic under consideration. Techniques such as free association may stimulate new thoughts. Yet, it seems insufficient that the ideas be merely "new," i.e., novel in a given discussion. Need not the ideas also be good? And what is a "good" idea anyway? In the context of interpretive discussion, a "good" idea is sometimes said to be one for which there is textual evidence. We will reflect further upon this possible criterion as we proceed.

In the next segment, the students read the exchange between Lord Capulet and Tybalt that occurs in act I, scene v.

*

CAPULET: Why, how now, kinsman? Wherefore storm you so?
TYBALT: Uncle, this is a Montague, our foe,
A villain, that is hither come in spite
To scorn our solemnity this night.
CAPULET: Young Romeo is it?
TYBALT: 'Tis he, that villain Romeo.

CAPULET: Content thee, gentle coz, let him alone.
'A bears him like a portly gentleman,
And, to say truth, Verona brags of him
To be a virtuous and well-governed youth.
I would not for the wealth of all this town
Here in my house do him disparagement.
Therefore be patient; take no note of him.
It is my will, the which if thou respect,
Show a fair presence and put off these frowns,
An ill-beseeming semblance for a feast.
TYBALT: It fits when such a villain is a guest.
I'll not endure him.
CAPULET: He shall be endured.
What, goodman boy! I say he shall. Go to!
Am I the master here, or you? Go to!
You'll not endure him, God shall mend my soul!
You'll make a mutiny among my guests!
You will set a cock-a hoop. You'll be the man!
TYBALT: Why, uncle, 'tis a shame.
CAPULET: Go to, go to!
You are a saucy boy. Is't so indeed?
This trick may chance to scathe you. I know what.
You must contrary me! Marry, 'tis time—
Well said, my hearts!—You are a princox–go!
Be quiet, or–More light, more light!—For shame!
I'll make you quiet. What!—Cheerly, my hearts!
TYBALT: Patience perforce with willful choler meeting
Makes my flesh tremble in their different greeting.
I will withdraw; but this intrusion shall,
Now seeming sweet, convert to bitt'rest gall.

MS: Now let's think about Capulet. What can you tell about his character from this scene? Larry.
LARRY: Well, he knows he has power. He is superior to Tybalt. But he is reasonable; he is not just wielding the power without reason.
MS: OK, some more. Martin.
MARTIN: I think that he's different from Tybalt in that he has got pride in himself. That's part of the reason he is saying that he doesn't want Tybalt to cause any trouble. Another reason is for

the honor of his family as a whole. But he's saying, "I don't want any trouble right now."

MS: Good. Edna?

EDNA: I think there's something behind what Capulet is doing. He is scheming or something. He's just, like, "Just let him be for now. Just for now, let him be." Either he is trying to build up to something by being nice to him and telling him to shut up and wait until later, or maybe he thinks Romeo is genuinely a good person and is saying like, "Why are you doing this to him?" Because Capulet has no individual dislike toward Romeo. He hears he's a good person. He knows that just because he's from the other family doesn't mean he's a bad person.

The reader may wonder why Edna says that Capulet is "scheming." Indeed, as we will soon see, Mrs. Spring has this question herself. Who is Capulet scheming against? And what is the scheme? Edna gives no reasons why she thinks Capulet is scheming. So, while she has offered a new idea about Capulet, it is not clear yet how the text supports it. So is it a "good" idea? The discussion continues.

MS: Very good. So now we are thinking about how Capulet responds to Romeo. How about how he responds to Tybalt? Elizabeth and then Jarvis.

ELIZABETH: This is kind of like what Edna said. First of all, Capulet is the man of the house and his word goes. He is also sort of concerned with his social view—with how people will look at him. He says, "Here in my house, not for anything would I make a fool of myself by embarrassing him in my house."

JARVIS: In response to how Capulet is reacting to Tybalt. He's taking the energy that Tybalt thinks he should be taking out on Romeo on him. He's arguing with Tybalt rather than arguing with Romeo. It's just strange that he's taking out all his energy on Tybalt rather than Romeo.

MS: Nice. Abby and then Edna.

ABBY: It seems that actually, at heart, Capulet is a good man. He has good moral feeling.

EDNA: The thing I was going to say was that one reason he might be being so nice to Romeo is that the prince doesn't want any kind of conflict between them, remember? So this would put him even further on the prince's side that he is being so virtuous in letting his reason rule over these petty fights.

Now, what has happened to Edna's suggestion that Capulet is scheming, that he is trying to accomplish some end surreptitiously? Have any of these speakers offered evidence to support it? Have they picked up the suggestion and tried to use it to make sense out of the events—something that often happens to good ideas? The answer to both questions seems to be no. Elizabeth says she is going to say something "kind of like what Edna says," but she does not. Instead, she makes the point that Capulet is concerned with his appearance and does not want to embarrass himself. She does not argue that he is scheming. Jarvis's main point seems to be that Capulet is taking out anger directed toward Romeo on Tybalt, an idea that does not refer to Edna's. Abby, it seems, is contradicting Edna's point when she says that Capulet is really a good man at heart—hardly the characteristic of a schemer. Even Edna herself seems to have dropped the point when she asserts that Capulet is acting rational—ignoring Romeo—so as to please the prince. Or, is his attempt to please the prince part of his scheme? Maybe Edna hasn't given up her idea after all. The discussion continues:

> MS: But what about Tybalt's raging response to Romeo? How does Capulet deal with it? Edna.
> EDNA: He is overzealous about it. And this goes along with his scheming. He even criticizes Tybalt somewhere.
> MS: But Tybalt was saying that it was bad that Romeo was there.
> EDNA: Capulet had self-control! With a couple of words, he [Romeo] could have just been taken away, or whatever. I think he [Capulet] is trying to cover up for something, or build something. Because he is being so overindulgent about it. You know, like if you catch someone in a lie and they get flustered and keep rattling on and on. He is doing that because he is covering up something he is caught between.

Edna is persistent. Capulet gets flustered and "rattles on and on" because Tybalt has caught him in a lie, she says. But what "lie" has he told? What is he trying to "cover up"? Edna has not explained herself. At the same time, she has not dropped her idea. Until it becomes clear that Edna's idea is supported by textual evidence, it is hard to call it a "good" one.[4]

Let us pause to contrast the Belden and Chalmers classes. As I have mentioned, the students in the Chalmers classroom have had much experience with interpretive discussion, while those in the Belden classroom have not. Nevertheless, the groups do not appear totally dissimilar. For example, in both places, we see students addressing the questions posed, and entering the conversation by agreeing, disagreeing, or otherwise modifying what others have said—each being a possible move. We have seen students in both groups free-associate and come to new ideas.[5] And in both places, some of the ideas put forth seem to be well grounded in textual evidence, while others seem not to be. True, the Belden students, as a rule, do not enter as spontaneously, nor are they aware of all the circumstances under which they may enter the discussion, it seems. The sheer amount of talk and the ease with which it flows sharply differentiates the groups. At the same time, students in Chalmers are not always following the rules even when they seem to be. And the fact that they are not raises questions about how seriously they are working to resolve the issues they address, despite the fact that they speak so easily.

Up until now, our focus, in trying to determine the characteristics of a "good" discussion, has been mostly on the students. Have they followed the rules for interpretive discussion? Have they offered new ideas? Have the ideas been supported by the text? Now let us shift attention to the teacher. Certainly, the things she does can be good or not so good as well. So let us watch as Mrs. Spring manages the situation with Edna:

MS: Keeping that possibility alive, look at what just happened right before Capulet starts to talk—bottom of page 67. Tybalt says, "It fits when such a villain is a guest. I'll not endure him." Then Capulet says, "He shall be endured. / What, goodman boy! I say he shall. Go to! / Am I the master here or you? You'll not endure him, God shall mend my soul!" Now, what is the specific thing Capulet is responding to here? Brian.

BRIAN: Well, he is fighting with himself because he is not sure that he is right. Maybe Tybalt is right. Maybe he is like wimping because he is enduring the enemy in the house and is doing nothing about it. He is losing self-control because he is not sure he is right and because he is not sure he is able to control Tybalt.

MS: Say that last point again. Brian.

BRIAN: Capulet is worried that he might not be able to control Tybalt.

MS: OK. Edna.

EDNA: I'm looking at something different. I think Capulet is responding to "I shall not endure him." Tybalt is saying, "I will not do this no matter what you say." And then Capulet is like, "What are you talking about? How can you talk to me like this? I am above you; I am your master; you don't have a right to say this to me." He is upset that his superiority is being challenged.

MS: All right. Kevin and then Jarvis.

KEVIN: It seems like he was forcing things into Capulet's mind. And Tybalt was like, "I want to get him back. I just have to put revenge on him." And Capulet is like, "Stop!" He is saying, "Well, according to Verona, I have heard that Romeo is such a good boy and that even if we do something to get revenge on him, it might backfire on us." So he is just saying, "Take it easy."

JARVIS: I think that Tybalt was trying to get Capulet all riled up and maybe he would change his opinion and go after Romeo. Tybalt knows that he is not the master of the house, because, obviously, it's Capulet's house. But he is trying to take control in Capulet's house because he doesn't like the idea that Capulet let Romeo have control by coming in the house. So Capulet gets all riled up when he is speaking because he is telling Tybalt that no one has control except me.

————

Mrs. Spring seems to respond to Edna's suggestion that Capulet is scheming by posing what she takes to be a "fact" question, one that can be answered definitively by pointing to a passage in the text.[6] What, she asks, is Capulet responding to when he gets upset with Tybalt? This question is vague but I take it to be a fact question since the teacher seems to be looking for a particular answer. Notice that when Brian gives the answer she is seeking—"Capulet is worried that he might not be able to control Tybalt"—she asks him to repeat it, almost as if to say: Yes, that is the right response. Here, the teacher's reasoning seems to be: If Capulet's anger is caused by fear that Tybalt will gain control, then his anger is not a consequence of having been discovered scheming or covering up something. It appears that the teacher is trying to direct the students toward evidence that contradicts Edna's claim.

When the teacher feels that an idea on the floor is unjustified by the text, it is common practice to direct attention toward the contradictory evidence. The discussant then must explain the evidence in a way that preserves the idea or else abandon the idea. Such a move by the teacher is much more effective than telling the student "You are wrong," for then the textual evidence provides the reason for the judgment, not just the judgment itself. How does Edna respond in this situation?

Edna says she is "looking at something different," and then argues that Capulet is responding to Tybalt's challenge to his authority. She seems to be saying precisely what Brian said, that Capulet fears that Tybalt may gain control. So, in fact, she does not seem to be "looking at something different." Has Edna acquiesced?.

Perhaps, but note that something new is beginning to happen to her idea. Ordinarily, "bad" ideas are dropped in interpretive discussions, as there is no textual evidence to sustain them. Here, however, Jarvis makes a comment that seems to build on Edna's apparently unsound idea. Tybalt wants control, Jarvis says, because Tybalt doesn't like the fact the Capulet "let Romeo have control by coming into the house." This remark suggests that Capulet gave Romeo control. If so, then perhaps Capulet has been scheming after all!

If Jarvis is picking up on Edna's idea, does this indicate her claim may be a reasonable one? Mrs. Spring and I pursue this issue in the conversation that follows. We also consider additional criteria for judging the quality of an interpretive discussion.

SHG: Do you remember how Edna said that Capulet grew angry because his authority had been challenged?

MS: Yes!

SHG: It occurs to me that maybe the idea fit in with her theory. After all, if Capulet had some plot or scheme that he was trying to pull off, then someone challenging his authority could interfere with his plans.

MS: Well, if you're right, then it confirms a worry I had about this discussion.

SHG: What was that?

MS: It seemed to me that some of the time these students really weren't listening to each other. Often, they just seemed to pick up on a word or part of some else's comment and just go off on their own tangents. Like Edna did.[7]

SHG: But remember what Kevin said towards the end? His idea was that Capulet was aware of Romeo's reputation in Verona and was cautioning Tybalt that an attack on Romeo might backfire and bring disgrace to the family instead of superiority or honorable recognition.

MS: Yes, that was an interesting idea.

SHG: I think one might argue that this very idea emerged from the conversation, and that it could not have occurred had Kevin not been drawn into what was said previously. In the first place, it portrays Capulet as trying to get control—the very claim that Edna made repeatedly. Secondly, this is a Capulet who is preoccupied with his public image and, perhaps most particularly, with his appearance to the prince—also a point the students were emphasizing. Finally, it is family rather than personal honor that concerns Capulet—a distinction that was made early on in the conversation.[8]

MS: And I suppose you would say that the same thing was
happening when Jarvis followed Kevin by arguing that Tybalt
was trying to get Capulet all riled up so he would assault Romeo.
SHG: OK, yes. Jarvis seemed to be building on the idea that Kevin
had just suggested—that Tybalt was trying to "force things into
Capulet's mind," as Kevin put it. Jarvis, taking what Kevin said,
suggests that Tybalt may be trying to provoke Capulet, hoping
he'll turn on Romeo. Only the whole thing backfired on Tybalt.

Here, Mrs. Spring and I consider a fourth criterion for a good interpretive
discussion, namely that the students listen carefully to one another and respond to what has been said. They are, then "building" upon each others'
ideas. We contrast this behavior with picking out a word or remark that someone makes and, taking it out of context, using it to go on to make a point that
one already wanted to bring up—to go off on a tangent. Mrs. Spring worries
that Edna has been doing this, thereby perverting one of the rules for entering
the discussion.[9] I argue that Kevin and Jarvis have been listening and building
on others' remarks, however. It seems that they have been drawn into the discussion in a serious way as they listened and participated. But Mrs. Spring
expresses a reservation, as she is not convinced that their ideas are well
grounded in the text.

MS: All right, maybe you are right that some of the students were
listening to each other better than it seemed they were. But I still
have a problem. It seems to me there is little evidence for the
claim that Tybalt is trying to manipulate Capulet. Tybalt just
seems to be mad, mad that he is not allowed to expose the
intruder. I don't see why we have to attribute any ulterior motive
to any of his statements. After all, Capulet seems to be
overreacting to Tybalt, as Edna said. What you have is Tybalt's
outrage, followed by Capulet's overly zealous response, followed
by more anger from Tybalt. So, even if Kevin and Jarvis are
talking and seem to be building on each other's comments, I'm
not certain they are seriously engaged, since their idea seems to
lack textual support.
SHG: But what about Tybalt's last comment, that what seems
sweet now will turn to bitterest gall? Doesn't that remark show
forethought and planning for future action? I find their idea
persuasive because it explains Tybalt's anticipatory speech at the
end. And if Kevin and Jarvis are right, it seems to suggest that
Tybalt has been trying to control the situation ever since he
spotted Romeo and will go on with the effort.

MS: Well, when Tybalt says that what seems sweet will turn to bittersweet gall, he seems to be saying that he will not forget this incident with Romeo. But he is just mad; he is not plotting to manipulate the future then and there. Of course, Shakespeare is fond of using such devices to alert the reader as to what is coming, but I don't think this means Tybalt is right now scheming to get rid of Romeo.

SHG: But Tybalt is persistent. He does not acquiesce graciously when Capulet explains, quite calmly, why he chooses to ignore Romeo's presence. Tybalt's continued resistance to Capulet, coupled with his remark about the sweetness turning to gall, suggests to me—as it did to some of the students—that he is trying to move Capulet, to provoke him into forcefully ejecting Romeo from the scene. My point is that Tybalt keeps on pressing Capulet, and there seems to me little doubt that this is the case. You aren't about to maintain that he gives in, are you?

MS: No, I grant that he repeats that he cannot endure Romeo— and after Capulet tells him to forget about it. But I am not convinced that he does this in order to provoke Capulet. He may just be expressing his anger. And as for the end—what seems sweet now will turn to gall—I'm not sure about that, I guess.

We have said that the interpretive discussion should generate ideas that are supported by the text. Kevin and Jarvis have come to a new idea—that Tybalt is trying to manipulate Capulet into turning on Romeo. The implication of that interpretation is that Tybalt, in his last speech about sweetness turning to gall, may be understood to plot revenge when he does not succeed. Mrs. Spring is not sure Tybalt is plotting revenge with that remark, and she rejects the suggestion that he was trying to manipulate Capulet throughout the scene. Even if she is right, would we say that the students have not had a "good" interpretive discussion since they have not produced an idea supported by the text?

Somehow, this suggestion seems inappropriate. For one thing, the students' ideas do have some textual support. Furthermore, they seemed to be building on one another's comments and moving the analysis of Tybalt's and Capulet's relationship forward. Finally, something very important seems to have happened in this conversation, which did not occur at all in the Belden discussion of "weaning," as I indicate to Mrs. Spring in what follows.

SHG: I'm not sure the criteria for a good conversation should be defined simply in terms of whether the ideas generated are supported by the text. In addition, it seems as though something has to happen to the content of the conversation.

MS: Like what?

SHG: It has to do with letting the truth about some topic emerge.

MS: The truth? What do you mean by "truth"?

SHG: When a conversation takes place, there is some topic, some subject, that is under discussion, right?

MS: I guess so, but what about the old college bull session? Does that have a subject?

SHG: Yes, if it is a conversation, then some subject emerges. It may be the men in the physics lab or the Viet Nam war, but there is some subject that is focused upon—maybe more than one. And as the conversation goes on, an object emerges, an idea that is created by the conversation itself.[10] This idea is not just an idea a particular participant has, although a particular person may express it. Rather, it is the product of the remarks. It is what I was calling the "truth" a minute ago.

MS: Maybe you could give an example. I mean did the students' discussion today have an "object," as you call it? And if so, in what sense was it "truth"?

SHG: Well, I would say that the product of their conversation, its object, was just beginning to emerge. You perhaps see its clearest formulation in Jarvis's last comment—the idea that Tybalt was trying to get Capulet all riled up so that he would go after Romeo.

MS: But why is that idea the "object" of the conversation? Haven't we just been disputing its truth?

SHG: We have been disputing whether Tybalt was trying to manipulate Romeo, yes. But that is our debate, not the students'. In other words, our conversation kind of began where theirs left off. But as we said earlier, this remark by Jarvis was really the outcome of earlier comments; it seemed to presuppose some and draw upon others, right?

MS: Well, I suppose one could say that Kevin's comment, which came right before Jarvis's provided a strong foundation for it, what with all that talk about Tybalt trying to manipulate Capulet.

SHG: Yes, and as we said, that idea seemed to follow from Edna's earlier statement that Capulet was scheming and trying to cover up something, and other remarks. So, you see, as the students talked, an object, an idea, began to emerge in the discussion, and this idea is the object of the conversation. And in my view, that object was created as discussants listened and responded to each other's remarks.

MS: But why pick on Jarvis's statement as the best expression of the "object"? Why not Edna's point that Capulet was trying to cover up something, or any other idea for that matter?

SHG: The "object" of the conversation has to respond to the question—implicit or explicit—that the group is trying to address. It is the question the discussants really care about resolving. In this case, the question came to be: Why does Capulet respond as he does to Tybalt? While I think you proposed the question initially, it came to mean: Why does Capulet become so angry with Tybalt? Since that's the question that seems to emerge, Jarvis's statement, which addresses it by drawing upon remarks made earlier in the conversation, seems to reveal the "object" of the conversation.

MS: But why do you want to say that this statement of Jarvis's is some sort of "truth"?

SHG: It is the idea that emerges out of these comments. In other words, it follows, logically, from other things that have been asserted in the discussion. It is a "truth" if we accept these other premises which have already been established.

MS: So to say it's a "truth" doesn't mean it's factually true, right?

SHG: Well it's not necessarily true outside the situation in which it arises. But it is true within that context. One could ask: Given all that was said in this discussion, does Jarvis's idea that Tybalt was trying to manipulate Capulet to turn on Romeo follow? It seems to me that the answer is yes, which is why I want to say that Jarvis seems to be expressing the "object" of the conversation.

MS: So how does this notion of the "object" of the conversation help us in defining the criteria of a good interpretive discussion?

SHG: It requires us to look at what happens to the topic of the conversation and ask: Did an object emerge? Did an idea which addresses the question people really want to answer, one which follows from what was said in the conversation, actually arise? It seems to me that those are important indicators of a good interpretive discussion.

The new proposed criterion—being able to identify an object of the discussion—has several advantages. First, instead of simply asking whether the ideas mentioned are justified by evidence in the text, it allows us to consider the relation between the participants' ideas and the question they are addressing. It assumes that the ideas should address the question. It therefore assumes that a genuine concern or issue does arise for the group[11] and that the conversation progresses to the point where the comments imply its resolution.

Furthermore, it makes clear the value of a coherent conversation. Since it focuses on the relation between the issue that concerns the group and the response that the group makes to the issue, it emphasizes the unique, creative, "product" that arises from the interpretive discussion. While the resolution may be judged deficient on another occasion, perhaps because other aspects of the text are then emphasized, it can nevertheless be recognized for what it is: the outcome of the serious thinking the group has done at a given time. To identify a genuine issue the discussants care to resolve, and to address it to the point where the remarks have clear implication for a resolution, is indeed an accomplishment. And the present criterion recognizes it as such.

We can see now that although the discussions at Belden and Chalmers do share some features, there is at least one striking difference. In the Chalmers classroom, students seem to have listened to each other well enough to construct a genuine issue—one they seemed to care about resolving. Furthermore, they reflect on it long enough for their comments to imply a resolution. As we have seen, the problem the group came to focus upon was: Why did Capulet become so angry with Tybalt? And the resolution they move toward—as evidenced by Jarvis's last remark—was: Because Tybalt was trying to provoke Capulet into turning on Romeo.

One might argue that the Chalmers students did not really identify an issue they cared to resolve, that they were just playing the "game" of discussion, working out an issue, and addressing it. Indeed, Mrs. Spring may have harbored this perception. Even if one holds this view, it seems that they came much closer to a genuine issue than did the students at Belden. Indeed, the Chalmers discussants seemed to get drawn into the topic as the conversation progressed, even if they did not really care about it at the beginning.

So one may ask: Why did the Chalmers discussion reach this point, while the one at Belden did not? Part of the answer seems to be that the Chalmers students are more facile at following the rules for interpretive discussion. They know what the rules are and they follow them, almost in spite of the teacher at times. Indeed, they know that the teacher's viewpoint is no more important than their own, once the discussion begins. Because they understand that only the rules of discussion constrain them, they pursue their ideas and interests freely, so long as they appear to conform to the rules. Edna knew that as long as she could see evidence in the text for her idea that Capulet was scheming, she need not abandon it, despite Mrs. Spring's hesitation. One might say that the rules protect the students from being dominated by the teacher's beliefs and preoccupations; participants are thereby freed to work toward issues of genuine concern.

The Belden students, by contrast, are inexperienced in interpretive discussion. While they are beginning to follow some of the rules, they are still unsure of these, as we observed in Conversation 2. They are, therefore, unsure about how to use the rules to work out questions about the play that they care to resolve. Furthermore, one important avenue to such questions is personal experience. The fact that I did not encourage the Belden students to talk about their experiences and interests may well have inhibited the formation of meaningful discussion topics; for I did not show them how to harness these concerns to the rules of interpretive discussion.

In the next five conversations, we return to the Belden school, where I struggle on. Unfortunately, things get worse before they get better. But they do get better! I begin to learn how to manage my own concerns and at the same time, help students use their experiences to raise and address genuine issues in the discussion.

PART TWO

How Are Students and Teachers Transformed through Discussion?

CONVERSATION 4
The "Phony" Issue

As we have seen, even when the teacher makes a serious effort, she may have difficulty helping students use their personal experiences to illuminate the meaning of a text; for the teacher comes to the discussion with assumptions and beliefs about how people learn and about the things that students should be gaining from the experience. As the discussion proceeds, thoughts and concerns arise in the teacher's mind: Do the students comprehend the "surface," factual level of the text? Are people really listening to the comments that others make and thinking about their suggestions? In previous conversations, we have watched the teachers struggle to understand and assist the students, all the while guided by their own convictions and beliefs about what is taking place.

In the following discussion, the Belden students actually raise a question about the play that they seem eager to resolve. As it turns out, the issue probably arose from their personal experiences, although I certainly don't see that possibility at first. Indeed, I was convinced that the students were not raising the matter out of genuine concern for it. Rather, I felt that they wished to test or frustrate me. It is not until I discuss the incident with Mrs. Prince that I begin to shift my perspective and allow that the students may have had a serious concern after all.

The reader may feel that my view of the students is unnecessarily rigid. Why do I cling so tenaciously to my narrow and probably erroneous perspective? To put it more generally: Why is it so hard for the teacher to see what the observer can grasp to readily? D. A. Schön[1] has argued that only by *reflecting* on their classroom practices can teachers come to understand the basis for students' comments and thinking, for when immersed in the flux of classroom interaction, the teacher's judgment is often colored by preconceived assumptions about the text and the students.[2] In my case, it takes the conversations with Mrs. Prince to facilitate reflection and a bring about a subsequent shift in view.

The question the students raised concerns the end of act I, scene v, of

Romeo and Juliet. The scene is still Lord Capulet's party, and Romeo, over-whelmed with love at his first sight of Juliet, questions the nurse about the girl's identity:

> *
>
> ROMEO: What is her mother?
> NURSE: Marry, bachelor,
> Her mother is the lady of the house,
> And a good lady, and wise and virtuous.
> I nursed her daughter that you talked withal.
> I tell you, he that can lay hold of her
> Shall have the chinks [plenty of money].
> ROMEO: Is she a Capulet?
> O dear account! My life is my foe's debt.
>
> *

The students had some trouble reading the passage aloud, and again I as-sisted them. Fearing that they had not grasped the text, I began the discussion trying to find out:

> SHG: Now, when Romeo says: "Is she a Capulet?" who is he asking about here? Mason?
> MASON: Juliet. Her mother.
> SHG: Actually, just before that Romeo had said, "What is her mother?"—line 113. That is what you are thinking of, I think, Mason. And the nurse says to Romeo, "Marry, bachelor, / Her mother is the lady of the house." So what does Romeo know, now that he knows the mother is the lady of the house? Myrna.
> MYRNA: That she is a Capulet.
> SHG: That she is a Capulet because it is Capulet's party, right?
> COLETTE: Right.
> MP: Thank you, Colette. And so Juliet is a Capulet, right?

It is interesting that although Mason presents two answers to my initial question—who is Romeo asking about when he says "Is she a Capulet?"—I do not ask him to clarify which position he holds. Instead, I anticipate the reason for his two-pronged answer by referring to a passage that, it seems to me, may have given him the idea of "mother." Once again, my fear that he did not understand interferes with my asking him to clarify himself. I am too ea-ger to assure him that his thinking has been acceptable! Also, I am eager to make sure they have grasped the one "fact" that the passage presents, namely, that Juliet is a Capulet. Myrna and Colette seem to grasp the "fact," but then the discussion proceeds in a way I had not anticipated:

MICHAEL: We don't know that.

SHG: We don't know that, Michael?

COLETTE: And Romeo is a Montague!

SHG: Wait a minute! Michael is saying that we don't know that Juliet is a Capulet.

MASON: Michael is playing the fool!

MICHAEL: No! Doesn't Romeo say "Is she a Capulet?"

SHG: Yes he does, Michael—line 119. Now when he asks this, does this mean he does not know whether she is?

MARCY: No.

SHG: Does he know or doesn't he know?

SYLVIA: He don't.

SHG: He doesn't know?

MARCY: He doesn't know for sure.

SHG: Wait a minute!

MICHAEL: He can't be sure just because the mother is the lady of the house.

We cannot be sure that Juliet is Capulet? It seems to me that if there is one thing we can be certain of in the play, it is that Juliet is a Capulet! After all, the main theme seems to be the senselessness and destructiveness of the feud between the two families, the Montagues and the Capulets. If Juliet is not a Capulet, the central issue of the play is dissolved. Could there be any possibility that Shakespeare intends us to question the girl's lineage?

Given my perspective, it occurs to me that the students have merely misread the text. Surely the matter will resolve itself momentarily:

MP: Yes, Myrna.

MYRNA: You know her mother is one.

SHG: If the mother is a Capulet, is there any way that Juliet is not a Capulet? Henry?

HENRY: When her mother got married, she could have kept her maiden name.

SYLVIA: Her mother could have just wished to be a Capulet. Then her daughter wouldn't be one.

SHG: James, what do you think about this? Is it possible that Juliet might not be a Capulet?

JAMES: Yeah.

SHG: You think she might not be one?

> JAMES: It's possible, but she is one, though.
> SHG: Is it possible that Juliet could have been a Montague?
> A chorus of "NO!!" fills the air. "That would be crazy!"

The students have no doubt that Juliet cannot be a Montague. Yet they doubt she is a Capulet. And they are right that in the passage they have just read, the nurse has identified Juliet's mother as the lady of the house; she does not say that the mother is "Lady Capulet." Henry argues that if the mother had not changed her name, Juliet would not be a Capulet, i.e., she would not have the name "Capulet." Sylvia ventures that the mother might merely have wished to be a Capulet, the suggestion being that she may have wished to marry Lord Capulet but did not. Even James allows that Juliet might not be a Capulet, although he thinks she probably is.

He thinks she *probably* is? I cannot believe my ears. At this point, the students have read all of act I, during which Juliet's mother has been designated "Lady Capulet" twelve times in the text. This fact alone should demonstrate that Shakespeare intends us to think that the woman is married to Lord Capulet and that their child, Juliet, is therefore a Capulet. Even if the couple were not married, there is no question that Juliet is the daughter of Lord Capulet, as the students have seen that in act I, scene ii, the young man Paris goes to Lord Capulet asking for his daughter's hand in marriage.

Given these facts, I am persuaded that the students are not serious when they ask whether Juliet is a Capulet. I feel they are testing me to learn how much nonsense, in the name of discussion, I will tolerate. The conversation continues:

> SHG: But could Juliet have been other than a Capulet? Myrna.
> MYRNA: Yeah. Her mother could have got married and didn't change her name. Then the mother wouldn't be another Capulet.
> SYLVIA: Yeah! If the mother didn't change her name, then the mother wouldn't be another Capulet.
> RICHARD: But she probably did change it.
> SHG: So you think she is a Capulet, Richard? You think there is no question about it? Why would she have to be a Capulet, Richard?
> RICHARD: Because you said so!
> SHG: Because I said so?

There it is again! My claim must be correct since I am the teacher. But can they possibly be sincere in appealing to my authority as a basis for concluding that Juliet is a Capulet? Surely they are putting me on! And can they really believe, as both Myrna and Sylvia have said, that Juliet's mother might not have changed her name, might not be a Capulet, and that Juliet might not then be a Capulet? I am more convinced than ever that these students are not really interested in resolving the question they have posed, that they do not believe it is a real question. Yet I had let them pursue the topic. Why had I done so? I take the matter up with Mrs. Prince after class:

SHG: To what extent were they serious when they told me Juliet must be a Capulet because I said so? Were they just egging me on when they said that? I thought they were. But I couldn't be completely sure.

MP: Well, I tend to think that even when they are leading you on, they are still serious.

SHG: Huh?

MP: Take the discussion of whether Juliet was a Capulet. My feeling was that they were not completely sure about that.

SHG: You aren't serious!

MP: No, I am serious! I'm not sure that they were. I mean look at page 69, line 119, where Romeo says, "Is she a Capulet?" Now it is not clear whether he is asking the nurse or whether this is a rhetorical question, is it?

SHG: Well, in the previous speech, the nurse has told Romeo that Juliet's mother is the lady of the house. This makes it pretty clear that as her daughter, Juliet must be a Capulet. So it seems pretty clear that it is a rhetorical question, especially since Romeo goes right on to say, "O dear account! My life is my foe's debt." He knows she is a Capulet and that this may cost him his life.

MP: All right, the students may have picked up on the incredulous aspect of Romeo's comment. To pose this question—"Is she a Capulet?"—after what the nurse has said suggests that he himself cannot believe what appears to be the case. So when the students ask whether Juliet is a Capulet, they may be echoing Romeo's disbelief.

SHG: Yes, but Romeo was certain that Juliet was a Capulet.

MP: His logic told him that, but he could not believe it at first, could he?

SHG: Well, it did seem to stun him.

MP: You see, my thought is that the students had some sense of Romeo's predicament here—that they played out the possibility that he himself may well have entertained only for an instant, namely, that perhaps by some miracle Juliet was not a Capulet. After all, if only she weren't, his troubles would be over.

SHG: Yes, but the point is that the text leaves no room for doubt
about this matter.
MP: And clearly, Romeo doesn't really question in the way the
students did. But wouldn't he have liked to hold out their hope?
SHG: Of course. But he saw it was impossible.
MP: Maybe these students are not as yet bound by the text.
Maybe they enter the discussion in a somewhat noncritical,
nonanalytic fashion. Maybe at moments they catch the spirit of
what is happening and fly away with it, depart from the text.
And the fact that they are having a discussion seems to encourage
these flights of fancy.

Mrs. Prince has raised an important point about the Belden discussants.
Their inexperience with interpretive discussion means, very simply, that they
are not used to following its rules. For them, there remains the possibility of
departing from the text to speculate about possibilities that textual evidence
cannot support. While we cannot be certain that they did identify with
Romeo's incredulity in the way Mrs. Prince suggests, she has indeed identified
a pattern that we find among young or very inexperienced discussants.

MP: But look, if you thought they were doing this to you, why did
you let the discussion go on?
SHG: That is a good question, and I'm not sure I know the
answer. Part of it was that at least they were talking—and talking
about the play. I mean, that is a lot better than staring into space
like James seemed to be doing much of the time or answering me
in monosyllables. Now that I think of it, I guess I let them
continue the topic because I believe that *if* they are going to get
into an interesting conversation, they have to begin somewhere,
they have to be talking. Once they are talking, then I can question
them, draw out implications, and hopefully come to a genuine
question—a real issue that they want to resolve.[3]

My inability to terminate the discussion of whether Juliet was a Capulet
seems to have arisen from my belief that if a genuine issue is to form in the
conversation, students must be talking. The discussion of whether Juliet was a
Capulet was one of the first spontaneous exchanges I had witnessed among
the Belden students. How could I extinguish it when I believed that from it a
real question might evolve?

MP: Well, that wasn't a bad strategy. But I guess you feel
frustrated because the issue of whether Juliet was a Capulet seems
to you to be a nonissue, right?

SHG: Exactly. So letting them talk and then trying to draw out implications of what they said didn't succeed in helping to bring them to a real question, one they really weren't certain about.

MP: But I think you are missing something. This issue of whether Juliet was a Capulet or not *did seem to be a real question,* at least for some of them.[4] Remember when someone said that Juliet's mother might not have changed her name when she got married, in which case Juliet would not have been a Capulet?

SHG: Yes, I was wondering about that logic, but for some reason I didn't question them about it.

MP: I have two ideas about what they were getting at. One possibility is that if Juliet's mother did not change her name, then Juliet, as her daughter, might not have the name "Capulet." They could have been thinking of single-parent situations in which the mother does not change her name.

SHG: Yes, but even if she didn't change her name, Juliet still had Capulet as a father, which makes her a Capulet.

MP: Now wait a minute. The text they were looking at—with the nurse and Romeo—says that Juliet is the daughter of the lady of the house. That doesn't mean she's Capulet's daughter does it? And this is the second possibility: that Juliet's mother may have had a child by another man. Again, maybe these students are bringing their own experience to bear on their interpretation of the text. And my guess is that a number of them know of women who have children who are not their husband's, children born of other fathers. So maybe Juliet's mother did not change her name, or even if she did, maybe Juliet was not Lord Capulet's child. In either case, one might say that Juliet was not a Capulet.

———

Mrs. Prince's comments point out an interesting possibility about the role that personal experience may play in a discussion. On the one hand, I have been extolling it as the basis from which meaningful contact with the text can arise. Yet, it can also happen that discussants impose their experience on the text in such a way as to block out events or ideas that are otherwise visible.[5] From my perspective, it appears that the students' personal experiences may have distracted them from recognizing an obvious "fact" in the text—that Juliet was a Capulet.

We have now identified three reasons why the students might have raised the issue about Juliet's lineage. The first, which I strongly suspect at the start, is that they were testing or trying to provoke me. However, they may also have had empathy for Romeo's position, or they may have raised the question because of their own personal experience with family relationships. Indeed, their experience may have brought them to "misinterpret" the text—to overlook the abundant evidence that Juliet was a Capulet.[6]

> SHG: Yes, but what about act I, scene ii, where Capulet has a
> discussion with Paris about Juliet. There, Capulet refers to Juliet
> as his child! So I just don't see any doubt about this matter.
> MP: I agree with you—so far as the actual play is concerned—but
> I still think the issue of whether Juliet was a Capulet must have
> been a genuine issue for some of these students. For one thing,
> some of them may not have been here for the reading of act I,
> scene ii, or they may have forgotten it from last week, right? I
> mean it is not a lengthy exchange between Paris and Capulet. So
> with attention focused on the conversation between Romeo and
> the nurse in act I, scene v, it seems to me quite possible that the
> students may have forgotten Capulet's discussion with Paris.
> SHG: Yes, that is possible, and I think some of them were absent
> the day we read that scene.

Again, Mrs. Prince seems to have a point. It takes some time and experience in discussions before participants become committed to the task of using their ideas to explain as much of the text as possible. In time, they will work to recall evidence from all parts of the play to argue for their interpretations.[7] However, I am still not convinced that they pursue the issue of Juliet's lineage out of genuine interest in it or lack of experience with interpretive discussion.

> SHG: But if the question about whether Juliet was a Capulet *was* a
> real question, why did it come up?
> MP: I don't know, really.
> SHG: Maybe the best way to answer the question is to think
> about what they had been talking about when the issue came up.
> As I recall, we were looking at act II, scene i, where Benvolio and
> Mercutio, Romeo's companions, are trying to coax him out of
> hiding. Romeo, of course, has leapt the wall around Juliet's house
> and does not respond to the summons. The question we asked
> was whether Benvolio, who had been at the party with Romeo,
> knew that his companion had seen and fallen in love with Juliet.
> As far as I can see, this is an interpretive question; it's not clear
> whether Benvolio knows or not.

To give the reader some perspective on the next phase of my conversation with Mrs. Prince, let us return to the classroom discussion to see how the

Belden students managed the question of whether Benvolio knew about
Romeo and Juliet. The following exchange occurred just before the students
raised the issue of whether Juliet is a Capulet:

SHG: So, has Benvolio seen that Romeo has fallen in love with
Juliet at the party?
MASON: Yes. It's in line 30 on page 73, act II, scene i.
SHG: What does Benvolio say here?
MASON: Benvolio says, "Blind is his [Romeo's] love and best
befits the dark."
SHG: Now look back at page 69, line 120, act I, scene v, the scene
of Capulet's party, where Romeo says: "Is she a Capulet? / O
dear account! My life is my foe's debt." And then what does
Benvolio say, Mason?
MASON: Benvolio says: "Away, be gone; the sport is at the best."
SHG: What does Benvolio mean here, Myrna?
MYRNA: He is saying that Romeo picked out the best one. He
picked the best one.
SHG: In the first part of the line, when Benvolio says "Away, be
gone," what is Benvolio saying to Romeo?
COLETTE: He knows it is going to be trouble.
SHG: He says, "Away." Colette says this means he knows it is
going to be trouble. What do you think of that, Myrna?
MYRNA: He is telling Romeo, "You are the boss."
COLETTE: No! He is telling Romeo to leave.
SHG: Well, Myrna, what does he want Romeo to do?
MYRNA: Forget.
SHG: Forget who?
COLETTE: Forget about Rosaline!
MP: Thank you Colette!
SHG: Now, when Romeo says, "Is she a Capulet?" who is he
asking about here, Mason?
MASON: Juliet. Her Mother.

What followed was the exchange we have seen before. So we see now exactly
what preceded the point where the issue of whether Juliet was a Capulet arose.
When asked whether Benvolio knows of Romeo's feelings toward Juliet, Mason says that he does know and cites evidence from act II, scene i. I, however,
do not question Mason about the line: I do not ask what Benvolio means or in
other ways explore the relevance of that line for our question, despite the fact
that is relevant. Here the student is responding just as he should—citing a passage to support his position—and I ignore him. Why? Because the evidence he

cites is not the evidence I had in mind. So focused was I upon the evidence in act I, scene v, that I bypassed Mason's passage altogether.

Furthermore, once back in act I, I do not ask Mason to interpret the passage that he reads but turn instead to Myrna. As it happens, Myrna seems to me to have little idea of what Benvolio is saying, and Colette quickly jumps in to correct her. Again I forego a chance to explore Myrna's thoughts and cling instead to the "correct" interpretation that Colette offers. As for Colette, she uses Myrna's remark that Benvolio is trying to get Romeo to "forget" in order to enter the conversation again.

MP: So why do the students raise the question of whether Juliet is a Capulet?

SHG: Well, OK, I guess I do think they are trying to give me a message—that they want me to realize how frustrated they are. What they mean is: "I am not getting enough from this. Please let's stop." These kids want to tell me that they cannot enter this world that Shakespeare has created, that they are on the outside, and that I am failing to open the door for them.

MP: So they didn't just raise this question about whether Juliet was a Capulet to entertain themselves, to enter into some activity that they could understand and participate in?

SHG: Well, let's say not *just* to entertain themselves! They did want to entertain themselves; they did want to talk about something they could understand and relate to. And they certainly know that I am going to listen to their questions and that above all I want them to talk. So they wanted to talk about something *they could talk about*—like whether Juliet was a Capulet. But they also picked this topic to let me know that the only thing they could talk about was a nonissue, that they couldn't really enter into the genuine issues of this pay. Which, as I said, was their way of telling me that I was failing to bring them into contact or dialogue with it.

MP: But in this instance, I am not convinced that they really were trying to tell you that you were failing when they raised the issue of whether Juliet was a Capulet. It does seem to me possible that their experience, and not their frustration, provoked the question about Juliet. This is what I said earlier. I mean if you knew families in which the children were not the children of the adults in the house, wouldn't you raise the question?

SHG: OK, let's assume that given their experience, the students did believe that Juliet might not have been a Capulet. Why did they make such an issue over this point?

MP: But isn't that always how we arrive at questions—our past experience throws us into a particular relation with the new events we encounter and makes us see some issues rather than others?[8] Given Romeo's question—"Is she a Capulet?"—plus the sympathy they may have had for Romeo's wish that Juliet not be a Capulet, I think the students arrived at the question of whether she was one.

So we are back to asking, as we did at the end of Conversation 3: Does a genuine issue for the students arise in this discussion? And does the conversation proceed far enough for an object to emerge, for there to be implication for its resolution, given what was said? If we can answer both questions affirmatively, then the discussion has met the last of the criteria we considered previously.

On the one hand, there now appears to be the possibility that the students did have a genuine question about whether Juliet was a Capulet. The problem with their question, however, is that given the text, even just act I, it cannot stand as a genuine issue; there is simply too much evidence to suggest that Juliet is a Capulet. So an object of the conversation cannot arise, for the question may be definitively resolved.

It seems we must conclude that the Belden students do not identify and pursue a genuine textual issue, even though they seemed to be drawing upon their personal experiences. And yet, one cannot say that there was no progress over their previous discussion. For unlike the conversation about "weaning," a spontaneous question that seemed to have had meaning to the students did emerge. Furthermore, we saw more evidence that students were following the rules of interpretive discussion, even to the point of seeking and finding appropriate textual references without the teacher's assistance (as Mason did when asked whether Benvolio knew that Romeo had fallen for Juliet). The discussion seems also to have moved students to new ideas, although the idea that Juliet was not a Capulet stands only if one disregards part of the evidence. Finally, it seems that the students were listening to each other somewhat more on this occasion.

SHG: Well, maybe you are right. I have to admit that after that discussion about Juliet being a Capulet, the students did begin talking more easily, I think—except for James. He just wouldn't budge. And I'm sorry, but that one kid just gets to me. You can't say I succeeded with him!

MP: I know what you mean. He just doesn't seem to want to contribute. He refused to read today again, and he seems only to

respond when called upon. If you leave him alone, he says
nothing. Of course, we are only just starting act II!
SHG: Well, I guess you are right. I need to have some patience.
And after all, something rather remarkable did happen after that
discussion about Juliet being a Capulet.
MP: What was that?

The exchange with the students had gone like this:

SHG: OK, if it is pretty clear that Juliet is a Capulet, then let's ask
one more question about Benvolio—
MICHAEL: I think he knows.
SHG: You think he knows what?
MASON: I think he does too.
MICHAEL: That Romeo likes Juliet.
SHG: Is that why Benvolio is trying to make Romeo leave the
party, Michael?
MICHAEL: Yeah!

I reviewed the exchange with Mrs. Prince and made my observation.

SHG: The fact that the students anticipate my question about
Benvolio and jump to respond indicates not only that the text has
come to have some meaning to them but that they have become
interested in responding to an interpretive question—a question
for which there is no definitive answer. This is a big step for even
two students to take.
MP: I think you are right about that. And maybe we will see
others take it as time goes on.

   In the next conversation, we watch as more Belden students begin to venture interpretations. The fact that they have already begun to do so suggests
that perhaps it was not a mistake to let them pursue the question of whether
Juliet was a Capulet after all. Perhaps it opened them up to the pleasures of
serious reflection.

CONVERSATION 5
The "Genuine" Issue

In this conversation, we see the Belden students discussing genuine questions concerning *Romeo and Juliet*. While their remarks still seem random and arbitrary at times, the questions they explore are ones not answered definitively in the text. What is happening to the students such that they are beginning to form and struggle with textual issues? And why does James, a student who for so many sessions refused to contribute to the discussion except when called upon, suddenly become an active participant? We ponder these questions in what follows.

The student are now discussing act II, scene ii, of the play, the famous "balcony scene" in which Romeo, hiding in the garden beneath Juliet's window, spies his love and speaks to her.

*

ROMEO: But soft! What light through yonder window breaks?
It is the East, and Juliet is the sun!
Arise, fair sun, and kill the envious moon,
Who is already sick and pale with grief,
That thou her maid art far more fair than she.
Be not her maid, since she is envious.
Her vestal livery [virginity] is but sick and green,
And none but fools do wear it. Cast it off.
It is my lady! O, it is my love!
O, that she knew she were!
She speaks, yet she says nothing. What of that?
Her eye discourses; I will answer it.
I am too bold, 'tis not to me she speaks.
Two of the fairest stars in all heaven,
Having some business, do entreat her eyes
To twinkle in their spheres till they return.
What if her eyes were there, they in her head?
The brightness of her cheek would shame those stars
As daylight doth a lamp; her eyes in heaven

Would through the airy region stream so bright
That birds would sing and think it were not night.
See how she leans her cheek upon her hand!
O, that I were a glove upon that hand,
That I might touch that cheek!

SHG: Now, if you look at Romeo's speech, James, do you think he is nervous? Here he is in love with this girl, Juliet, whom he sees at the window. But he is not supposed to be there, right? Romeo isn't supposed to be there in Juliet's garden?
COLETTE: Right!
MP: Thank you, Colette. Now James, do you think that Romeo is worried about being there?
JAMES: No.
SHG: How come he isn't afraid?
JAMES: He is in love.
SHG: He is so in love that he doesn't fear anything? Does everybody agree with that? Do you feel that Romeo is nervous at all about being there?
MARCY: Nope.
SHG: He feels pretty comfortable? What about Juliet? How does she feel? Marcy.
MARCY: She daydreams.
MARVIN: She feels beautiful!
SHG: Where do you think she says that, Marvin? Is it line 33, page 75, where Juliet says: "Romeo, Romeo! Wherefore art thou, Romeo"? See line 33? Is that where she is feeling beautiful, Marvin?
MARVIN: I don't know.
SHG: It is interesting that they are in a dangerous situation, but does anybody feel any danger? James says no, Romeo is so in love that he doesn't feel any danger at all.
COLETTE: He don't.
SHG: OK, Colette, what about Juliet? Does she feel any danger?
COLETTE: Yeah.
SHG: Where do you get the idea that she feels some danger?
COLETTE: Let me find it.

I am taking no chances today. I begin right off with an interpretive question: Do either Romeo or Juliet feel anxious about Romeo's presence in the garden? While one has to interpret the speeches to address the issue, there is plenty of evidence to go on, and I hope the students will relate their comments to it. Do they do so? Marvin and Marcy both say that Juliet feels no anxiety about Romeo's presence, that she "feels beautiful," as Marvin puts it. But they do not feel compelled to defend this claim with lines from the play. Even when I direct Marvin toward what seems to me to be supportive material, he refuses to focus on and interpret the passage. Colette, on the other hand, goes seeking evidence for her view that Juliet feels anxious. Very soon, Colette calls out:

COLETTE: Page 76, line 65.
SHG: OK, Colette. Why don't you read it?
COLETTE: Juliet says:

> How camest thou hither, tell me, and wherefore?
> The orchard walls are high and hard to climb,
> And the place, death, considering who thou art,
> If any of my kinsmen find thee here.

SHG: What is she saying here?
COLETTE: If her people find him there, they are going to try to kill him.

Colette has focused the group on lines that seem to contradict Marvin and Marcy. The passage she reads does not indicate that Juliet is "daydreaming" or "feeling beautiful." The evidence she presents shifts attention to the opposite resolution, namely, that Juliet is anxious about Romeo's presence in the garden. James pursues the topic.

JAMES: They are going to kill him, if they catch him!
SHG: Interesting, James. So would you say it sounds like Juliet is worried about Romeo's being there—from these lines?
JAMES: Yes!
SHG: So does Romeo get worried? You said he wasn't worried at first because he was so in love. After Juliet makes this statement, which Colette just read here, does Romeo get nervous?
COLETTE: No.
SHG: You say no, Colette? Well if you say no, find some lines to show us he is not anxious after that.
COLETTE: Right at the bottom.
SHG: Wait, Colette, let James and Sylvia find it.
COLETTE: Page 75.
SHG: Just mark it for a second, then you can go to it when we are ready.

Colette is playing the game.[1] She does not spontaneously seek a passage to support her position, but she moves to do so when asked. Meanwhile, James is getting drawn into the issue on the floor:

> JAMES: He never gets scared.
> SHG: He is not afraid, James? He never gets frightened?
> JAMES: He is not afraid of Juliet.
> SHG: What is he afraid of?
> JAMES: She is frightened if they catch him.
> SHG: Is *he* afraid of anything?
> JAMES: Not right now.
> SHG: He doesn't get frightened even when Juliet says, "If my kinsmen catch you, it is death for you." He still isn't afraid, James?
> JAMES: He knows he shouldn't be out.

Why does James say that Romeo is "not afraid of Juliet"? Where does he get any idea that he might be afraid of her? This comment seems to me all but arbitrary and I find it quite confusing. Likewise, why, in response to my question about whether Romeo fears anything, does James respond that Romeo "knows he shouldn't be out"? How does that comment address the question? While these remarks strike me a little bizarre—indeed, I take the first one up with Mrs. Prince after class—I am impressed that James seems to be drawn into the issue of whether Romeo and Juliet are afraid. So I turn James's attention to a passage in the play, hoping that he will begin to do what Colette has done, that is, work to support his interpretations with textual evidence. But Colette disrupts my efforts:

> SHG: What does Romeo mean when, right after Juliet says, "If my kinsmen, if any of them find thee, this is a place of death for you, Romeo," and then Romeo says, "With love's light wings did I o'erperch these walls"—
> COLETTE: That's what I said! That's my place!
> SHG: OK, Colette, why don't you read it.
> COLETTE: Romeo says:
>
>> With love's light wings did I o'erperch these walls,
>> For stony limits cannot hold love out,
>> And what love can do, that dares love attempt,
>> Therefore thy kinsmen are no stop to me.[2]
>
> What he is trying to say is that he is not afraid. They can't stop him because he is so in love.
> SHG: Marcy, why is Romeo not afraid?

MARCY: He believes that nobody can keep him from the person
he loves.

SHG: So he is stronger than all this hate between the families?
Does Juliet, Marvin, does Juliet agree with Romeo? Look at the
next line there. Does she agree that love is stronger than all of
these barriers of hatred?

MARVIN: I don't know.

SHG: How about looking at line 70. See what line 70 says? Juliet
says, "If they do see thee . . ." What does she say?

COLETTE: They will kill him.

I have turned James's attention to Romeo's lines— "With love's light wings I
did o'erperch these walls"—but when Colette bursts in that this is the passage
she has been waiting to read, I give her the floor, leaving James in the middle of
the exchange. Now, for several sessions I have been struggling in hopes that
James would participate in the discussion freely and actively. Why, then, when
Colette finishes, do I question first Marcy and then Marvin? Why don't I return to James, even if only to ask him whether he agrees with Colette's
interpretation? Why don't I return to the issue James raised earlier, namely,
whether Romeo fears Juliet? Have I given James the message that I am really
not very interested in his ideas?

SYLVIA: Juliet says, "They will murder thee."

SHG: All right, Sylvia.

SYLVIA: Maybe she's trying to get Romeo killed.

JAMES: Is she trying to get Romeo killed??

SHG: Is she, James? Go ahead and read the line.

JAMES: "If they do see thee, they will murder thee."

COLETTE: Meaning if they do see him, they will murder him.

SHG: OK, Colette. So what is Juliet saying to Romeo? Myrna.

MYRNA: You had better hide. If they catch Romeo, he's just as
good as dead.

JAMES: He had better leave before they catch him.

When Sylvia says that Juliet may be "trying to get Romeo killed," James is
incredulous. How can such a thing be possible? His response to Sylvia is to
gesture toward the text, and I invite him to read the line. Before he has a
chance to interpret it, Colette jumps in and does it for him. But James is not
put off. He interprets Juliet's remark for himself— "He [Romeo] had better
leave before they catch him"—and seems to recognize that this evidence does
not support Sylvia's suggestion that Juliet wishes harm to Romeo. So James's

interpretation of Juliet's feelings has moved him not only to reject Sylvia's suggestion emphatically but to seek appropriate textual evidence for his own view. In the next exchange, he goes on to describe Romeo's attitude toward Juliet.

SHG: OK, now James says that Juliet wants Romeo to leave. Do you think that is what she is saying, Marcy? Do you think that is what she wants?
MARCY: No, I think that she's just letting him know that if they find him they're going to kill him.
MP: All right. She has told him now twice, hasn't she? She says, listen, if they find you, you are dead and gone. Now, how does Romeo respond to that? Look at the next line that Romeo says, page 76. James, could you read those lines and tell us what Romeo is saying?
JAMES:
> Alack, there lies more peril in thine eye
> Than twenty of their swords! Look thou but sweet,
> And I am proof against their enmity.

He means that even if they fight him, he will come back.
SHG: Great! If the kinsmen attack him, he would still come back to the garden another time?
JAMES: He would find a way to come back.
SHG: So nothing can stop him.

I am quite certain that James does not understand the word "enmity," and I find his interpretation a little off the mark. Where does he get the idea Romeo is saying he will return no matter what? Once again, I do not ask him to explain his comment—a pattern of mine that I discuss with Mrs. Prince after class. Instead, my spontaneous response is "Great"—great that he has read the lines and that he has ventured an interpretation immediately. I know I should ask James to explain his comment, but the moment is passed, and the discussion is beginning to move on its own, sweeping James and others with it:

SHG: What do you want to say, Marvin?
MARVIN: Juliet loves this Romeo guy. Who wants to kill him?
SHG: Who would want to kill him: She said, "my kinsmen." James.
JAMES: They're the royal servants.
MARCY: No, her kinfolks.
MP: Mason?
MASON: It could be her brother. We would never know.
SYLVIA: It *is* her kinfolks—her daddy!

SHG: What are kinsmen?

SYLVIA: Her kinfolk!

SHG: People who are related to her, right? Now that could be the servants as well. That is, people who serve are often relatives. Marvin?

MARVIN: Why do they want to kill him?

SHG: Myrna.

MYRNA: Because he is a Montague. They hate Montagues; Montagues are their enemy.

Here we see that James and other students, who have thus far been on the periphery in these discussions, are raising and addressing questions about the text. Marvin asks who wants to kill Romeo. Marvin's is a "fact" question, as there seems to be one answer, which Myrna states clearly. But by posing the question, he shows that he has become interested in understanding what is happening in the play. Furthermore, others are eager to address his question—another sign that they have been drawn into the conversation. Notice that they do not hesitate to explore the meaning of the word "kinsmen." This time, there is no request to seek the dictionary's help, and the associations to the word arise spontaneously: "Royal servants," suggests James; "Kinfolk," venture Marcy and Sylvia; "Her brother," says Mason. I try to draw their ideas about the word together and the discussion rolls toward another formation of the issue that has begun to grip us:

MP: Well, one thing I noticed about Juliet is that she never says, "Go home." This goes back to the discussion between Colette and Marcy. Juliet never really says, "Go away." Why doesn't she tell Romeo to go away?

COLETTE: Because she is in love with him.

SHG: So she is in love, Colette, but she knows he is in danger. Still, she doesn't tell him to leave.

COLETTE: Right.

MP: She wants him to be there?

COLETTE: Right.

MARCY: They love each other.

MP: They love each other but she never tells him to go. Don't you think that is interesting? If you love somebody, and they come to your house, and they are in danger if they stick around—may get hurt—but you never tell the person to go. Isn't that interesting? Colette.

COLETTE: If she don't tell him to go, she's trying to get him hurt.

SHG: Do you think she is trying to get him hurt? Sylvia.

SYLVIA: No, she's in love and she wants to see her man. If he
leaves and gets hurt, she might never see him again.
MARCY: I think she's trying to tell him to come over to her house.
SHG: So she wants him to come in, Marcy?
MARCY: Yeah.
SHG: But doesn't she worry about it?
MARCY: She said, if they see him outside they are going to get
him. She is trying to give him the idea to come into her bedroom.
JAMES: She wants to hide him?
MARCY: No, she doesn't. She wants to get married.

It has happened. There is a genuine textual issue on the floor, one raised by
the play that the students care to resolve. Mrs. Prince posed the question initially: Why doesn't Juliet tell Romeo to leave the garden? Yet, as she says, the
question was actually raised by an earlier exchange between Colette and Marcy. How have the students been drawn into the dilemma?

Part of the answer may be that in the above sequence, Mrs. Prince makes an
important move. She asks the students to consider what they would do if they
were in Juliet's position. Would they tell a lover to leave, knowing that he or
she was in danger? As the students begin to ponder their own experience
aloud, they make statements which contradict their earlier interpretations of
the play.[3] For example, Colette reasons that Juliet is trying to harm Romeo,
since if she were not, she would tell him to leave. The idea that Juliet wishes
Romeo harm certainly contradicts Colette's earlier claim that Juliet loves the
young man. To Colette's suggestion that Juliet wants Romeo to be hurt, I respond by asking Sylvia what she thinks of that possibility. Sylvia rejects the
idea, arguing that Juliet loves Romeo, wants to see him, and fears that she will
not see him again if he does get hurt. Sylvia's comment raises the possibility
that Juliet does not tell Romeo to leave because she wants to hide him in her
bedroom—a new suggestion. To this idea, Marcy says no, Juliet wants Romeo
in her bedroom not to hide him but because she loves him and wants to marry
him, pure and simple.

We have on the floor two opposing views about why Juliet does not tell
Romeo to leave the garden: Colette says that the young girl wants Romeo
harmed; Sylvia says Juliet wants to see Romeo and fears his being harmed.
Marcy and Sylvia further disagree about why Juliet wants Romeo in her bedroom. As the conversation continues, Mrs. Prince presses the students to keep
thinking about what they would do in Juliet's situation. Interestingly enough,
Marcy is not dissuaded from her position, despite the fact that her view of
what she would do seems to contradict it.

MP: It is still interesting to me that Juliet didn't say, "Go away." If you really loved somebody, wouldn't you tell your loved one—
JAMES: Juliet is fourteen years old!
MP: But wouldn't you say to your lover, "Please run away. I will talk to you tomorrow"?
COLETTE: Uh-huh.
SYLVIA: Uh-huh.
RICHARD: I wouldn't.
COLETTE: Better than for him to be dead!
MARCY: I would rather see him safe.
SHG: So would you send him, Marcy?
MARCY: I would send him so fast.
MP: Now James is suggesting something interesting when he says that Juliet is only fourteen years old. Do you think Juliet doesn't tell Romeo to go because she is so young?
COLETTE: Yeah.
MP: Let's take this a little further. Is it possible that young love can be a little selfish? What do we mean by "selfish," Henry?
HENRY: Keeping things to yourself.
COLETTE: Concerned only with oneself.
SHG: So, Colette, is she thinking about him or herself?
COLETTE: I think she is thinking about him.
MYRNA: Both.
MARCY: Yes, both. She wants him now because her love might get killed.
SHG: So what you are suggesting, Marcy, is that Juliet wants the pleasure of the moment while she can get it. Is that what she is doing?
COLETTE: No, it's just like you said. She is trying to tell him to wait until they get older.
MP: Is she?
COLETTE: Yeah.
MARCY: No, they're so in love that they—if they are that in love, they couldn't wait.[4]

Although Marcy says that if her lover were in danger she would "send him so fast," she emphatically denies that Juliet is doing this. When Colette suggests that Juliet is trying to get Romeo to wait, Marcy insists that the young girl is too much in love to wait. Perhaps James's comment that Juliet is fourteen has inspired two different views of her. Colette imagines her telling Romeo to wait until they are older, while Marcy insists that the lovers cannot wait, perhaps, as Mrs. Prince has suggested, because they are so young. While

Colette seems to feel that Juliet is "thinking about" Romeo out of concern for
his welfare, Marcy says it is because she wants to have her lover now.

How is one to explain the fact that for the first time, the Belden students
have become genuinely engaged in textual issues during this discussion? Why
did James become an active participant, despite my lack of encouragement at
times? Why did Marcy reach such strong convictions about Juliet's motives?
Mrs. Prince and I pursue these questions in the following conversation:

> SHG: It seems to me that James was like a different person today. I
> wonder what happened to him? He was actively contributing
> throughout the discussion.
> MP: Maybe he somehow felt he really had a lot to say.
> SHG: But how did he reach that conclusion, I wonder. Not that it
> isn't true, of course, but why today?
> MP: You know, now that I think about it, it seems as though every
> time he said something you asked him a question about what he
> said, or you related it to what others had been saying, or you
> asked him a new question. So that what he said had a place in the
> conversation, and he could see that.
> SHG: Why don't you give me some examples. I've rather
> forgotten what I said to him.
> MP: Well, at the beginning you asked whether Romeo was afraid
> when he was in the orchard, and James said no, that Romeo was
> too much in love.
> SHG: Yes, that was a good answer. There was textual evidence to
> support it, but James really had to interpret what Romeo said
> and did to arrive at his conclusion.
> MP: And the next thing you did was to ask for the evidence. It
> seems to me that move took James's suggestion seriously—made
> others think about his point further. And since there was evidence
> to support it, everyone could see that James had made a
> contribution.

The first point is, then, that responding to students' comments in a serious
manner—relating them to what others have said, asking for textual evidence
to support the view, questioning its meaning, for example—encourages the
student to participate in the discussion. Yet, the fact remains that those very
moves on the part of the teacher may have little effect if the participants do not
see the importance of their contributions for themselves. They need to see that
what they have said really does advance the discussion. It may well be that
James began to participate because he saw that some of his contributions—for

example, that Romeo was not anxious about being in the garden, that Juliet was fourteen—helped to explain what was happening in the play.

If the inference about James is correct, then we must raise anew the dilemma that we encountered in Conversation 4: How does the teacher handle the situation in which a student's comment seems to be totally random, off the wall, and unlikely to make a contribution to the group's reflection upon the topic under consideration? Isn't is possible that close scrutiny of such remarks may only humiliate the student?

SHG: Well, I'm glad I did something right. Because there were several moments when I just had to ignore what James was saying.

MP: Why did you do that?

SHG: Because some of the things he said were simply random, totally off the wall.

MP: Which of his remarks do you have in mind?

SHG: Well, the first strange thing he said was that Romeo was not afraid of Juliet. Where did he get the idea that Romeo might be afraid of Juliet, anyway? I just didn't see any hope of a real issue here and I didn't want him to feel discouraged with himself.

MP: But look at Romeo's first speech in the scene, the one we began with today. See line 10, where he spies Juliet on the balcony and says, "It is my lady! O, it is my love! / O, that she knew that she were!" And then he says: "Her eye discourses; I will answer it. / I am too bold; 'tis not to me she speaks." Doesn't it sound as though Romeo might be afraid of Juliet?

SHG: Well, he certainly was hesitant to speak to her at that point. But do you think James saw that? I mean, we read that speech but we didn't even discuss it.

MP: Then after Romeo hears Juliet's "O Romeo, Romeo! Wherefore are thou Romeo" speech, he says: "Shall I hear more or shall I speak at this?" That sounds pretty hesitant to me.

SHG: OK, so you think James's idea that Romeo might be afraid of Juliet did come from those lines in the play?

MP: Right! And if not, then where did it come from?

It is very hard to imagine that some things students say are serious contributions, that they are offering a suggestion that they believe others should think about. Often, it seems as if there is no reason, no evidence that can be brought forth, for the idea and that it cannot possibly advance the conversation in some way. In the preceding exchange, Mrs. Prince has pointed to evidence in the play I had not noticed during the discussion, evidence that supports James's idea that Romeo might be afraid of Juliet. In so doing, she raises the question of whether there is such a thing as a totally random idea. Her "theory" about the matter follows:

> MP: You know, I'm more convinced than ever that there really is no such thing as totally random, arbitrary comments in these discussions. It seems that anything someone says has to come up for some reason. That is, there has to be something about the situation that makes it arise, makes it pop into one's head.[5] Even if James was bored and "just talking" when he said that Romeo was not afraid of Juliet—meaning, talking without careful reflection—his remark must have been in response to some other thoughts or ideas that were part of this situation, right? So if he didn't get the idea of Romeo's being afraid of Juliet from Shakespeare, there must have been something in the situation that raised the idea. And the fact is that Romeo does seem hesitant, almost fearful, of addressing Juliet in the speeches that open act II, scene ii.
>
> SHG: But I still can't believe that James really understood this play as well you seem to be suggesting.
>
> MP: I'm not saying he did "understand" certain things. I can imagine a lot of questions about it he would have had difficulty answering. But maybe he was getting more than we think. Because that strange-sounding, off-the-wall comment may really be coming as a consequence of reading what Shakespeare writes, even though it doesn't seem like it.

If Mrs. Prince is right, then it would seem to mean that even arbitrary-sounding remarks that students make in an interpretive discussion might profitably be explored.[6] That is, the students could be questioned about the meaning of these comments and asked to provide evidence to support them. For the strange suggestions—the ones that seem most unlikely to further the discussion—may be the very ones that open up whole new perspectives on the issues. What would have happened to the conversation if I had asked James what made him think that Romeo was afraid of Juliet? Or if I had asked Sylvia, when she first made an effort to comment, why she thought Juliet wanted to harm Romeo? As Mrs. Prince and I have begun to realize, these suggestions may not have been so arbitrary as they first seemed.

But while we may reason that students ought be questioned about their "off-the-wall" remarks, teaching is not always driven by such reasoning, as the next exchange makes clear:

MP: So, say again why you did not ask James to explain what gave him the idea that Romeo might or might not be afraid of Juliet.

SHG: I was afraid to do it! I mean I didn't see any evidence that could allow us to discuss the matter. And I didn't want to question James in a way that would make his contribution look silly, for fear he would never speak again! So I just let it drop.

MP: But we have already seen that there is some evidence that Romeo may have been afraid to speak to Juliet, which means that James might have come out better than you thought, had you questioned him.

SHG: Yes, but I didn't see that evidence! I just thought the remark was off the wall!

MP: So you didn't want to take a chance on making him look silly.

SHG: Right!

MP: But doesn't the conversation we have just had suggest you should have taken that chance, that even though you don't see the evidence, it may well be there, since that idea must have come from somewhere?

SHG: Maybe. But I don't think I have enough faith yet! I mean our theory—that anything someone says in discussions like this comes up because it fits somehow, somewhere, with other things that have been said—is just a theory. Meanwhile, there are my gut-level beliefs about what makes people participate.

MP: Such as?

SHG: Such as that students will not participate if they don't feel good about the things that happen to the comments that they make. And James is so sensitive and so easily discouraged! Furthermore, if I didn't see any evidence for Romeo's being afraid—or not being afraid—of Juliet, how could I expect James to find it?

MP: Are you saying that if you didn't see the evidence, he wouldn't be able to either?

SHG: Right. I mean it's a hard thing for Colette and some of the better students to do.

MP: But that doesn't mean James couldn't have done it.

SHG: I suppose not. But I was afraid that he would fail, so I didn't

try. I admit it. But are you saying I should have had more
courage?
MP: I think that's what our earlier conversation about Romeo's
hesitation in speaking to Juliet suggests, yes.
SHG: So you would have questioned James, knowing he might
have had nothing to say, felt embarrassed, and given up?
MP: I'm not saying I would have questioned him. I understand
why you did what you did. And indeed, your tactics worked; he
remained an active participant to the end. And especially when
you don't see how to help him find evidence that will support his
idea, you tend to let it drop rather than rubbing that in—
SHG: Right.
MP: Yet, I do think our "theory" suggests we ought to have a little
more faith! And who knows, James might have found that
passage!
SHG: Maybe, but somehow, I doubt it.

    While I can see Mrs. Prince's point, I have a hard time imagining myself
questioning James as she suggests. And yet there was Marcy, who, like James,
insisted on an interpretation of Juliet that did not seem to be supported by the
lines we had been reading. Nowhere does Shakespeare indicate that Juliet was
eager for Romeo to enter her bedroom. In Marcy's case, our questioning
seemed to sustain and deepen her convictions about Juliet's motives rather
than undermine them. How did that happen?

SHG: Let's forget about James now and take another example. I
have to say that at first, I was surprised to hear Marcy insisting
that Juliet was trying to lure Romeo into her bedroom. This is
certainly not what Shakespeare says in the text.
MP: Are you really telling me Marcy's idea doesn't make any
sense? I mean if there was anything Juliet probably wanted, it
was to get Romeo into her bedroom, especially as their
conversation went on. Now, I admit that Juliet doesn't invite him
in, but is there any doubt about what she desires?
SHG: OK, I admit that Marcy has certainly made a powerful
suggestion about Juliet's motives, one that seems consistent with
what we know of her character and situation. I wonder how
Marcy came to hold that view of Juliet with such conviction?
MP: Perhaps it was my question about what they, the students,
would do if they were in Juliet's situation. It seems as though
Marcy's personal experience gave her this sense of Juliet's desires,
don't you think? After all, they are both fourteen!

SHG: Yet Marcy said that she would send her lover away, which is not what Juliet did.

MP: True, but Marcy had no trouble explaining why Juliet behaved as she did. As she put it, the couple was too much in love to wait! Doesn't that idea seem to arise from Marcy's own ideas about the power of passion?

SHG: Perhaps. I remember when I asked Marcy whether Juliet wanted to hide Romeo in her bedroom, and she insisted that no, Juliet wanted to marry him. Maybe that's what she, Marcy, would have wanted to do with Romeo!

MP: At the same time, the idea that Juliet is madly in love with Romeo and wants to marry him is certainly consistent with the characterization of Juliet that Shakespeare presents. So Marcy is not ignoring the play in favor of her experience.

It may be that by projecting and reflecting on her own feelings about Juliet's situation, Marcy gained a perspective on Juliet. Given her perspective, the student had no hesitation in rejecting the possibility that Juliet wished Romeo harm, or that she wanted Romeo in her bedroom in order to hide him, or that she was telling Romeo to wait. These ideas are inconsistent with Marcy's intuitions about Juliet's motives. In rejecting the suggestions, she seems to deepen her conviction that Juliet wants Romeo to come into her bedroom, and for one purpose only!

Perhaps questioning students about their assertions, even the strange, random-sounding ones, might benefit the discussion in the long run. If Mrs. Prince had not asked the group members what they would have done in Juliet's situation, Marcy might never have arrived at a perspective that, in fact, made more plausible her initial conviction about Juliet, a conviction that had seemed unfounded. Treating the odd comment as though it has some basis of support may allow the students to discover the appropriateness and usefulness of their own intuitions. It may then teach them—as well as the teacher!—to have patience and respect for ideas that seem barely tolerable. For such ideas often turn out to open a new and powerful perspective on the text and upon life as we know it.

Before moving on, let us note that the Belden students are making great progress with interpretive discussion. They are becoming used to its rules, as they are now willing to address interpretive questions whose answers are indeterminate. They are seeking and finding evidence in the play to support their interpretations, and doing so spontaneously at moments. The discussion we have just observed moved the participants to new ideas, and often ones that were supported by the text, although they did not always seem to be at first. The students also seemed to pay greater attention to each other's statements, even moving to respond to the questions or ideas that arose.

The product of this progress, it appears, is that for the first time, the students have begun to invest themselves in the conversation to the point of forming and addressing genuine textual issues. The question of why Juliet does not tell Romeo to leave the garden is a case in point. The group's reflection on the issue was sustained enough for several possibilities about its resolution to emerge and be evaluated. For example, by the end, Sylvia, and perhaps others, seems to have given up the idea that Juliet wanted Romeo to suffer harm. While no clear "object" or resolution seems to be implied by the thinking of the group, several participants have begun to form convictions about the matter.

Mrs. Prince, too, is also changing, it seems. Although somewhat inexperienced with interpretive discussion, my co-leader has begun to raise interpretive questions with the students. She is relating these to questions that ask discussants to draw upon their personal experiences and views. Furthermore, the outcome of her questioning seems to be that the students are deepening their interest in and feel for the events in the play.

In the next conversation, we watch the Belden students actually use their personal experience to form a textual issue that they wish to resolve. While I continue to struggle against my tendency to "protect" them from humiliation, thereby ignoring their most provocative remarks, I too make some progress.

CONVERSATION 6

The Group Emerges

In this conversation, the Belden discussants begin, for the first time, to act like a group. Among other things, this means that they engage in conversation that moves them along, conversation that draws them into the play in a way that has not been true in the past. In addition, both the students and I do things that we have not done before.[1]

For example, the first thing we see is that Colette opens the discussion by posing a question about Juliet—a question that seems to raise a genuine issue, given the text. Since the question comes from the student, I am in a new position: I may either take the part of discussant and try to address it, or I may work to clarify the issue for the group. When later in the hour we move on to analyze a speech by Friar Lawrence, the priest who marries Romeo and Juliet, I again find myself doing things I had not done previously, such as paraphrasing lines for the students and pushing them to reach an interpretation I have in mind. The students, for their part, pursue the analysis with an energy and determination they had not exhibited on previous occasions.

Why do these changes occur? And are they changes for the better or worse? Mrs. Prince and I take up these questions at the conclusion of the student discussion. At the same time, we consider another issue that has also arisen, namely, Mrs. Prince's role in the conversation.

At the start of class, the students are still focused on the balcony scene in *Romeo and Juliet*, act II, scene ii. Romeo and Juliet, having declared their love to one another, make plans to unite in matrimony. We have read the scene on a previous occasion, so discussion opens immediately, this time with a student question:

COLETTE: Why was Juliet so eager to get married?
SHG: Now, that is an interesting question, Colette. And it's kind of funny, because on the bottom of page 77, act II, scene ii, line 116, Juliet says:

> Although I joy in thee,
> I have no joy of this contract tonight.
> It is too rash, too unadvised, too sudden;

> Too like the lightning, which doth cease to be
> Ere one can say it lightens. Sweet, good night!
> This bud of love, by summer's ripening breath,
> May prove a beauteous flow'r when next we meet.
> Good night, good night! As sweet repose and rest
> Come to thy heart as that within my breast!

Now, is Juliet talking about the marriage contract when she says this? Marcy?

MARCY: Yeah.

SHG: Do you think so? And what is she saying about the marriage contract, right there in that place, Marcy?

MARCY: She ain't ready to get married.

SHG: Right there? What does she mean, Sylvia, when she says it is "too rash, too sudden" Is she still talking about the marriage contract there?

SYLVIA: I don't know.

SHG: James, do you think she is talking about the marriage contract at the top of page 78 when she says, "It is too rash, too sudden"?

JAMES: Yeah.

SHG: So how does she feel about getting married, James?

JAMES: All I know is that she wants to get married and get it over with.

SHG: Then why does she say it is "*too* rash, *too* unadvised?" "*Too* sudden"?

JAMES: Why?

SHG: Yes, it is very strange.

JAMES: She hasn't got her head on straight.

SHG: That's what it seems like, doesn't it? Michael, do you see the problem? On the top of page 78, she is saying it is "too rash," but then later on she comes back to Romeo again, do you see that? She has been inside and—

MICHAEL: She's confused!

SHG: James and Michael say she is confused. Look at line 144 on the bottom of page 78. Juliet says:

> If thy bent of love be honorable,
> Thy purpose marriage, send me word tomorrow,
> By one that I'll procure to come to thee,
> Where and what time thou wilt perform the rite;
> And all my fortunes at thy foot I'll lay
> And follow thee my lord throughout the world.

So here she seems to be saying: If you are really serious, you had
better tell me what time and when. So how is she feeling about
this? James and Michael say she is confused. Is that right,
Colette?
COLETTE: She wants to hurry up and get it over with.
SHG: But what is she in such a big rush about, Colette?

What is this we see? A student posing the first question in the discussion?[2]
That is something we have not seen in these conversations. And is that the
leader, SHG, interpreting some of the lines in Juliet's speech for the students? I
do not interpret the entire speech, of course, but to interpret any of it is a departure from my former practice.

Now, because Colette opened the discussion with a question, I have the option of addressing it as one of the discussants or trying to clarify it so that
others may understand and respond to it. I am caught a little off guard, but
Colette's question strikes me as sound, given the text. On the one hand, Juliet
asks Romeo to set the time and place of the wedding; on the other hand, she
sees the marriage as a rash move whose prospect "gives her no joy."

Seeing its rashness, why, indeed, is Juliet in such a rush to marry Romeo? I
awkwardly question the students to expose the dilemma that Colette has identified.[3] Many of the questions I ask draw attention to lines that underscore the
issue. My activity requires me to the interpret the lines so as to determine their
relevance to the problem. The lines I paraphrase for the students—Juliet's request that Romeo establish the time and place of the wedding—likewise
emphasize the dilemma. My newly assumed goal—to clarify the issue for the
group—seems to have moved me into action I had heretofore avoided, namely,
interpreting some of the lines.

Another way to respond to Colette would have been to ask *her* to explain
why she had raised the question. Might she not have identified the passages
that had prompted it? Perhaps I should have tried this tack. But my eagerness
to support the conversation, to provide the students with evidence that will
deepen their queries about and engagement with the play, has moved me to
focus the students on what seem to be relevant passages. I continue in like
manner:

SHG: Look at the top of page 79. Would you read those two lines
again, Sylvia, to see if it helps us?
SYLVIA: "And all my fortunes at thy foot I'll lay,/And follow thee
my lord throughout the world."
SHG: What is she saying she is going to do?

SYLVIA: Follow him.
MARCY: She wants to be with him—
JAMES: Do whatever he says.
SHG: Why is she so eager to be with him, to follow him
throughout the world, do whatever he says?
COLETTE: She loves him.
SHG: She loves him, Colette? But this has been pretty fast, right?
Yes, James.
JAMES: They will run away so nobody will be hurt.
SHG: Are you saying they are going to sneak off?
JAMES: Yes.
SHG: This is a sort of secret thing, then.
COLETTE: I hope not because they're really going to kill him if he
sneaks off and marries her.

Notice that Colette's reaction to the plan of "sneaking off" contradicts
James's idea that "nobody will be hurt." On the contrary, she says, they will kill
Romeo if he sneaks off with Juliet. Colette's comment thereby shifts the issue
before the group. The issue we now face is: What will happen to the couple if
they sneak off? rather than: Why is Juliet in such a rush to marry Romeo? As the
leader, I might return the conversation to the original question. Do I do so?

SHG: So you are saying, Collette, that if he sneaked off and
married her, they would really come after him, right? So instead
of being safe and being able to get away, they would be in more
trouble?
COLETTE: I don't know.
SHG: Is this a good idea that Romeo and Juliet have here,
Colette?
SYLVIA: Yes.
JAMES: Maybe to them, but not to others.
SHG: Why is it a good idea to them, James?
JAMES: Because they are in love.
SHG: But is it dangerous?
JAMES: Not to them.
SHG: If they are in love and trying to get away, is this a smart
thing to do? You are saying that for them it is, because they will
be free, right, James? Even with everybody chasing them and
everything?
JAMES: They won't have to answer to anybody.
SHG: I see, so they can do what they want. They will be free. But
what are you saying, Colette?

COLETTE: If somebody took my daughter and ran off and got married, I would kill him!

I do not return the group to Colette's original issue. Why? because we seem to be moving toward a shared issue, one that several in the group are helping to form. Such an issue is one the group may care more about resolving. In a sense, I seem to be encouraging the discussion to take its own course instead of imposing one, that is, I ask questions that draw out the students' ideas rather than forcing them to stick with a particular problem—a departure from my usual approach.

As the discussion continues, it becomes more compelling. The new issue— What will happen to the couple if they sneak off and get married?—acquires intensity when Colette projects herself into the role of a father whose daughter elopes with a man. "I would kill him," she declares. In drawing upon her beliefs about a father's reaction to the situation, Colette polarizes the issue before the group in a very dramatic way. James has been arguing that the lovers will be free if they run off; Colette, given her sense of a father's response, declares they will be in mortal danger. She asserts that the father in such a situation would pursue the couple, not just leave them to enjoy each other. Here is a clear example of how beliefs that arise through one's personal experience—in this case, perhaps, Colette's experience of seeing fathers respond— can focus and intensify the discussion of a literary text.[4] I support the growing controversy by emphasizing the difference between what James and Colette have said:

SHG: You would kill them, Colette? So you don't think that this plan of sneaking off to get married is a good idea? You think they are going to be in more trouble doing it this way? What would you suggest that they do in this situation?
COLETTE: I think they should tell someone.
SHG: Should Juliet go to her father and say, "Hey, I'm not interested in Paris, but there is someone else I am interested in"?
COLETTE: Yeah! He can't do nothing!
SHG: So you think she would be better off if she went and told her father about it instead of trying to sneak off?
COLETTE: Right.
MARCY: Just because he couldn't stop them anyway.
JAMES: He could stop them, but he probably has someone else to stop them. But, I think he'll be very upset with her if she tells him.
SHG: So he would be even more upset if she came back and said she was married?

SYLVIA: To him [Romeo], because he is a Montague and she is a Capulet, and Montagues and Capulets don't get along.

The issue has shifted slightly again and become even more focused. After Colette's declaration that she, as a father, would kill a man who eloped with her daughter, the suggestion comes that perhaps the couple should tell the father before the marriage occurred. Again, I follow the issue as it seems to be evolving and present the dilemma that the group has now raised:

SHG: Would the father be more upset to know before or after the marriage?

JAMES: After.

SHG: You say "after," James? Why?

JAMES: They were talking to her before. Plus, eating, he would spit out his food at her.

SHG: So that is what happens if she tells him before, right? What about if she tells him afterward? What would he do, James?

JAMES: He would be bent out of shape!

COLETTE: Uh-uh, he would kill Romeo for marrying his daughter.

SHG: James, I am still not sure what you are saying. Would it be worse if she told her father before or after the marriage?

JAMES: Anyway it goes is bad.

SHG: So it wouldn't make any difference. Colette says it might be worse afterwards because Capulet might want to kill Romeo. Do you think that is right, Sylvia?

SYLVIA: If she tells him she is going to get married, he will be hurt. He will say, "Why didn't you tell me before?" She would get a lecture.

MARCY: So that is why she wouldn't tell him?

SYLVIA: Yeah. He would probably talk her to death so she would miss her wedding!

SHG: Aha! So Capulet would really try to keep her away from Romeo, right?

COLETTE: I think if they married, and then she told her father, he would try to keep her away from Romeo.

The students in this group seem to have identified an issue they are eager to discuss. How can one tell? A clear sign is that they reiterate their claims and appear to resist a change in view. Here, Colette insists that it would be worse to tell Capulet after the fact. When Sylvia argues that he would try to keep Juliet from marrying Romeo if he knew beforehand, Colette counters that Capulet would still try to separate the couple if he found out afterwards. On the one hand, the students seem not to be listening very carefully to one another. On the other hand, for the first time, at least some of them are engaged in a textual issue deeply enough to insist on being right.

The eagerness of the students persists as we move into act II, scene iii, where a very different sort of exchange occurs. Here, I engage them in some close textual analysis with surprising results. At this point in the play, Romeo goes to Friar Lawrence and asks him to perform the marriage rite. Romeo is no stranger to the friar, who has watched the young man pine over women before. At first he refuses Romeo's request, but at last he gives in. After we read the scene aloud, I pose the following question to the group: Why does the friar agree to marry Romeo and Juliet? Some discussion ensues, and I then direct attention to a passage in the text:

SHG: OK, now let's look at page 84, line 90, act II, scene iii.
Sylvia, why don't you read for us and tell us what the passage means.
SYLVIA:
    In one respect, I'll thy assistant be;
    For this alliance may so happy prove
    To turn your households' rancor to pure love.
SHG: So why does the friar agree to marry them?
SYLVIA: 'Cause he respect him.
COLETTE: No.
MARCY: So this will make him happy.
SHG: What is an alliance?
COLETTE: In the dictionary.
SHG: When people get together. So "for this alliance"—
SYLVIA: If they get married, they will be a happy couple.
SHG: And they might do what?
MARCY: Have kids.

On the one hand, it appears that some of the students are responding much as they seemed to do when we discussed the meaning of the word "wean." That is, Colette suggests we turn to the dictionary for help with the word "alliance," and Marcy makes what appears to be an unreflective guess when she says that Romeo and Juliet may have kids when they marry.

On the other hand, there are important differences between the present discussion and the one on "weaning." To begin with, this time, after I pose the question of why the friar agrees to marry Romeo and Juliet, three students respond without prompting. Furthermore, they respond to each other—Colette says Sylvia is wrong—as well as to me. So eager is Sylvia that she jumps to use my definition of "alliance" to answer the question of why the friar decides to marry the lovers. Indeed, her point—the friar agrees to marry Romeo and Juliet to make the couple "happy"—seems to extend Marcy's idea that the wedding will make Romeo happy. In general, the students seem to be listening more carefully and interacting much more freely than they were in the "weaning" conversation.

Furthermore, my behavior on the present occasion has changed as well. The question I pose is a genuine question. It is not clear, from the text, why the friar agrees to marry Romeo and Juliet. In the earlier discussion, the question that I asked about the word "wean" was a factual question, it is answered definitively by the dictionary and indeed, is fully explained by the nurse in her speech. In addition, when I ask what the word "alliance" means, I do not forbid Colette to consult the dictionary, as I did when she wanted to look up "wean." Indeed, I define the word myself before she has a chance to read the definition. What accounts for these changes in the students and teacher?

One possibility is that the question I have posed—Why does the friar agree to marry Romeo and Juliet?—may be one that at least Sylvia, Colette, and Marcy recognize as a genuine problem. Sometimes students respond to a question more readily if they realize that it is a real question, that the teacher is not sitting there with the answer in mind. As for my responses, it may be that the question set the priorities for me. If my concern was to resolve the issue, then looking up or debating the meaning of the word "alliance" was merely a distraction. Perhaps the willingness of the students to pursue the question about the friar propelled me beyond defining "alliance." My next move was to take the students into some further textual analysis:

> SHG: OK, What about the next line, "Turn your households' rancor"?
> MARCY: Make your households come together and be friends.
> SHG: Possibly, Marcy.
> MICHAEL: They will come together and chill out!
> MP: Come on, listen to what Michael is saying!
> SHG: So what is your idea about why the friar might agree to marry them, Michael?
> MICHAEL: What did I just say?
> JAMES: If they are married, they love each other, some day his mother and father and her mother and father might call a truce and everybody will be friends. They'll go to a party—
> SHG: So, he would marry them not just to bring these two people together but to bring the two families together?

MICHAEL: There you go!
SHG: Is that what you are suggesting here?
COLETTE: That's what the whole book is about!

Once again, it feels to me as though we have reached a milestone. Although I believe that the students do not understand the word "rancor," they are able to interpret the friar's statement, nevertheless. Indeed, they seem not to be put off by the appearance of a foreign word as they forge ahead to explain the lines. The discussants may be listening to each other better, too. James elaborates the interpretation first proposed by Marcy and reasserted by Michael: he explains the friar's line in detail, and he delivers his analysis with care and conviction. James, like the other speakers, seems to think he is "right" this time, and not because either I or Mrs. Prince have so indicated.[5] As Colette defends the interpretation by justifying it in terms of the entire play—another important move that we have not seen the Belden students make before—she indicates recognition of the ultimate authority in interpretive discussions: the text.

Inspired by the students, I draw their attention to a passage that seems to me to support their idea about why the friar agrees to marry Romeo and Juliet. While my intention was to show them evidence for their claim, the reader should realize that this move threatened to jeopardize the discussion. Why? Because I am about to ask the students not only to interpret a passage but to make a particular interpretation, namely, one that will lend support to their idea about the friar. While experienced discussants cannot be persuaded to accept an interpretation simply because the teacher holds it, the Belden students may allow themselves to be guided by my cues rather than what they read.

SHG: OK, Colette, bringing the two families together could solve a lot of problems. Now, there is one place that might suggest your idea about the friar has some sense to it. Look back on page 81, line 15. Marvin, would you like to read those lines over again?
COLETTE: I'll read them!
SHG: No, Colette. Go ahead, Marvin.
MARVIN:
    FRIAR: O mickle [much] is the powerful grace that lies
    In plants, herbs, stones, and their true qualities;
    For naught so vile that on the earth doth live
    But to the earth some special good doth give;
    Nor aught so good but, strained from that fair use,

> Revolts from true birth, stumbling on abuse.
> Virtue itself turns vice, being misapplied,
> And vice sometime by action dignified.
>
> SHG: So what is he saying about herbs and plants?
> JAMES: And stones!
> MARCY: They think and breathe!
> SHG: Let's take this apart. "That nothing is so vile." What do you think "vile" is, Henry?
> HENRY: Violent and precious.
> MP: No.
> COLETTE: I am going to look in the dictionary.
> SHG: If something is "vile," what is it? Have you seen that word?
> RICHARD: Things smell vile.
> SHG: OK, things smell vile, Richard.
> COLETTE: (reading) "A very foul thing or bad."
> SHG: Yes, you see, if something is "vile," it is bad, unpleasant. So let's put this together: Nothing is so unpleasant—Come on!— For nothing is so bad that—
> JAMES: What did we say "vile" meant?
> MARCY: Horrible!

What is this? Once again I am telling the students the meaning of words in my great eagerness to get into the text interpretation. I even ignore the "precious" association that Richard makes to the word "vile," so great is my determination. I have no patience with what I take to be their guessing—Marcy's suggestion that plants, herbs, "and stones" think and breathe—and press on virtually in spite of the students.

> SHG: For nothing is so horrible "that on the earth doth live,/But to the earth some special good doth give." What does that line mean? Who should give something special—
> SYLVIA: They should. They should give something special to the priest.
> COLETTE: No.
> SHG: What has the friar just been talking about here?
> SYLVIA: Them.
> MARCY: Love.
> SHG: James?
> JAMES: Somebody gives—
> SHG: That is a start. Go on: There is nothing on the earth that is so—
> JAMES: Somebody gives something special to Romeo and Juliet!

More guessing: "Them," and "Love," are the responses to my question, "Who has the friar just been talking about here?" "Somebody gives something special to Romeo and Juliet," declares James. Believing that the students have not yet seen what I wish them to see, I refocus the attention:

SHG: Sometimes when you cannot figure out what a couple of lines mean, it helps to read on a little bit and then you can go back. So let's just read on to the end of these lines and see if that doesn't help us. Next, the friar says:
> Nor aught so good but, strained from that fair use,
> Revolts from true birth, stumbling on abuse.
> Virtue itself turns vice, being misapplied,
> And vice sometime by action dignified.
So what can happen to good things, Marcy?
MARCY: They can turn bad.
SHG: OK, that opens up the whole thing. And what is he saying at the end, Marcy, right after that: "Virtue itself turns vice," meaning what?
MARCY: I don't know.
SHG: It's just what you said.
SYLVIA: Turns bad!
SHG: OK, Sylvia. Vice is bad, right? "Virtue itself turns to vice, being misapplied." Misused. So if you take virtue and use it the wrong way, it becomes bad, right? Look at what he says right after that. James, what does the last line say—"And vice, sometimes by action dignified"?
JAMES: Sometimes it can be wrong.
SHG: So sometimes what could happen to bad things, James?
JAMES: They turn good.

Do the students grasp the friar's point here? That is the question in my mind. Notice that I have identified the point they should grasp! Despite the fact that Marcy cannot put the phrase "Virtue itself turns vice" into her own words, she says that good things "can turn bad," according to the friar. Both James and Sylvia seem to have understood the elements of reversal here: Sylvia says that good turns to bad, and James says that bad things can turn good. While the lines may seem a little fuzzy to the students, it appears to me they can now return to the friar's earlier comment about the plants and understand it better:

SHG: Yes. Now let's go back to the line about the plants. I know it

sounds funny, but this is how you figure out puzzling lines
sometimes. I'm at line 15:

> FRIAR: O much is the powerful grace that lies
> In plants, herbs, stones and their true qualities.
> For nothing so vile that on the earth doth live
> But to the earth some special good doth give.

So what is the friar saying about the bad plants, herbs, and
stones? Colette?

COLETTE: I don't know.

SHG: Marcy, look at those lines, now. What is he saying about
bad plants? What can be true about all bad plants?

MARCY: They can be good plants.

JAMES: All of the bad plants and herbs and stones, there could be
something special to them.

SHG: There could be something special to them, something good
to them. Right, James. Wonderful!

———

While Colette seems to have lost interest—perhaps she cannot yet see the
connection between her original idea about the friar and the present analysis—I must confess to the reader that at this moment in the discussion, I was
elated. I had confronted the students with a complicated passage and some, at
least, had stuck with the analysis until they had figured it out. James, in fact,
had corrected his earlier interpretation. He was now saying that there was
"something special" to the bad plants, not that somebody was going to give
something special to Romeo and Juliet." All I could think was that Marcy,
James, Sylvia, and perhaps others who were silent seemed to have grasped the
basic idea of the passage, which indicates progress from the start of the
exchange.

Unfortunately, the bell rang before we had a chance to discuss how the
friar's comments about the plants related to his decision to marry Romeo and
Juliet. I would like to think that the students saw and still cared about the
connection. Such thinking may be wishful, but one thing was certain: The
Belden students seemed never to have cared so much about the conversation
as they had on this day.

We have witnessed striking changes in both the students and their leader.
Each has done things we have not observed before. Now the question is: Why
did these changes occur on this occasion? And were they all for the good?

There is also another issue before us. Perhaps the reader has noticed that
Mrs. Prince was unusually silent during the student discussion, speaking only
twice the entire hour. Why has she not participated more? Has she been trou-

bled or confused by the preceding? Was she distracted with other matters? In what follows, she and I discuss the issue, as well as the question of why the students and I were responding so differently to one another.

SHG: You were certainly quiet today. Was I talking too much?

MP: I wouldn't say you were talking too much, but you did some things I've never seen you do, and I wasn't sure what to make of it all.

SHG: What are you thinking of?

MP: Well, to begin with, I have never seen you interpret the play for the students, actually tell them what some of the lines meant. I have also never seen you push certain interpretations on them through your questioning. Did you realize that you did both of those things today?

SHG: Yes, I know I did.

MP: Do you think that was such a good idea? I thought your idea was that discussion should draw the ideas out of the students, find out what they think Shakespeare means, not give them our interpretations or push them toward certain ones.

SHG: I agree with you. But I don't think I did any great damage today.

MP: Why do you say that?

SHG: Because the students participated very eagerly in this discussion. I mean, wasn't it striking that as soon as we started talking, Colette asked that question about why Juliet was in such a rush to marry Romeo? I don't think our discussions have ever begun with a student question.

MP: I guess that's true.

SHG: It seems to me the students are getting more involved with the play, more eager to understand what is happening.

MP: Well, they seemed to become very concerned about the problem of whether Juliet should tell her father about Romeo before or after the marriage.

SHG: Yes, and that was their issue—one which seemed to open up when they began to draw upon their personal experience with family relationships.

MP: But something bothered me about the rest of the discussion.

SHG: What was that?

MP: Well, as you say, when the students were discussing why Juliet was so eager to marry Romeo, they were drawing on their experiences of family relations and feelings. That was fine. But later, when they were discussing the friar's lines, they seemed to leave their entire world out of the discussion. It almost seemed as if it was no longer their conversation.

SHG: What do you mean?

MP: I mean you posed the questions. You asked why the friar agreed to marry Romeo to Juliet, and you directed the students to the end of the scene where the friar talks about turning their households' rancor to love. Then you focused them on the friar's earlier discussion of the plants.

SHG: Yes, I was quite directive when we got into the friar's speech. But I questioned them about the plant passage in the way that I did so that they would see more evidence for their point about the friar. Remember how they said that he agreed to marry Romeo and Juliet so as to bring the two households together? I thought his lines about the plants gave further evidence for that view, which is why I directed them there. I wanted them to see that relevant evidence.

MP: But it seemed that you wanted them to interpret the lines in a particular way instead of drawing out what they saw in the passage. I didn't know how to contribute under those circumstances, so I let you proceed with your agenda.

SHG: Yes, I suppose I was a little heavy-handed.

MP: Why didn't you ask them to find other passages that supported their view and just let them make the interpretations?[6]

SHG: You may be right. But it is interesting that despite my heavy-handedness, they were willing to stick with me and try to interpret the passages I directed them to even though they hadn't posed the issue that was on the floor—the one about why the friar agreed to marry the lovers—or identified the passages. That's the part that amazes me. I wonder why they were they so willing to analyze the details of the friar's speech.

MP: Well, it's true, most of them made a serious effort with it, I think. Maybe they are beginning to understand what they are supposed to do in the discussion. Or maybe they are just trying to please you.

SHG: You may be right about both of those suggestions. On the one hand, they do seem to be learning the rules that they are supposed to follow in having a discussion, and they are learning what happens when you follow those rules. So they are more willing to take a chance, to try to analyze passages when I ask them to do so, even though they may not see the point of looking at a particular place at first. Then too, I think they were trying to please me, do what I want them to do. But there again, I think we have a change that needs to be explained. Why, all of a sudden do they want to please me?

MP: Well, you are a nice lady and they are getting to know you.

SHG: Yes, but I think there is more to it than that. I mean I think I was trying to please them more, too. For example, I was trying to do things that would support their thinking, things that would minimize their frustration and encourage them to talk. I think that's why I was working so hard to show them how to use the text to explore their ideas. Remember how, at the very beginning, I didn't ask Colette to explain her question about why Juliet was so eager to marry Romeo? Instead, I took the students right into the parts of Juliet's speech that point up the dilemma that Colette had identified. I wanted to show them how to sustain and deepen their question without making them go through the difficult job of digging out the supportive evidence themselves, which is not easy to do sometimes.

MP: But you might have asked Colette to explain her question a little more, I think. I mean, I am not so sure it was inspired by the conflicting aspects of Juliet's speech. Maybe Colette just wondered why Juliet was in such a rush to marry Romeo since they had only just met.

SHG: You are right. I could have asked Colette to talk about the source of her question. But you see, I want them to connect their ideas and questions about the play with the lines themselves. I want to help them to realize that the text can give them more ideas if they look at it. And I think it is working.

MP: What do you mean?

SHG: Maybe they are finding that when they look at the play more closely, when they pay attention to the lines I show them, they do get more ideas. And it feels good to get ideas.

MP: Well, it's true that even with the discussion about the friar, they got more interested in it as it went along. Except for Colette. She seemed to fade out by the end.

SHG: Well, it's too bad the bell rang because we didn't have the chance to relate the analysis of the friar's speech about the plants back to the point they had made about why the friar married Romeo and Juliet. Perhaps we lost Colette because she lost sight of the connection. Even so, the group is really beginning to feel like a group.[7] The students want to please me and I want to please them. I am working to draw out and support their ideas, and they are responding to my efforts so that their ideas really are getting out on the table. It seems that they are discovering the rewards of discussion.

MP: That's interesting. Now that I think about it, maybe the students were willing to analyze that passage about the plants for so long because of what happened when they were asked to explain those lines of the friar's about the households' rancor turning to love.

SHG: What do you mean?

MP: Well, you had asked why the friar agrees to marry the lovers. Then you directed the students to that passage about the marriage turning the households' rancor to love and they figured it out, don't you remember? Marcy said it first, that the households would become friends. Then Michael said they would "chill out." Then James explained Marcy's point, and Colette pointed out that this interpretation fit in with what the whole book was about.

SHG: So together those students had figured the meaning of the passage and its relevance to the question. That is what happens in a group that is functioning like a group!

MP: Right.

SHG: And your idea is that this experience made them willing to look at another passage, almost as though they knew now that they could get something out of a passage they didn't see much in at first?

MP: That's my guess.

SHG: And I suppose they were further encouraged when I told them that the passage we were next going to consider seemed to support their idea about why the friar had agreed to marry Romeo and Juliet. After all, who among us doesn't want to see more evidence that our ideas or interpretations are good ones?

MP: Maybe.

When she says "Maybe," Mrs. Prince suggests that perhaps she is not totally convinced by our argument. Perhaps she still worries about pushing the conversation to the point where students' experience cannot even come up. She may also think that if the teacher does too much interpretation for the discussants, they may become inclined to let her do more and more. And if she tries to push certain interpretations, discussants may become focused on trying to discover what she thinks is right rather than the lines themselves.

While these are reasonable concerns, there is no question that, from my point of view, the discussion was more effective than it had been. Indeed, the fact that the students and I were conversing with each other so much more productively seemed to render some of the discussion rules irrelevant at moments.

In the next conversation, we watch as Mrs. Prince takes the floor in no uncertain terms and at one point asks the students to consider their own ideas so as to judge the appropriateness of Shakespeare's. Her move occurs after a discussion in which the students, rather than using their experience to generate textual issues, employ the play of *Romeo and Juliet* to reflect on a topic of serious concern to them apart from the text, namely, premarital sex.

CONVERSATION 7
The Evaluative Discussion

We now watch two very different sorts of teacher-questioning—the one interpretive, the other evaluative. In the case of the first, the students are asked to analyze the text, to try to determine its meaning. When called upon to evaluate the text, the teacher asks the discussants to compare their ideas on a topic with Shakespeare's: Do they agree with his?

The topic that concerns the students today is premarital sex. They get into the subject after they are asked to reflect upon the actions of Romeo and Juliet and a puzzling comment that the friar makes to the couple. Sensing their keen interest in the topic, Mrs. Prince uses the analysis of the play to draw out the students' feelings about engaging in sexual relations before marriage.

Once again, there is disagreement between the teachers about what should take place in the discussion. This time, I am the one who is reduced to silence at one point, as I am unsure how to contribute to the evaluative part of the conversation. In the aftermath, Mrs. Prince and I consider the merits of the evaluative questioning. Was it appropriate? Did it benefit the students?

The group has now reached act II, scene vi, of *Romeo and Juliet*. Here, Romeo and Juliet come to Friar Lawrence so that he may perform the rite of marriage. After we read the brief scene aloud, I open the discussion with a question about one of the friar's remarks:

SHG: OK, now, when Juliet enters the friar's cell, where Romeo is standing with the friar, she says: "Good evening to my ghostly confessor." And the friar says: "Romeo shall thank thee, daughter, for us both." Why does the friar say this?

MYRNA: Thank who daughter?

SHG: OK, Marcy, who is the friar talking to?

MARCY: Juliet.

SHG: Is that right, Myrna?

MYRNA: Isn't he talking to Romeo?

SHG: Well, he says, "Romeo shall thank thee, daughter, for us both." So, who is he talking to?

JAMES: Juliet.

SHG: James says, "Juliet."
MYRNA: Oh, Juliet. That's right.

Notice that even though Myrna asks me who the friar is talking about when
he says, "Romeo shall thank thee, daughter," she submits to questioning without resistance. Other students respond to questions about the issue and even
volunteer to address it. I am pleased that they seem willing both to pose questions and to try to resolve them for themselves, instead of demanding that the
teacher tell them the answer.

SHG: OK, so what does the friar mean here, Myrna?
MYRNA: I guess the friar is Juliet's father.
MP: Say it again! Who is the friar? Myrna wasn't here last time.
COLETTE: He is the priest.
JAMES: He is the father.
SHG: Right, James. He is going to marry her, right?
JAMES: The justice.
COLETTE: Right.
SHG: So when the friar calls her "daughter," does he mean
literally that this is his daughter, Marcy?
MARCY: No, he means like in church!
MYRNA: Ain't nobody in church call me daughter!
MP: No, Myrna? Would a priest be likely to call somebody in the
congregation a daughter?
MYRNA: No.
MARCY: Yes.
MP: Sylvia is the daughter of a minister, so does he call everyone
in the church "daughter," sometimes?
SYLVIA: Uh-huh.

Here, it is clear that Myrna, Marcy, and Sylvia are drawing directly on their
personal experiences to answer the question of why the friar refers to Juliet as
"daughter." It is also interesting that their experiences contrast with one another. Myrna says that the priest in her church does not refer to women as
"daughter," while Sylvia and Marcy disagree. The differences in their personal
experiences give these students very different perspectives on the text before
them, for what strikes Myrna as puzzling seems perfectly understandable to
the other two girls.

Again we see more evidence of the students' willingness to participate in the
conversation. Although Myrna is unsure who the friar is, she volunteers the
suggestion that he's Juliet's father. And even after she (mistakenly) says that

the friar was addressing Romeo, Myrna is willing to try out her ideas, even if tentative. The other students are quick to correct her, but do so in a cooperative spirit. They seem to take some pride in understanding what is happening in the play. Then Marcy raises another question:

> MARCY: Do Romeo and Juliet go to bed?
> SHG: No, not yet, Marcy.
> MARCY: Well, it sure sounds like that. "Thank thee, daughter, for us both."

Marcy's question is interesting for several reasons. First of all, she, like others in previous conversations, is beginning to raise questions about the meaning of the text.[1] In the second place, Marcy follows her question by reading the text passage that suggested the query to her. Here, she shows evidence that she is learning to share her thinking with the group, a pattern one finds in experienced discussants. Perhaps because the students have been asked to present evidence from the text for their ideas, they are now beginning to do so spontaneously. Furthermore, Marcy's question springs from a serious interest she brings to the discussion, as the reader will shortly see. Indeed, the strength of that interest—which others share—may account for the fact that Marcy's question seems to set up the topic that sustains much of the subsequent conversation.

> SHG: To get a little clearer about what the friar means by his puzzling remark, let's look at Juliet's response to him. Juliet says, "As much to him, else his thanks is too much." Look at the note. It says "As much to him" means: "the same greeting to Romeo." What is that same greeting to Romeo? James.
> JAMES: I do.
> HENRY: Thank you.
> SHG: That is interesting. "I give the same greeting to Romeo or else his thanks is too much." Or else what? Marcy, what do you think that is all about?
> MARCY: I think she says that—I forgot.
> MP: Go ahead, Marcy.
> SHG: Marcy, how do you think a woman can thank a man for giving himself to her?
> JAMES: By saying "I do," like I just said.
> MP: All right, James!
> SYLVIA: By giving yourself back to him.
> SHG: OK, Sylvia, by giving yourself back to him in what way?
> SYLVIA: Oh!

> JAMES: By saying "I do"!
> MP: Sylvia, not James!

My thought here is that if the students see how Juliet takes the friar's puzzling line, they may get some ideas about what he means. James seems to have no question about the meaning of Juliet's response and indeed, about the friar's remark. He says, several times, that Romeo and Juliet will thank each other by saying "I do." Perhaps because of the conviction with which he repeats his point, neither Mrs. Prince nor I question James about what he means, which we surely should have done, as his comment is not transparent. Instead, we focus attention on Marcy, who after all, made the first interpretation of the friar's comment. We want her to examine that interpretation in light of Juliet's remark. Marcy is a little unsure of how to respond, but Sylvia's "Oh!" suggests she realizes the point that Marcy first intuited, namely, that the friar may be anticipating the consummation of the marriage. Colette is also reaching Sylvia's conclusions:

> COLETTE: Well, giving him [Romeo] love would make him happy.
> MP: Michael, can you explain what Colette just said? Michael, why don't you tell us about it?
> MICHAEL: She is talking about stuff that's dirty.
> MP: Can you tell us what the dirt is? Colette, do you think she was talking dirty? I want to know! Are we all thinking the same thing?
> SYLVIA: They're going to do it.
> MP: But they are getting married, aren't they Sylvia?
> MICHAEL: Romeo should have thanked the priest by saying "thank you"; but instead he is going to thank her later.
> JAMES: Yeah!

Looking at the text, one might ask whether Shakespeare is drawing attention to the sexual aspect of the relationship between Romeo and Juliet or to their feelings of love and care for one another. The students seem to think it is the former: Michael says that Juliet was "talking dirty." What gives them this impression? I return the group to the text:

> SHG: But the friar says, "Romeo shall thank thee, daughter for both of us." According to this idea, what is happening here? If Romeo is going to thank her for both of them, right? For both the friar and Romeo?
> SYLVIA: He can't thank both of them!
> SHG: Well, except in what sense, Sylvia?

SYLVIA: He can't thank the friar in the way that he is going to thank Juliet.

SHG: All right. It is the friar who says, "Romeo is going to thank you for the both of us." So Romeo is going to do something for both of them, right?

SYLVIA: How can he do that?

COLETTE: He is going to do something nasty for that man!

———

Colette is the first to have an idea about how Romeo could thank Juliet for himself and the friar: He is going to "do something nasty for that man," which seems to mean having sexual relations with Juliet on behalf of the friar. Colette's idea seems to come in response to Sylvia's question of how Romeo can act for the friar. Mrs. Prince's response to Colette's suggestion departs from the text and takes the students directly into an examination of their ideas about sex and the clergy:

———

MP: Come on! Priests don't do what? What is one of the things that priests don't do?

MARCY: Have sexual contact!

MP: They don't have any sexual contact, do they?

MYRNA: Priests have sex. Some do.

JAMES: I say all of them do!

MP: All right, James. But a friar in a Catholic church is what is called a celibate, right? That is, a person who doesn't engage in sexual relations. That is part of the vow, right? Not all priests and ministers are like that, obviously.

———

Notice that the discussion is no longer focused on the friar's remark. Instead, the students are exchanging their ideas about whether priests have sexual relations or not, ideas that must have arisen from personal experiences of some sort or other. From priests, Marvin and Myrna go on to the sexual habits of nuns:

———

MARVIN: Nuns don't have sex, right?

MYRNA: I know a nun that has kids.

SHG: But basically the Church—the Catholic church—doesn't allow it, Myrna.

MP: Myrna, can we go over the rules for a moment? The rules say no, but there is an exception to every rule, right?

MYRNA: It ain't no law!

SHG: It is the Church law. They are supposed to be celibate.

One might wonder why I fail to question the students about their views instead of presenting them with "facts" about church regulations. On what basis do the speakers make their claims? Do others agree with the positions that have been expressed? And if these views on the sexual habits of priests and nuns are correct, what does it suggest about the meaning of the friar's puzzling remark? Should we take it as sexual innuendo or not?

Perhaps the reason I do not so question the students is that it seems to me the discussion is moving further and further from the text all the time. While I am all in favor of using personal experience to illuminate the play, and vice versa, I feel distinct discomfort when it seems to me that the Shakespeare has been abandoned altogether. My "factual" responses to the students may be motivated by the desire to terminate their commentary about priests and nuns and get back to *Romeo and Juliet*. But things are out of my control:

MP: Now, what did you call sex, Myrna?

MYRNA: Called it "dirty."

MP: Is it still "nasty" after you get married, James?

JAMES: No.

MP: Sylvia?

SYLVIA: No.

MP: Does marriage suddenly legalize something that you just considered nasty?

CHORUS: *Yes!!*

MP: Is it still nasty?

CHORUS: *NO!!!*

MP: One person! Henry?

HENRY: I don't say anything.

MP: OK, I guess it is just the girls. Colette, you said it was nasty. Is it suddenly not nasty after you get married?

COLETTE: No.

MARCY: I didn't say it was nasty.

MP: You didn't, Marcy?

MARCY: It all depends on who you do it with.

MP: When is it nasty?

JAMES: NEVER!

MP: Just a minute, James.

MARCY: When you are not going with them.

MP: What is missing when you are not going with them? There are no feelings. There is no love there, right?

SYLVIA: Yeah!

MP: When you are not in love, then is it different?

COLETTE: Yeah!

MP: So what I am trying to say is that I think Shakespeare is taking something out of the back alley and bringing it out in the open. Is it really something "nasty"? Or is it something for married people to do? Or, what is it for? Do the boys feel differently than the girls?

SHG: James, can you come back to the table and finish the conversation? Your teacher has asked a question. I couldn't hear what you were saying.

JAMES: No, man. I ain't got all day!

MP: James, what are you saying?

JAMES: They do it when they're ready!

MP: OK, what does it mean to be ready? Before or after marriage.

HENRY: Whenever!

MP: What was Shakespeare's view?

JAMES: Nope!

SHG: You don't think that is what Shakespeare is saying?

JAMES: Well, I don't feel that way! Not at all!

MICHAEL: Neither do I!

MP: I think this is interesting because the boys feel one way and the girls feel another.

JAMES: We don't really care who they are. We just take 'em.

MP: And, Sylvia, do you disagree with James?

SYLVIA: I care because—

JAMES: We don't care at all. We just want to be satisfied.

COLETTE: You are nasty!

Mrs. Prince has seized an opportunity to pursue the subject of sex with the students. She has observed their keen interest in the topic, and she seems to have an interpretation of Shakespeare's position that she wants the students to consider. She says, "Shakespeare is taking something out of the back alley and bringing it into the open." Perhaps the fact that Romeo and Juliet choose to marry rather than to sleep together out of wedlock suggests to Mrs. Prince that premarital sex is unacceptable, according to Shakespeare.

Here, the teacher does not question the students in order to interpret the playwright. Rather, she wants them to express their own views and consider them in light of the playwright's, that is, in light of her interpretation of Shakespeare's position. She is impressed by the fact that some of the girls seem to think sex before marriage is "nasty," while the boys disagree. What is Shakespeare's view? she asks. Does he believe that under some circumstances it is not "nasty" to have sexual relations? What are those circumstances? And is his view shared by the students?

Such questioning of the students by the teacher might be called "evaluative." Why? Because the intent is not to interpret the author's position but to evaluate it in light of one's own view. Evaluation requires the discussants to express their positions on an issue and compare them to what they take to be the author's position, perhaps judging its adequacy. In this instance, Mrs. Prince seems to hope that the students will also judge their own ideas in light of what she takes to be Shakespeare's.

Evaluative questioning is likely to arise when the discussion brings up an issue about which members of a group have strong feelings, apart from the text. In this instance, the author's view is taken as one among many and provides a springboard for investigation of others' perspectives—generally those of the discussants. Now the question is: Since evaluative questioning may not remain focused upon the text, is it appropriate in an interpretive discussion? Furthermore, was Mrs. Prince simply interested in the student evaluations of Shakespeare's ideas, or did she wish the discussants to reach a particular conclusion? In other words, was the teacher "moralizing"? Mrs. Prince and I take up these questions in what follows.

SHG: What did you think of the student conversation at the end there? Were you satisfied with it?

MP: I think it was good. Why? How did you feel about it?

SHG: Well, all I can say is that you asked a lot of questions I would not have asked.

MP: Such as?

SHG: I don't think I would have asked the students whether they thought that sex was still dirty after marriage, for example.

MP: Why not?

SHG: Because it felt to me like the purpose of the questioning was to make a point to the students about premarital sex, not to find out what they thought about it.

MP: That is not quite true. I did care about their ideas, and in fact, it was their idea—that sex was "nasty"—that I asked about. But yes, you are right: there was something beyond my questioning besides simply finding out about their ideas. I wanted them to consider Shakespeare's view, to think about whether it made sense. You have no idea the difficulties these kids get into because they don't think about the consequences of early sexual experience in a mature way. How many students have I lost to motherhood before their time?

SHG: Well, I guess it troubled me that you wanted the students to consider the text in a certain way rather than trying to figure out what it was saying. Asking the students to evaluate Shakespeare's position on premarital sex assumes that it was clear, and I'm not so sure that it was.

MP: What do you mean? The fact is that Shakespeare has the lovers get married before they have sex. It is as if this pure, innocent love would no longer be pure and innocent if they slept with each other out of wedlock. That says to me that from Shakespeare's point of view, the love of these two young people could only be powerful enough to bring the two feuding households together if it were sanctified by marriage, and marriage in the Church! That's a powerful message about sex and marriage, isn't it?

SHG: Well, you have a point. But it seems to me that Shakespeare's primary concern is with the love between the couple, not sex and marriage. That feeling of love is pretty powerful if they want to tie themselves together in matrimony so quickly! They might have chosen to sleep together first, but they didn't. And that choice, that desire to be married first, is what tells Friar Lawrence that this is serious and genuine love, a love that could unite the Montagues and the Capulets. So it is the feelings that Romeo and Juliet have for each other that move the friar to certain actions, and those very feelings, rather than the fact of the marriage itself, may be what make sexual relations between these two characters acceptable.

MP: But what about the Friar's comments to Romeo in the earlier scene—scene iii, which I am looking at again, now, line 67: "Young men's love then lies / Not truly in their hearts but in their eyes." Does this sound like the friar trusts young love in the way you are suggesting? He sounds pretty skeptical to me. I don't think it's Romeo's love for Juliet that persuades the friar to marry the couple as much as his hope of healing the strife between the families.

SHG: Yes, but look at lines 81 and 82, same scene. Romeo says, "Thou chidst me oft for loving Rosaline." And Friar Lawrence says, "For doting, not for loving, pupil mine." So clearly, the friar felt Romeo had been doting over Rosaline, that he was not really in love with her. The friar says nothing against love here, or even young love.

MP: Look, I see your point to some degree—

SHG: But the fact that we are arguing about Shakespeare's view of premarital sex makes clear why it is dangerous to ask students to evaluate it.

MP: Well, this is where we disagree. I grant that there may be some question about Shakespeare's position. But the fact is that I did not see the point you are making about it until we had this discussion. Given my view of Shakespeare, I think it made perfectly good sense to ask them to compare their views to his. What was wrong with that?

SHG: But it is like you forgot all about trying to figure out what Shakespeare was really saying.

MP: I think that may be right. We were no longer trying to figure out his view. But if we hadn't done that, we would never have gotten to the students' views. And after all, what are we reading this play for anyway? Isn't it to help the students draw out their own ideas so that they can think about them?

SHG: Yes, that's right. But the question is: What is the best way to draw out their ideas? Is it to ask them to look at the author's or to forget about the author?

MP: It just seems to me that there comes a point where you have to forget about the author in order to pay attention to what you, yourself, really think.

SHG: Maybe so. But if you forget about the author too quickly, you miss the insights that the text offers. I mean now that I think about it, Marcy's position was not too different from the one I was attributing to Shakespeare. If she had realized that, she might have used the play to help her defend her view.

MP: What do you mean?

SHG: Didn't Marcy say that sex before marriage might not be nasty, that it depended upon who you did it with and how each person felt about the other?

MP: Yes, and Sylvia and Colette agreed that if you loved the person, then it made a difference.

SHG: Well, that was my point about Shakespeare's view. He might have been saying that the pure and innocent love that existed between Romeo and Juliet justified the friar in marrying them, even though it was dangerous. And if their powerful love justified such action, might it not also have justified their sleeping together before marriage? If Marcy had seen this possible interpretation, then she might have used the example of Romeo and Juliet to argue for the importance of love in the sexual situation. As it was, all she could do was give her opinion that love was important.

MP: But do you think that if we had continued to interpret Shakespeare's view, Marcy's would ever have come out? I'm afraid I don't. It was only after I began asking them when and if they thought sex was nasty that they started thinking about their own beliefs.

The issue between Mrs. Prince and myself is a complex one. If one puts the text aside to explore the students' own beliefs, then one may miss important insights that the text has to offer. On the other hand, if one stays focused on the text, the discussants' views on issues of vital concern to them may go unexamined. In what follows, we continue to worry the problem. In addition, we tackle another one: If the teacher leaves text interpretation in favor of evaluation, then what should the goal of the discussion become? To decide whose view is right? To persuade students of certain views? I worry that Mrs. Prince has tried to impose her view on the students rather than eliciting theirs.

SHG: All right, I think there is something to what you say. I mean we might not have heard all the different perspectives that the students expressed had you not asked them about their views on premarital sex. And the fact that you emphasized the contrast between the boys' and girls' view may have allowed each group to push its position more fully.
MP: So you think I was right to ask all those questions?
SHG: I think you got their views out on the table. Or did you?
MP: What do you mean?
SHG: Now that I think about it, I wonder: Did James and the other boys really believe all those things they were saying about just wanting to be satisfied and not caring who they slept with? Maybe that was just "macho" talk. And did Colette ever explain why she thought sex outside of marriage was "nasty"? I can't recall that she did. Even Marcy did not tell us why she thought premarital sex was acceptable if the partners loved each other. So maybe we really didn't get their views out on the table.
MP: Look, it seems to me that we learned a lot more about their ideas than we would have if I hadn't asked them those questions, if we'd just stuck to Shakespeare. Even if James was talking "macho," there are people who feel the way he and Michael described themselves as feeling. So it was a view that needed to come out on the table. As for Colette and Marcy, well, maybe I should have asked them more about why they held the views they expressed. But at least we got it started.
SHG: But why didn't you ask them to clarify themselves?

MP: Well, in the case of Marcy, I felt I knew why she thought that being in love—having feelings for your partner—made a difference. I mean her idea made sense to me. As for Colette, I'm not so sure why she said sex was nasty.

SHG: OK, I could be all wrong about this, but my sense was that you didn't question Colette because you were eager for them to consider what you called "Shakespeare's view"—the view that sex was not "nasty" between married people. It seemed to me that you were really more interested in having them accept Shakespeare's view than in finding out about Colette's.

MP: As I said before, I admit that I wanted the students to at least consider Shakespeare's position—that is, what I took to be Shakespeare's position. And yes, that was more important than asking Colette the reasons for her views. Now are you saying I was wrong to ask them to think about what Shakespeare was saying, to see how it would apply to their own lives?

SHG: Well, it seems to me one thing to ask them to evaluate Shakespeare's position. But you were trying to get them to agree and act accordingly, right?[2]

MP: Maybe not.

SHG: Maybe not? I remember when you asked them whether marriage legalized something they considered "nasty," and they yelled "Yes!" Then you asked them whether it was then "still nasty!" and they all yelled "No!" Then you asked again if it was suddenly "not nasty" after marriage and Colette immediately said "No." The way the exchange ran, I had the sense that you wanted certain answers from the students and that they knew it and were giving you what you wanted. And those answers seemed to indicate they were agreeing with Shakespeare's view, much as you wanted them to do. I guess it sort of felt as though you were moralizing, trying to indoctrinate the students.

MP: OK, I guess it did sound that way at that point. And as I keep saying, I wanted them to consider Shakespeare's view. If anything will make them think twice before becoming sexually involved, I'm for it. It kills me to see them throw their futures away. Still and all, the more I think back on the conversation, the more I think there is something you are missing.

SHG: What is that?

MP: Marcy said that sex before marriage was acceptable if the couple was in love, right?

SHG: That's right.

MP: And James and Michael said they disagreed with

Shakespeare, remember? And then they stated their "macho" position, as we have called it.

SHG: Yes, that's right.

MP: It seems to me that the students could not and would not have told me about their views if they had not thought I was open to them. In other words, I don't think they would have said much if they had thought I was trying to indoctrinate them.

SHG: Yes, but James was about to talk out of the room as he spoke. Maybe he thought you didn't really care about what he had to say. In fact, earlier in the conversation, we never asked him what he meant when he kept saying "I do" in response to our questions about the friar's puzzling remark. Remember that? So maybe he thought we were not so interested in his views, that we only wanted him to think in a certain way.

MP: But the fact is that he did stay and tell us his position, and he expressed it with a lot of feeling, too.

SHG: That's certainly true.

MP: And Michael agreed with him, as did some of the other boys who did not speak but nodded.

SHG: True enough.

MP: Which says to me that they know I do care about their ideas, even if I hold a different position and try to get them to consider it.

SHG: OK, and I have to admit you did help Marcy to defend her idea that sex before marriage might not be nasty under certain circumstances.

MP: That's right. I wouldn't have done that if I just wanted her to think that it was nasty. In fact, that's really where the whole discussion started.

SHG: What do you mean?

MP: Colette and Myrna kept insisting that sex was something nasty. But as I said to them, it seems to me that Shakespeare is taking sex out of the back alley and saying that it is not nasty under some circumstances. I really wanted them to think about those circumstances.

SHG: Which is somewhat different then asking them to agree that only sex after marriage is legitimate. Is that what you are saying?

MP: Yes, that's right.

———

I am coming to realize that Mrs. Prince may not have been trying to indoctrinate the students, after all. Although she wants them to consider a particular position that she believes Shakespeare holds, it is not as though she cares nothing for their views. Perhaps the fact that they express differing opinions with such vehemence suggests that they believe their teacher cares what they think, regardless of whether she agrees with the position.

The question remaining for me, however, is whether Mrs. Prince could have explored the students' views in greater depth had she asked them to interpret Shakespeare's text rather than evaluate it. Might not the discussants' opinions have come out as they tried to determine the view of premarital sex expressed in the text? Perhaps, too, the students would have had a better basis for reflecting on their views had they learned more about Shakespeare's, for he could have helped them to form supportive or critical arguments.

In Conversation 8, we take our last look at the Belden students. Before doing so, we reflect back on the turning of the soul that seems to have occurred—for both the students and the teachers—and ask how the transformations have come about.

CONVERSATION 8
Getting It "Right"

We are making our last visit to the Belden classroom. My claim is that we have witnessed a transformation[1] in these students, a turning of the soul, if you will. To see that this is the case, it is helpful to review the changes among the students since Conversation 1. In so doing, we will see not only that the discussants are responding differently than they did at first but that their vision has been "turned" so that they are finding meaning in the play and gaining some perspective on aspects of their lives, beliefs, and values. Indeed, their vision of the discussion opportunity seems not to be what it was. After we consider the students, we will turn to the teachers and the question of their transformation.

As the reader may recall, Conversation 1 indicated that the Belden discussants bring a wealth of powerful, personal experience to the classroom. Yet, we saw them bypassing those feelings and experiences in their initial discussions of *Romeo and Juliet*. Indeed, at first they showed little interest in the text and were not drawing on their own interests and feelings and values effectively. Gradually, over the time we have observed, the students have come to draw more and more on their personal backgrounds and beliefs as they explore the play.

We remember that Conversation 2 focused on what the word "wean" meant. The discussants had difficulty interpreting—even attending to—the speech in which Juliet's nurse describes the girl's weaning. Many responded to my questions with what seemed to me to be guesses or with the deflating "I don't know." Few tried to build upon others' remarks, even when invited to do so. Indeed, they seemed not to know the rules for participating in discussion. When they did respond to questioning, they often appealed to the teacher's authority rather than thinking aloud about questions they could not readily resolve. And when told that the meaning of the word "wean" could be found in the text itself, one student hurried for the dictionary instead. Many in the group remained confused about the nurse's account of the weaning, and they never arrived at a shared focus or concern—an issue they wanted to resolve. They made virtually no attempts, even when requested to do so, to support their views with lines from the text, and what "evidence" they gave was general. In short, the students seemed to have little interest in the play or the conversation, and I spent much of the time trying to determine whether they had grasped the factual events and storyline.

In Conversation 4, we began to see some change. True, I continued to worry about whether the students were grasping the text at a factual level. Why? Because they insisted that Juliet might not be a Capulet. To raise this question, it seemed to me, meant either that they were simply misreading or that they were trying to provoke me. However, as the discussion of this matter progressed, the students did not once respond "I don't know" to a question, nor did I hear many guesses. While the issue of Juliet's lineage seemed to me phony, the students seemed to take it seriously. They began to express their opinions by responding to the comments of others. They seemed to be thinking aloud and were raising new ideas about the matter, as when Henry suggested that upon her marriage, Juliet's mother might not have changed her name. This time the students did arrive at a shared focus; they seemed truly eager to defend the possibility that Juliet might not be a Capulet. Yet, one of them still maintained that the girl "must be" a Capulet because I, the teacher, had said so!

While the students were involved with the play in Conversation 4, they did not raise a genuine textual issue, since their question about Juliet was answered definitively by the work. They did not seem to be bound by the evidence in the text, since their question was based in part on what seemed to be wishful thinking that they attributed to Romeo. Indeed, their empathy with Romeo—which suggested to some that he might well wish Juliet were not a Capulet—seemed to cloud their perception of the text as it limited their focus. Nevertheless, the issue had arisen in part because Michael noticed that Romeo does ask "Is she (Juliet) a Capulet?" (act I, scene v). Here, then, was evidence that the students were beginning to look at the text and to draw on it to defend their ideas.

In Conversation 5, the students reach a genuine textual issue they wish to resolve, namely: Why did Juliet not tell Romeo to leave the garden, even though he was in danger by remaining there? The question was posed by Mrs. Prince, who drew it out of the discussants' comments. While there were still arbitrary "guesses" and "I don't know's" in this conversation, the students show increased willingness to listen to and build upon others' remarks. Some students were willing to free-associate in order to come up with new ideas. This time, there were no appeals to the teacher's authority.

While Marvin refused to seek textual evidence for a point he made, Colette did do so when asked. And James spontaneously moved to support his position with a line from the play. In general, then, students were beginning to ground their remarks in the play itself. As concern with the text increased, the discussants seemed to be swept along by textual issues. In the debate between the students over why Juliet did not tell Romeo to leave the garden, seven students—James, Colette, Sylvia, Richard, Marcy, Henry, and Myrna—pursued the matter with intensity, along with the two teachers. Furthermore, some—like Marcy, who insisted that Juliet was trying to lure Romeo into her bedroom—seemed to be drawing on personal experience to elaborate ideas about the characters and their actions.

As we saw, Conversation 6 gave evidence that the students in the Belden classroom were beginning to function as a group. While there was still some guessing about the answers to questions and students replying that they "did not know" on four occasions, there were several significant changes. To begin with, Colette opened the conversation with a question: Why was Juliet in such a rush to marry Romeo? To this, students offered conflicting interpretations. Together, we evolved an issue that they clearly cared to address, namely, whether Capulet would prefer to hear about Romeo's marriage to Juliet before or after its occurrence. Here, then, was a genuine issue for the group that had been raised by the students themselves, not by the teacher. Furthermore, there were no appeals to the teacher's authority. On the contrary, some seemed to take great pride in thinking they were right, that they knew what the text was saying. We saw this particularly when several worked together to interpret a line from Friar Lawrence's speech that spoke of turning the Montague and Capulet households' "rancor to love."

The students' attitude toward the text had shifted, it seemed. Not only did they interpret a passage together, but they appeared certain that they were right and proud of their accomplishment. They then persevered with the analysis of the friar's "herb" speech, which was difficult for them, until they were able to make some sense of it. That they were willing to work at this difficult passage showed a great change from the attitude they had displayed toward the nurse's speech about weaning Juliet in Conversation 2. Finally, the appeal to personal experience once again had a dramatic effect on the discussion: Colette's assertion that she would "kill Romeo" if he eloped with her daughter set up the issue of whether Capulet would prefer to hear about the marriage before or after its occurrence.

In Conversation 7, there was not one "I don't know" response from the discussants, nor were there instances of what seemed to be guesses. The students continued to pose and pursue resolution of questions: What does the friar mean when he says "Thank you, daughter?" asks Myrna as we finish reading the scene. Again, there is no appeal to the teacher's authority. On this occasion, the students disagree with the teacher: "Sure sounds like [Romeo and Juliet are going to bed]," says Marcy to me. The reader may recall also that the students did not hesitate to express their opinions of "Shakespeare's view" of premarital sex. And once again, the group arrived at a shared focus, which began with the attempt to interpret the meaning of the friar's puzzling remark to Juliet. This time, the issue became an evaluative one: Was sex before marriage acceptable, and if so, under what circumstances?

While I pose the issue about the meaning of the friar's comment to Juliet, it is Marcy who raises the matter that captures everyone's attention when she asks whether Romeo and Juliet are going to sleep together. Her question arises directly out of the play, and she quotes the relevant line in posing it. Although there is an evaluative portion of this conversation, it seems that the students' concern with and sensitivity to the text has greatly intensified since Conversation 2. In addition, the willingness to share, compare, and otherwise discuss personal views has certainly not diminished, as evidenced by the discussion of sex before marriage. On the contrary, the play seems to have provided a basis for discussing a topic of great concern to the students and Mrs. Prince.

We have witnessed, then, genuine alteration, if not transformation, in the Belden discussants—a turning of the soul, if you will—in that they are now approaching the interpretive discussion opportunity much differently than they did at first. They are also finding more meaning in the play than was the case initially and perhaps more meaning in at least some aspects in their own lives. Art, says the philosopher Gadamer, "is the raising up of . . . reality into its truth."[2] It is not that the students have come to agree with Shakespeare, or even that they have "properly understood" the play. Rather, in reading and discussing it, they have drawn on their personal experience to interpret texts; and the text, then, has become a basis for reflecting on life's experiences. In short, their use of the discussion opportunity is not what it was at first.

As final evidence that these discussants are now engaged with the text much differently than they were at the start, let us consider an argument that occurred between them as they were discussing act III, scene ii. In this instance, the students not only argued over the meaning of the lines and worked together to interpret them, but they were more insistent that they be heard and understood than in previous discussions. They seem to feel more intensely than ever before the importance of both gaining from and contributing to an analysis of the play.

In scene ii of act III, Juliet's nurse tells the girl that Romeo has killed her cousin Tybalt and that as punishment, he has been banished from their town of Verona. Upon learning that Romeo has been exiled, Juliet cries:

*

JULIET: "Tybalt is dead, and Romeo—banishéd."
That "banishéd," that one word "banishéd,"
Hath slain ten thousand Tybalts. Tybalt's death
Was woe enough, if it had ended there;
Or, if sour woe delights in fellowship
And needly will be ranked with other griefs,
Why followed not, when she said, "Tybalt's dead,"
Thy father, or thy mother, nay, or both,
Which modern [ordinary] lamentation might have moved?
But with a rearward [rear guard] following Tybalt's death,
"Romeo is banishéd"—to speak that word
Is father, mother, Tybalt, Romeo, Juliet,
All slain, all dead. "Romeo is banishéd"—
There is no end, no limit, measure, bound,
In that word's death; no words can that woe sound.

———

SHG: Now, how does Juliet feel about the fact that Romeo is banished?
MARCY: She doesn't feel too good about it.
SHG: What makes you say that, Marcy" Where does she say that?
MARCY: Hmmmm.
MICHAEL: Maybe she keeps saying "banished" because he left without saying anything.
SHG: OK, but then she says, "Romeo is banished[1]—To speak that word / Is father, mother, Tybalt, Romeo, Juliet, / "All slain, all dead." What does she mean when she says that?
HENRY: If he goes away, all of them will die. If somebody sends him away.
MP: Henry says that if they send him away, all these people are going to die. OK. That is what Henry is saying. Now is that what she means?
COLETTE: No.
RICHARD: It does to her. If Romeo goes, it's like all of them are dead.
SHG: You are saying, Richard, that she feels, if Romeo is banished, she feels that all these people are dead. That is how bad it is. Henry you had a very interesting idea. What do you think of

what Richard just said? Is that different from what you were
thinking?
HENRY: Not really.

At this point in the conversation, Henry says he hears no distinction between his interpretation and Richard's. Perhaps he has not listened carefully
to Richard. Yet when Mrs. Prince asks Henry to reconsider what he has just
said, he shifts his claim:

MP: Did you understand what he said? Is it like what you said or
not the same?
HENRY: No, it ain't like what I said. Un-uh.
SHG: It isn't? Well which of you is right, do you think?
HENRY: I don't know.

Does Henry change his response to our question about Richard's comment
because he realized they had two different ideas? Or does he change because
we are questioning him on the matter? If the former, why does he have no
opinion about which interpretation is right? At this point, it is not yet clear
that Henry is really thinking much about the conversation. Things now
continue:

MP: Are you all clear on the two ideas they had?
MYRNA: I ain't clear on the ideas.
SHG: Let's ask each of them to say again what they said. Some of
you maybe didn't hear Henry, some of you maybe didn't hear
Richard. OK, Henry, what was your idea about what Juliet was
saying here?
HENRY: That if they send him away, all of them will die.
SHG: If he goes away, all of these other people are going to die.
JAMES: So what are you saying Richard?
SHG: Yes, Richard, what was your idea?
COLETTE: It is the same thing.
RICHARD: No, I said that to her, Romeo is—you all listening
now? I said if Romeo is banished, she feels like all of them are
dead.

When Myrna says she is not clear about Henry's and Richard's ideas, she
indicates that thus far she may not have been listening too carefully. But in
saying she is not clear—rather than remaining silent—she suggests that she
wants to know what was said. The fact that James asks Richard to state his
idea, once Henry repeats his, indicates that he too is getting drawn into the

conversation and wants to know what others were saying. When Colette asserts that Richard and Henry are saying "the same thing," she indicates that she also wants to participate in the discussion and perhaps that she has been listening and has made a judgment about the similarity of the two ideas. So the evidence before Richard, as he is about to make his statement, is that there are at least six people—Myrna, James, Henry, Colette, and the two teachers— who are waiting to hear his view. And he wants to be heard, it seems: "You all listening now?" he says before he begins. It seems important to Richard that he be properly understood; and it seems important to others that they get his position clear. The conversation moves on:

> SHG: Give me a bit more.
> JAMES: He said that if Romeo is banished, then all of them are dead.
> RICHARD: I said *that's how she feels. That's how bad she feels.*
> You know what I am saying?
> COLETTE: No we don't.
> MYRNA: We know what Henry is saying, though.
> MARCY: So you are saying her father and mother and she and
> Romeo be dead if he is banished.
> RICHARD: I'm saying *that's how she feels!* If all of them are dead,
> you know how bad she would feel. *That is how she feels if Romeo
> is banished. Do you understand now?*
> MICHAEL: OK.

James and Marcy do something we have seen the leaders do many times but these participants only infrequently: they repeat back to the speaker what they heard him saying. Now in this instance, both James and Marcy seem not to have understood Richard, at least he seems to feel they have not, as he forcefully reasserts his position each time. But the fact that some participants are trying to say back to one another what they have heard indicates a growing desire to understand the speaker. It also indicates that they know how to find out if they have grasped the point.

Now the reader may suspect that perhaps Colette and Myrna, and perhaps James and Marcy as well, are not really trying to understand Richard. After all, his point seems to be stated quite clearly, at least from the observer's perspective. Do Colette and Myrna really fail to grasp it? Maybe they are trying to provoke Richard, much as they seemed to be trying to provoke me the day they insisted that Juliet might not be a Capulet. Let us see what the next segment of the exchange suggests:

> COLETTE: She is saying that Romeo killed all those people?
> SYLVIA: No, no, no, Colette!

SHG: Richard, go ahead and explain it again.

RICHARD: I already explained it.

MP: Tell her why her idea is wrong.

RICHARD: You got it, Michael, you know. You tell'em.

MICHAEL: It's not my idea.

MP: Did you hear what Colette just said, Michael?

MICHAEL: What did she say?

COLETTE: I said that Romeo killed—that she thinks Romeo is banished because she thinks he killed all those people.

MARCY: She feels alone if Romeo is gone.

SHG: OK, Marcy, and Richard was saying before that Romeo's being gone makes Juliet feel as bad as if—

RICHARD: *As if her father and Tybalt is gone!*

SHG: —*as if* all these people were killed. That was his point. That is how bad she feels. OK, so she is not too happy about this.

Colette seems to be genuinely confused about Juliet's speech: "She is saying that Romeo killed all those people?" she asks. "No, no, no," says Sylvia, indicating that she thinks Colette has misunderstood. At this point, Colette seems to be trying to interpret the text rather than grasp Richard's interpretation. Her doing so may have made it difficult for her to attend to Richard's remarks, which may explain why she has not grasped his point. Marcy, however, is now repeating Richard's point: "She feels alone if Romeo is gone." Perhaps Marcy is looking at the text and interpreting it for herself, or perhaps she is repeating what she thinks Richard was saying. In either case, Marcy's and Richard's interpretations are very close to one another. So Marcy, and it seems Colette as well, were drawn into the debate over the text rather than trying to provoke Richard. And what of the others?

SHG: Now Henry, what do you now think of Richard's idea here?

HENRY: I think he was right.

SHG: So you agree with it?

HENRY: Uh-uh.

SYLVIA: I'm saying that—

MP: Go on, Sylvia—

SYLVIA: That she will feel bad if her mother and father and Tybalt were dead, right?

COLETTE: Do she think Romeo is dead?

HENRY: No, she doesn't think that, Colette!

COLETTE: What I'm trying to say is does she think Romeo did it?

SYLVIA: Did what?

MYRNA: Did what?

> COLETTE: Killed all her people?
> HENRY: Her people aren't dead!

Notice what has happened here. Henry seems to have been persuaded that Richard's interpretation is correct—which means that he, Henry, was wrong. Evidently, the conversation has convinced Henry that he was not right at first. Furthermore, he corrects Colette in a way that suggests he is quite sure of what did and did not happen. So he seems to have formed a new and clear interpretation of Juliet's remarks. James has now dropped out, which may mean that he understands Richard and thinks, like Henry and maybe Myrna, that his interpretation is correct. Colette and Sylvia are the only ones who continue to pursue the topic. Why? Perhaps it is because both of them are still feeling confused. Sylvia asks whether Juliet will feel bad if her "mother, father, and Tybalt are dead," suggesting that she is trying to grasp what is happening. Colette asks whether Juliet thinks that Romeo killed her family members, and she seems to be struggling generally to understand the text.

If my interpretation of the student conversation is correct, then it suggests that either the discussants were not trying to provoke Richard initially, or that if they were, they gave up this effort. They seem to continue talking either to get or give help in figuring out what the text means. Indeed, the conversation seems to have a cooperative spirit and ends on a note of consensus that one might not have anticipated from this group at one time:

> MP: Right, she feels that alone. Go on. Do you understand now, Colette?
> SHG: So, what does it mean for Juliet if Romeo is banished? Henry.
> HENRY: She can't see him, I guess.
> MARCY: Her heart is being broken.
> SHG: OK, her heart would be broken if she can't see him. Sylvia.
> SYLVIA: Now she will be a virgin on her marriage day!

It comes as no great surprise that Sylvia returns to the issue of sex. Indeed, these students, like others their age, seem to fixate upon that theme in *Romeo and Juliet*. And by focusing on the play, they have drawn out of themselves feelings about a subject that is otherwise difficult to discuss in a way that allows perspective and control. Sylvia's comment that Juliet will be a virgin on her wedding day seems to echo a universal fear that one may, for some reason, remain sexually unfulfilled. And to lay that fear upon the table opens the possibility for reflecting upon and coming to grips with it.

My claim, then, is not that the Belden students have become mature discus-

sants in the space of twelve weeks and one Shakespeare play. Rather, I would
say that they have experienced that turning of the soul I have described: they
have begun to find meaning in the play and use it to draw out feelings and
beliefs that they have. We have seen them come to the text looking to grasp
what it says; they have worked to make sense of it, which means developing
and defending interpretations of its lines, listening to, correcting and modifying others' interpretations, and drawing on their own experiences to form the
interpretations. The discussants now practice many of the rules for participating in interpretive discussion (criterion one of a "good" interpretive discussion; Conversation 3), come up with new ideas about the meaning of the work
(criterion two) that they defend with textual evidence (criterion three), form
genuine textual issues that they wish to resolve (criterion four), and listen
more carefully to each other, at least at moments (criterion five). Finally, the
discussion excerpt we have just seen suggests that these students are beginning
to pursue the discussion of textual issues to the point where an "object" of the
conversation is emerging. Given Richard's interpretation of Juliet's speech,
some conclusions about the meaning of the play follow necessarily. Indeed,
Henry informs Colette, in no uncertain terms, that Romeo cannot have killed
all of Juliet's family. His conviction about this point arises from his belief that
Juliet means to say simply that Romeo's banishment feels to her as bad as if her
entire family had died.

Now, what of the teachers, Mrs. Prince and myself?[3] Have we, too, been
changed, perhaps transformed, through the discussion experience? We, like
the students, seem to respond to the situation much differently in later conversations than we did first. So what has happened to us?

Thinking back to Conversation 1, the reader may recall that I was keenly
aware of the racial and social differences between myself and others at the
Belden School. Indeed, I was self-conscious to the point of not asking students
about phrases I was unsure of at the time (e.g., "having her picks and
chooses"). At first, too, I was stunned by the students' comments—by the dramatic nature of their experiences, the power of their descriptions, and their
willingness to share their feelings and personal histories with a stranger. Indeed, I was so taken aback that it was difficult for me to respond effectively to
the discussants initially. At the same time, Mrs. Prince, who seemed to know
her students well, encouraged them to participate, reading aloud from their
papers about times they took revenge (or thought of taking it). She interacted
easily with the students and seemed to have powerful relationships with them.

The self-consciousness—the sense of difference that I felt—persisted for a
time. Although I was aware of the wealth of personal experience these students

brought to the discussion situation, I had difficulty at first in helping them relate these experiences to the text. In Conversation 2, there were many instances when I ignored the opportunity to explore students' beliefs and values (for example, when Sylvia said that Juliet's mother ought to be beaten for not knowing the girl's age). I also failed to question students if I believed they could not support their responses with evidence from the play, as I feared they would not speak again. I was preoccupied with whether they were grasping the factual events in *Romeo and Juliet* and with my own convictions about teaching and learning. Recall, for example, how I sustained a discussion on the word "wean," believing that the students would gain confidence if they saw that they could determine its meaning from the nurse's speech. In that discussion, Mrs. Prince said little, except to correct students or draw them out, often trying to move them, it seemed, to the "right" answer. Indeed, the unified, almost choral responses that greeted her questions about the meaning of the word "wean" at the end of the discussion suggested that she was pushing hard for group consensus.

In Conversation 4, I began to relax and question the students about their ideas more fully. Indeed, I seemed to have been exploring their personal experiences and values without realizing I was doing so: When I asked the discussants why they thought Juliet might not be a Capulet, I did not realize that their reasons sprung from life in their own families. Instead, I worried that they were trying to provoke me, perhaps for boring them. I continued to be concerned about whether they were grasping the text—the issue of whether Juliet was a Capulet seemed either designed to provoke or the result of factual misunderstanding—and was still afraid to question students about their erroneous remarks. When Mason said that Romeo's line "Is she a Capulet?" referred to Juliet's mother, I quickly explained how he might have thought that instead of asking the student to explain himself. Mrs. Prince again said little, working mostly to encourage the students to participate.

In Conversation 5, I remained fixed on the task of interpreting the text, just as I had been in Conversations 2 and 4. Yet this time I deliberately asked students to draw on their beliefs about human relations so as to interpret the play (why Romeo is not worried as he stands in Juliet's garden). The questions I posed were now largely interpretive, and I seemed less preoccupied with students' grasp of the play at the factual level. I still hesitated to question students when I did not see evidence for their claims, as when James suggested that Romeo might have been afraid of Juliet.

For the first time, Mrs. Prince took a more prominent role in the discussion. She posed an interpretive question to which the students responded at length (why Juliet does not tell Romeo to leave the garden and go home). While there is some possibility that the teacher had an answer in mind to this question when she asked it, the text gives no definitive answer, so we could sustain a discussion of it. Mrs. Prince drew on the students' personal experience and values by asking them how they would respond to Juliet's situation.

By Conversation 6, I myself was finally working to draw out the beliefs, values, and ideas that were based on students' experiences outside of the classroom. Indeed, when Colette began the discussion by raising a question ("Why was Juliet in such a rush to marry Romeo?"), I tried to clarify the question and helped it to evolve until the group arrived at an issue it seemed to wish to resolve (whether Capulet would prefer to hear about Juliet's marriage to Romeo before or after it occurred). To form this question, students drew on their understanding of family relations. While I continued to stress the interpretation of the text, I did things I had never done before in the discussion, such as interpreting lines for the students, defining words for them, and encouraging a particular interpretation of the friar's "herb" speech. I sustained a long analysis of a single passage, something I had not done with such determination since Conversation 2; but this time I did it with the students instead of despite them. Mrs. Prince, however, was virtually silent through the discussion.

In Conversation 7, it was I who was silent. While I began the discussion by focusing the students on interpretation of the play, I did not work to draw out their personal experiences. Indeed, when they began discussing the sexual habits of nuns and priests, I responded with "factual" information about the policies of the Catholic church instead of questioning the students about their positions. I also found myself giving a negative answer to Marcy—instead of questioning her—when she asked whether Romeo and Juliet go to bed. My style seemed to have changed!

Meanwhile, Mrs. Prince had a lengthy exchange with the students in which she asked them to evaluate "Shakespeare's view" of premarital sex. In so doing, she questioned them about their own views of the matter. It seemed to me that she was "moralizing," trying to get the students to take a certain position on the issue. Both of us, then, were behaving somewhat differently than we had previously.

Now the question arises: Did Mrs. Prince and I undergo transformation? Or did we simply respond somewhat differently on different occasions, perhaps because of changes in the situation? I am not certain of Mrs. Prince, but I would have to say that in my own case the former seems a better description than the latter.[4] While I began with firm convictions about how to help the students read and enjoy *Romeo and Juliet,* I found myself drawing on these less and less as time went on. It is not that I made a conscious decision to change. On the contrary, I simply found myself doing things differently than I had done them with other groups in other circumstances. So, for example, I did not decide to interpret passages for students or give them definitions of words or push them toward certain interpretations. These things simply happened.

Not only was I behaving differently, but I found I was deepening my encounter with the play and with these students as time went on. I saw things in the lines that I had not seen before. And as we talked, I saw things in the students and in myself that had remained hidden until then. My self-consciousness, my sense of difference from the others, had evaporated, and I had become a member of this group exploring *Romeo and Juliet*. Indeed, the changes in my behavior seemed to allow me to gain more from the situation than had been the case at first.

It does not seem to me that the teachers in the Belden classroom taught the students to come to the discussion experience very differently over time, or that the students caused the teachers to change—or perhaps become transformed.[5] Rather, it seems more useful to think of the Belden classroom as a changing situation. Playing the game of interpretive discussion moved the entire situation—the students, the teachers, even the rules of the game themselves. Let me explain this point.

An interpretive discussion does not occur until people become bound by its constraints. If one is a discussant, then one responds to the leader and the other discussants in certain prescribed ways, some of which were indicated in Conversation 3. If one is the leader, then one follows certain other practices. In playing the game, both discussants and leaders give themselves up to it: that is, their purposes become the purposes identified in the game of interpretive discussion—for example, that of making interpretations of the text. The interpretations that emerge from the discussion are an outcome or product of observing its constraints.

As people become players in the game, their participation is altered. Over and over, we watched as students and teachers were drawn into the conversations. That is, they began following its rules and were swept away as things happened—things which opened up the meaning of play, their ideas about themselves, and others' ideas about them. As they attached more ideas to the text, they connected its events with ideas and events they had experienced elsewhere in their own lives. In so doing, they began to see their lives, or moments in their lives, in perspectives that the play provided. They also began to see the play itself in perspective.[6]

In Conversations 9 and 10, we return to the Chalmers classroom. Once again, we will witness what may be a turning of the soul that seems to take place as these students and their teacher work to interpret the play. While the apparent alteration looks different from that which we have seen at Belden, it is in its own way equally remarkable.

PART THREE

How Do Students Learn to Build an Interpretation?

CONVERSATION 9
Getting It "Wrong"

Let us now return to the students in the Chalmers School classroom, whom we last observed in Conversation 3. The reader may recall that at that time, their teacher, Mrs. Spring, was concerned that the discussants were neither listening carefully to each other nor making defensible interpretations of the text. When the group was discussing act I, scene v, and trying to determine why Capulet became so angry with Tybalt, for example, their teacher was hesitant about Edna's contention that Capulet was scheming. Likewise, she was unconvinced by Jarvis's claim that Tybalt had been trying to manipulate Capulet into confronting Romeo at the party.

The problem of how to help students learn to build sound textual interpretations is a pressing one for anyone who teaches through interpretive discussion. Indeed, we have seen the teachers at Belden as well as Mrs. Spring struggle with it. Recall, for example, the time when Marcy insisted that Juliet wanted Romeo to come into her bedroom, or the day when several of the Belden students maintained that Juliet might not be a Capulet. The question of how to help discussants build sound interpretations is an ongoing issue that resists simple, formulaic resolution. Why? Because the problem arises from the very nature of the discussion itself. On the one hand, a central goal is to help students interpret texts for themselves. The teacher's role is to ask questions that draw out the students' ideas about the meaning of the text. What, then, is the teacher to do when the discussants form interpretations that seem inappropriate, that seem to overlook or misconstrue portions of the text? One might think that she could stop questioning and simply "tell" the students the "correct" answer.[1] Is this the case? And if not, has she no choice but to allow the "misinterpretation" to stand?

On this occasion, Mrs. Spring, an experienced teacher with experienced discussants, encounters great frustration in trying to resolve these questions. The reader will see that although both students and teacher follow the rules for building interpretations, the teacher worries that some of the students are misunderstanding the play. And if they "misunderstand" it, can they be learning what they should from it? Mrs. Spring manages the situation as she sees fit, but without satisfaction. After the student conversation, she and I reflect on the dilemma.

We rejoin the Chalmers students as they are discussing act III, scene i of *Romeo and Juliet*. In this scene, Tybalt, who is Juliet's cousin, kills Mercutio, Romeo's friend, whereupon Romeo slays Tybalt. In the following discussion, it is Benvolio, Romeo's cousin and close friend to Mercutio, who receives closest scrutiny. Indeed, Benvolio's opening speech is the subject of great controversy. He says:

*

BENVOLIO: I pray thee, good Mercutio, let's retire.
The day is hot, the Capels are abroad,
And, if we meet, we shall not 'scape a brawl,
For now, these hot days, is the mad blood stirring.

──────

MS: Larry, do you have a question?
LARRY: Two things. Benvolio seems to be always like calm and reasonable. Not caught up in the furor of the fight. The other thing that strikes me is that he seems to know that the Capulets are around, and they should avoid a fight because their tempers are hot. He knew that the Capulets were mad about them [Romeo, Mercutio, Benvolio] coming to the party [act I, scene v].
MS: OK, a very nice point about this kind of reasonable, kind of thinking things through. Trying to keep cool. Believing he [Benvolio] cannot change characters, he says: "let's get out." Edna.
EDNA: Maybe one of the reasons Benvolio is saying that to Mercutio—"Let's go, let's go"—is because he knows, himself, he can't avoid the fight. In a way, Tybalt is right, in the beginning [act I, scene i] when he said, "You mean to make peace when you are drawing your sword." It's true, it's almost instigating it even more. Benvolio is like, "Stop, I have a sword."

──────

At this point, two conflicting visions of Benvolio are beginning to emerge. Larry has argued that the young Montague seems to be reasonable and thoughtful, while Edna asserts that he "can't avoid the fight," that he seems to be instigating it. These students have learned that when conflicting interpretations arise, one seeks evidence in the text for support or refutation. In other words, one tries to use the interpretation to explain events in the work. Larry proceeds to do precisely this:

──────

MS: Larry.
LARRY: Yes, but I mean in act II, scene i, Juliet's garden, where

> Mercutio and Benvolio are trying to get Romeo out of the bushes,
> Benvolio knows it's a situation that could explode into a fight.
> Because we know Mercutio has a quick temper, and if Romeo
> gets offended, then he and Mercutio are going to fight. He
> [Benvolio] is saying, "Don't talk about Rosaline like that because
> that's going to cause a fight."

Larry has used his interpretation of Benvolio—that he is reasonable and
trying to avoid conflict—to explain why he attempts to silence Mercutio in
Juliet's garden. Since the interpretation works to explain Benvolio's actions in
act II, scene i, that passage seems to support Larry's view.

One way to respond to Larry's point is to reinterpret the passage he has
cited, that is, to explain those events using an alternative account. Abby next
proceeds to do just that:

> ABBY: He [Benvolio] thinks he has the power to say, "You can't
> talk about it?"
> MS: Now, let's look at the line. It is page 73—
> ABBY: Benvolio thinks he knows better than anyone else. He
> steps in where he shouldn't. It's not his business.
> MS: Line 22, Abby. When Mercutio is saying—

What Larry sees as supportive of Benvolio's temperate qualities Abby takes
as evidence that he is trying to control situations. Benvolio's behavior with
Mercutio in Juliet's garden, says Abby, shows that Benvolio is pushy, "that he
steps in where he shouldn't." Abby, then, is reinterpreting the passage that
Larry cited to support her contrasting interpretation of Benvolio.

At this point in the conversation, Mrs. Spring is trying to intervene, but
without success. Twice she asks Abby to actually read a line in the passage to
which she is referring. Abby reasserts her view after Mrs. Spring's first request
and the teacher is again cut off after the second one. The situation here is typ-
ical. Think of the Belden discussion in which James kept insisting Juliet meant
to say "I do" when she was greeted by the friar's remark that Romeo would
thank her for them both later. James seemed unable to entertain any other
idea. As soon the out-of-turn speaker finishes, Mrs. Spring tries again:

> MS: What is it that Benvolio is after? What does he care about?
> Does anybody have any evidence?
> LARRY: I just wanted to say that I don't think he's all just trying
> to take power. At the beginning [act III, scene i] he says, "I pray
> thee, good Mercutio, let's retire." So he's just trying to do it for
> the general goodness instead of trying to take control. I mean

who would say, if they were trying to take control, "I prey thee"?
He's just saying, "Please stop."
MS: OK, Martin.
MARTIN: Yeah, he's pleading with him.
MS: So it sounds like a request. And even the words, "I prey
thee," is certainly not an order, not a command. It is gently said.
Very nice.

As Mrs. Spring indicates in her response to Larry and Martin, they have responded to her request for evidence appropriately. They have cited a passage and interpreted it, explaining why the evidence is evidence for their position.

Judging from her response, Mrs. Spring seems to feel comfortable with Larry's and Martin's interpretation of Benvolio. She does not ask them to consider the passage more closely, nor does she redirect them toward other evidence. In so doing, the teacher exerts direct control over the discussion, it might seem.

However, the control is only apparent. For the other students do not take Mrs. Spring's response to Larry and Martin as an indication that they are "right." Indeed, Janeen and Abby move on to interpret another part of act III, scene i, which they believe supports a different view of Benvolio:

MS: Janeen.
JANEEN: I think Benvolio does not want to fight because he is
scared, not because—
ABBY: Yeah! He is scared of his own person being hurt!
MS: Can you support that, Janeen?
JANEEN: Later in the scene when Mercutio and Tybalt start
fighting, Romeo says, "Draw, Benvolio; beat down their
weapons." It seems that Benvolio did do it [i.e., did draw his
sword] only after Romeo said to do it. So Benvolio didn't want to
get involved.
MS: OK, so we have the possible question of the definition of
cowardice, because we certainly see—

Here, Janeen makes a new point about Benvolio: that he is actually a coward. Her evidence is taken from later in act III, scene i, when Romeo tells Benvolio to break up the fight between Tybalt and Mercutio by drawing his sword and forcing them apart. Mrs. Spring seems to accept Janeen's evidence for saying that Benvolio is a coward. But once again, the teacher's response has no effect upon Larry, who, as we shall see, finds Janeen's suggestion "ridiculous." The evidence he points to comes right after Benvolio's opening speech, as Mercutio responds:

> MERCUTIO: Thou art like one of these fellows that, when he enters the confines of a tavern, claps me his sword upon the table and says, "God send me no need of thee!" and by the operation of the second cup draws him on the drawer [draws his sword on the waiter], when indeed there is no need.
> BENVOLIO: Am I like such a fellow?
> MERCUTIO: Come, come, thou art as hot a Jack in thy mood as any in Italy; and as soon moved to be moody [angry], and as soon moody to be moved [quick tempered].

LARRY: What Mercutio was saying about Benvolio would have been ridiculous if he had been a coward. Mercutio was saying, "You're the one who is always starting up fights." That could have been wrong, but it would have been completely ridiculous if Benvolio was really a coward.

Notice that the role of the teacher is minimal in these exchanges. The students are clear about how to justify their claims, and they proceed to identify and interpret the evidence as they see fit. That the teacher agrees or disagrees with the interpretation goes almost unnoticed by the students, it seems. On the one hand, the students have gained a freedom from the teacher that allows them great latitude. At the same time, they do not respond to the teacher's guidance at moments when she is eager for them to do so.

There is a very real sense, then, in which the leader of an interpretive discussion gives up control of the group. This is not to say that no one has control but rather that the control shifts from the teacher to the constraints of the discussion itself. We have seen the shift beginning to occur at Belden. For example, the students no longer appeal to the teacher as the authority in disputes over the text. Recall, also, how in Conversation 7, Marcy followed her question about whether Romeo and Juliet were going to sleep together with the line from the play that inspired the question, as if to dispute my response that the couple was not yet going to bed. These students have begun to realize what the Chalmers discussants already know well: They are free to assert their ideas—no matter who agrees or disagrees—as long as they can support them with evidence from the text.

Now, the shift in the location of power in the interpretive discussion can cause tension to mount between student and teacher, as we see in the next exchange:

MS: Reed.
REED. I think he [Benvolio] doesn't want to get in trouble with the prince. Also, he talks about the voice of reason. He says, "By my head, here comes the Capulets." It just seems that Benvolio thinks more about what will happen to him after the fight than during it.
MS: Beautiful quote: "By my head," suggesting certainly that he is thinking in the situation: "Let's talk, let's do anything, but let's not fight in public."
EDNA: I have two things to say. First, with "by my head," Benvolio might mean, "by the danger of losing my head." Also, when the scene starts, there is more than just Benvolio observing the fights between Mercutio and Tybalt and then Tybalt and Romeo. At the end, when the citizens come in with the prince and the other people, Benvolio says, "Oh noble Prince, I can discover [reveal] all / The unlucky manage [course] of this fatal brawl." There are other people there who could have told what happened, but Benvolio uses the chance. He wanted to be outward and have the power of telling people. He wanted to be the center of attention.
MS: What the prince says—I am looking at page 104, lines 152–153—
ABBY: I can tell you what happened! On page 103 Benvolio jumps out of everyone and says, "I will tell you what happened." That just shows that he wants to be the center of attention and have people focus on him.

While Mrs. Spring seems comfortable with Reed's reference to and interpretation of Benvolio's "By my head" line, she seems less content with Edna's growing conviction that Benvolio is seeking personal power. As soon as Edna finishes, the teacher tries to focus attention on a passage in the text, a passage Abby jumps to interpret before the teacher has a chance to finish her question. Mrs. Spring perseveres, however:

MS: Do you assume that the prince trusts Benvolio's answer or not, Abby?
ABBY: Well, there are twenty other people there, or a couple. It doesn't matter how many. But they have observed the entire thing. It doesn't say they exit anywhere. So you can assume that they are all still there.

> MS: If I were in a room with Tybalt, Benvolio, and Mercutio, or if
> you were, who would you ask to tell the story, of the ones named?
> Would you ask Benvolio?
> LARRY: Yes, because he is not involved in the fight. He is neutral.
> EDNA: But he doesn't want to risk his own life. He isn't willing to
> jump in. Also, Benvolio is the kind of person who walks into a
> bar and then pulls a sword on the waiter. How likely is it that the
> waiter is carrying a sword? How likely is it that the waiter is
> going to be able to fight back? Why doesn't he fight someone
> else? Why wouldn't he fight another person who has a sword?
> MS: But we don't see a single example of Benvolio hurting
> someone.
> EDNA: But he pulls his sword and says, "I have the power."

Mrs. Spring seems to be trying to shift Abby's and Edna's view of Benvolio:
"If you were in a room with Tybalt, Mercutio, and Benvolio, who would you
ask to tell the story?" she asks; "Does the prince trust Benvolio's answer?"
Finally, in what seems to be mild desperation, she says: "But we don't see a
single example of Benvolio hurting someone." Her remarks suggest that the
teacher is unconvinced that the evidence supports the position that Edna and
Abby espouse.

The students, for their part, seem to give little thought to their teacher's
question. Instead, Edna takes up—without a defense for so doing—Mercutio's line that Benvolio is like the man who draws his sword on the waiter. It
is as if Edna has taken Mercutio's description of Benvolio as a statement of
fact! As the Abby and Edna reassert their interpretation, their teacher again
tries to question them:

> MS: Abby.
> ABBY: He doesn't care what he does. He wants to give the
> impression of power.
> MS: But I think we need to think about what Shakespeare did and
> why. Edna.
> EDNA: In a way, he's very much like Tybalt but he doesn't have the
> courage to fight.
> MS: Who would you rather have in your household, Edna—
> EDNA: We're not outwardly told that Benvolio is a nice, trusting
> person. He's with Mercutio and look at what they do. They go
> around gallivanting to private parties they're not invited to. They
> pick fights.
> MS: They do? I don't think that Benvolio picks fights.
> ABBY: Well, they're sitting there and saying something is going to

happen, we're going to end up in a fight. He is assuming, he doesn't say, "You had better get out of here, because you are going to get into a fight." It's like, we have to get out of here.

The two students continue to insist that Benvolio is cowardly, power-hungry, and aggressive. When Mrs. Spring asks them for evidence, they cut her off. When she says she can think of no example in which Benvolio picks a fight, Abby equates "sitting there and saying something is going to happen" with picking a fight. The teacher's questions and comments suggest that she still finds Edna's and Abby's perspective on Benvolio unconvincing.

It seems, then, that Mrs. Spring is facing a dilemma. On the one hand, she is asking the students to interpret the text for themselves, and she is giving them the opportunity to build a defense for their interpretations. She does so by calling on the students repeatedly and allowing them to explain why given events in the play support the picture of Benvolio that they are trying to paint. On the other hand, the teacher seems uncomfortable with the view of Benvolio that Edna and Abby have been advocating. Are these discussants misinterpreting the play? Mrs. Spring seems to think they might be. Now, if she cuts off their thinking in one way or another because she thinks they are wrong, then she undermines the goal of the interpretive discussion—the goal of helping the students to interpret the text for themselves. At the same time, if she does not succeed in eliminating the misinterpretation, then the students seem not to have learned what they should from the play.

As indicated previously, the dilemma is similar to the one I faced in Conversation 4, when the Belden students insisted that Juliet might not be a Capulet. It seemed to me that in that instance, the group was grossly misinterpreting the play, either because people were overlooking obvious evidence or because they were testing me by insisting upon the preposterous. If I terminated the discussion, then I would be undermining their effort—one of their very first— to grapple with the lines and interpret the text for themselves. At the same time, by allowing the conversation to continue, I seemed to be permitting a gross misinterpretation to stand. As the reader may recall, Mrs. Prince eventually convinced me that the students could well have seen a genuine issue where I saw none. But what of Mrs. Spring in the present situation? She and I discuss it in what follows:

MS: That was frustrating! I mean, did you ever think of Benvolio as power-hungry? Trying to get all the attention? Trying to mess around in other people's business? And just as senseless was the idea that he didn't want to get involved because he was cowardly.

Furthermore, none of my questions worked. When I asked them,
"Who would you ask to tell you what happened: Mercutio,
Tybalt or Benvolio?" the students all but ignored me!
SHG: Well, if you thought they were so far off base, why didn't
you just say so—tell them the truth about Benvolio?
MS: You saw what they were doing! It is clear that if I "told them
the truth," as you put it, they weren't going to hear it as the
"truth" unless my point fit into what they already believed. You
saw it: they just ignored me and went right on to say what they
had to say. If I tell them something that is inconsistent with or
contradicts that which they already accept, or if my "truth"
doesn't in some way make more sensible or meaningful that
which they already think, it isn't going to stick. I might as well be
talking to the trees. So telling Edna and Abby that Benvolio is not
power-hungry or whatever is meaningless until they can see it for
themselves—at which point they don't need me to tell them! All I
can do is point them to passages which I think raise questions
about their interpretation.[2]

Here, Mrs. Spring has come face to face with a fact about discussants at
times, a fact that can be advantageous or disadvantageous, depending upon
the situation. Once the students realize that the text, not the teacher, is the
authority, the teacher loses power; she cannot tell them the "truth" if the
"truth" they see in the text differs from the one she sees. It's not that she cannot
stop questioning and start telling; it is rather that the students may not hear
her if their interpretations differ from hers. Why did the students cling so to
their position?

SHG: But it seems they wouldn't even attend to the passages you
directed them towards, nor would they answer your questions.
Why was that, do you think?
MS: Well, as far as the questions are concerned, it seems to me
that they didn't see the point of addressing them. They were
working hard to defend the idea that Benvolio was power-hungry
and wanted to get all the attention. So why should they worry
about irrelevant matters like: "Who would you rather hear the
story of the fight from: Benvolio, Romeo, or Mercutio?"
SHG: I suppose that question might have seemed irrelevant to
Edna and Abby—
MS: Yes. They just got onto that interpretation of Benvolio and
from then on, all they were open to was evidence that they could
use to defend it. It was as though they started playing the game—

following the rules for making an interpretation—and got completely drawn into it.[3] The more they sought and found evidence for their position, the more they resisted contrary evidence.

SHG: But now you are saying something different. Now you are saying that they were closing themselves off to—defending themselves against—evidence that might contradict their interpretation.

MS: Yes, that's right. I mean they wouldn't really think about questions that might yield contrary evidence, nor would they think about such evidence when it did, somehow, get on the floor. Take, for example, the point that Larry brought up about act I, where Montague asks Benvolio to give an account of the fight that has occurred in the streets. Here was excellent evidence for the point that Benvolio might be an objective source of information, one that others could trust. But that was evidence that Edna and Abby had no use for. You notice they never made any comment about that passage.

SHG: So, the points in the discussion they hung on to seemed to be ones that they could somehow use to build their interpretation, to add to its meaning. Each new idea that they were willing to entertain had to somehow fit in with the rest of the interpretation.[4]

MS: Right!

SHG: But I ask you: If you were in the midst of such a creation, would you entertain additions that might dash it to the rocks, undoing all your hard work?

Our hypothesis, then, is that sometimes you cannot tell discussants a "truth" that contradicts their beliefs because they are too busy playing the game of interpretive discussion—so busy that there is no place in their thinking for a question about their understanding. When they are engaged in building an interpretation, they are relating beliefs to one another; then only the beliefs consistent with those already accepted may be woven into the fabric, while other ideas are ignored. And why not? After all, it is no mean accomplishment to construct an interpretation, even one that leaves significant points in the text unexplained.

Now, sometimes discussants are able to build interpretations while at the same time entertaining questions and evidence that contradict their explanations, especially when they are making an interpretation to resolve some question that is broader than the interpretation itself. Then the discussants are likely to treat their budding theories more tentatively than did Edna and Abby. As a result, they accept the need to modify their ideas as the evidence before them indicates, rather than ignore the evidence. But Edna and Abby are not at this point. They have no larger question they wish to resolve using their interpretation of Benvolio; so they resist all suggestion that their interpretation should be altered or abandoned.

Once again, we note a parallel with the discussion of the Belden class on the day that it argued that Juliet might not be a Capulet. My feeling then was that the students did not really believe the position they were advocating. Mrs. Spring does not seem to feel that Edna and Abby are deliberately trying to frustrate her, but she wonders why they insist on supporting so preposterous a position.

MS: But the question is: Why put something together that is so preposterous—Benvolio is power-hungry and aggressive!
SHG: Look, one question here is why their view seemed so preposterous to you—
MS: You mean you don't think it was preposterous?
SHG: Right now, it doesn't matter what I think of their view. The question is why it seemed so unlikely to you. If we understand that, then we will understand where your dilemma with these students came from. And that, after all, is the problem—your feeling of frustration. So let me ask you a question.
MS: What is that?
SHG: How many times have you taught this play?
MS: Maybe twelve or fifteen!
SHG: And you find it a powerful and moving work, right?
MS: That much needs saying?
SHG: And my guess is that a good bit of the power that you feel when you reread those lines and ponder those characters each time comes from the fact that the personalities and issues are so clear and alive to you, perhaps as a result of having had many conversations over many of the lines and aspects of the play.
MS: That's true. And part of what excites me is that I still see things I have never seen in the drama. For example, I had never noticed that in act I, scene i, Montague asks Benvolio for his account of the street fight that has occurred.
SHG: Which means that Benvolio, as a character, has acquired an additional touch of meaning for you, right? The fact that he was asked for his version of the fight by his uncle, Montague, is something you have now coupled with the many other facts

about Benvolio that you have noticed before. So your picture of him continues to take shape.

MS: I guess that's right. When Larry brought up that point about Benvolio in act I, I remember comparing it with his volunteering to describe the brawl in act III. If you think about it, the evidence in act I suggests that Benvolio couldn't be power-hungry and aggressive. If he were, how could he be counted upon to give an accurate rendering of incidents in which fights occurred? And if he couldn't be counted on to give an unbiased account, why would his uncle have asked him what happened?

SHG: All right, let's accept your reasoning about the matter. It seems to me that your view of Benvolio is providing you with a perspective—a context, if you will—to which you relate the fact that he is asked to describe a street brawl to his uncle in act I and volunteers to do so in act III. Your perspective, acquired over much time and many discussions, allows you to interpret these new observations in a way which seems to directly contradict the idea that Benvolio was power-hungry and aggressive.[5]

MS: So, the point is?

SHG: The point is that the intensity of your negative response to Edna and Abby's interpretation comes, I think, from the power of your own view of Benvolio, which was once again strengthened by today's discussion.

MS: But the fact is that my perspective makes a whole lot more sense than the one Abby and Edna were urging. I mean, it explains many more of the things that Benvolio and other characters do in the play. That is why I couldn't really take their position seriously.

SHG: Well, there is no question that their perspective seems to be based upon a more narrow focus than yours.

MS: Right. For example, they did not seem to think about the role that Benvolio played in act I, scene v, where he was urging Romeo to leave the party so as to avoid conflict. Does that look like a person who is trying to gain control? Like a person who picks fights? Of course not!

Given Mrs. Spring's testimony, we gain some ideas about why she felt such frustration with Edna and Abby's interpretation. Not only did it violate a view of Benvolio that the teacher had been constructing for many years, but in addition, her own perspective had been strengthened by some new evidence that Edna and Abby had found, evidence that they used to support a conflicting interpretation. Furthermore, the teacher says that she could not entertain

that conflicting perspective as a serious alternative to her own because it over-
looked events in the play, such as Benvolio's actions at Capulet's party, which
were better explained by her interpretation.

So we have some ideas about the source of Mrs. Spring's feelings. But what
about the students? Why was their perspective not broader? Why was their
focus so much narrower than their teacher's? We have said that they seemed
not to relate their interpretation of Benvolio to a question they wished to resolve. What, then, was the course of their thinking?

SHG: You know, it is not surprising that the students didn't think
of these other places in the text—
MS: As if they didn't remember them!
SHG: But maybe they didn't remember them. Perhaps we only
remember things that have meaning, that we connect to our
current thoughts. If we don't make those connections, then we
don't remember.[6] So there has to be a basis for connecting past to
present thought or we don't remember the past.[7]
MS: I'm not sure I am following this now.
SHG: Think about what Abby and Edna were remembering. As
we said, Edna noticed that Benvolio jumped out in front of all the
people who were gathered there—in act III, I am talking about
now—and declared that he would tell the story of the fight. Now,
everyone in the class was looking at the scene, but Edna is the one
who noticed that Benvolio volunteered to tell the story when
there were other observers present. Maybe she makes this
observation because of the perspective on Benvolio that she is
constructing. I doubt that she would have spotted his action here
had she not been looking for evidence that he was power-hungry,
agressive, and seeking attention.
MS: There may be something to what you say. I have to confess
that I hadn't noticed that Benvolio offered to tell the story until
Edna pointed it out.
SHG: It seems to me that we remember what is meaningful to us,
what we can connect to our present interests. And Edna was, at
that moment, busy constructing a particular interpretation of
Benvolio which opened a fact in act III—his volunteering to tell
about the fight—to her attention.[8] Had Edna and Abby had
some question in mind to which they tried to relate their
interpretation of Benvolio, they might have remembered other
events in the play as well.
MS: Actually, my sense was that Abby and Edna came upon their
view of Benvolio as power-hungry and aggressive for the first

time in this discussion. The fact that they were able to make sense
of things that Benvolio did using this perspective may have been
what excited them so much about it. I mean it is not easy to come
to even a tentative interpretation that you can try out in the way
they were doing.

Why, then, did some students focus on only those events that provided them
with evidence for their interpretation? The suggestion is that they could not
remember any others, as these were not opened to them by their current
interest, namely, defending their perspective on Benvolio. The many conversations about *Romeo and Juliet* Mrs. Spring has had over the years—conversations that have no doubt shown Benvolio from a number of perspectives—are
missing from the students' experience. The events in the play that they notice
depend on the nature of the one interpretation that they have just begun to
entertain. Unlike Mrs. Spring, they do not have the benefit of a time-tested and
probably more comprehensive perspective, one that allows them to recall
many more events of the play.

So now the question arises: If the students have a limited perspective, what
is the teacher to do if that perspective seems to be an inadequate one, one that
cannot explain many of the events in the play satisfactorily? This was precisely
my question about the Belden students when they insisted that Juliet might
not be a Capulet. Should one do nothing and hope the students' interpretations shift of their own accord? Mrs. Spring and I reflect on the problem in
what follows:

> MS: What is to be done if the students leave this classroom with
> an erroneous vision of the play and Shakespeare's message? What
> have they learned in such a case?
> SHG: Well, one thing we can say is that they have begun to do the
> job that they are supposed to do when reading the play, right?
> They have begun to construct a story that allows them to connect
> the events in the play to one another in a meaningful way. That
> means they will remember those events, that the story they use to
> connect them will allow them to bring the events up so as to,
> perhaps at some point, connect them to their lives.
> MS: Yes, but that story about Benvolio was all wrong—
> SHG: Wrong? By what criteria? It is not your story—
> MS: It is not Shakespeare's story!
> SHG: Well perhaps not, I agree. But is yours Shakespeare's story?
> MS: Look, I don't claim to have any corner on his view. What I

do know is that those two girls have made an interpretation of
Benvolio that cannot really stand up to the text in its entirety.

SHG: You may well be right about that. But don't they now have a
view to modify at least? And won't there be another class
tomorrow?

MS: Yes, but the question is, what should I do then? I can't tell
them the truth, as we said a long time ago. They won't hear it.
And they won't entertain conflicting evidence—that much we
have seen. They even resist the questions I ask to get them to
rethink their perspective.

SHG: Maybe you ought to just forget about Edna and Abby.
Maybe things will straighten out.

MS: Maybe. But what they need is a new perspective on Benvolio,
another way of looking at him.

———

We have seen Mrs. Spring in a situation that everyone who teaches through
interpretive discussion is bound to encounter. Although the Chalmers students are much more experienced than their counterparts at Belden, the
problem is present at both places. And indeed, I saw it in both schools on
many occasions. Recall that my resolution of it at Belden in one instance—to
simply let the students pursue the topic that seemed to me phony—may have
opened them to more appropriate conversation about the play in the future;
for after that day, they began to grope with genuine textual issues much more
eagerly.

In the next conversation Mrs. Spring tries with her class once again, and
this time, with more satisfying results. Not only do the students' interpretations seem more sensible to her, but for the first time, we see these discussants
drawing on their personal experiences in ways that seem to deepen their discussion of *Romeo and Juliet*. Indeed, the fact that the conversation brings
personal feelings and experience to bear upon the play may help to explain
why the interpretations become more appropriate.

CONVERSATION 10

Getting It "Right" (Again)

The following conversation occurred the day after the one we have just seen. The difference between the two sessions is striking, as the reader will shortly see. What accounts for the change in the student responses on the two successive days? Mrs. Spring and I take up this issue at the conclusion of the classroom conversation.

Having told the class that she now wanted to focus on Romeo in act III, scene i (the same scene they had discussed the day before), Mrs. Spring called the students' attention to the following passage:

*

TYBALT: Romeo, the love I bear thee can afford
No better term than this: thou art a villain.
ROMEO: Tybalt, the reason that I have to love thee
Doth much excuse the appertaining rage
To such a greeting. Villain I am none.
Therefore, farewell. I see thou knowest me not.
TYBALT: Boy, this shall not excuse the injuries
That thou hast done me; therefore turn and draw.
ROMEO: I do protest I never injured thee,
But love thee better than thou canst devise
Till thou shalt know the reason of my love;
And so, good Capulet, which name I tender
As dearly as mine own, be satisfied.

MS: Now, what values is Romeo showing here, and why? Sarah.
SARAH: Well, it has to be about Juliet. He is saying, "I love you more than you know; I value your name a lot." He is just saying that he loves Juliet.
MS: OK, beautiful. Abe.
ABE: In a way, Romeo is caring about the family like Tybalt does, but in another way. Because Tybalt is now his in-law; he loves him and cares about him. But Tybalt, because Romeo isn't a Capulet, he hates him.

MS: Beautiful—that love has now expanded Romeo's family to include what was formerly the enemy. Beautiful!

Today, Mrs. Spring begins the discussion by asking: "What values is Romeo showing here?" In other words: What does Romeo show that he cares about in this speech? The students respond appropriately: Juliet, says Sarah; Tybalt and the others in the Capulet family, says Abe. In both of these responses, the speaker takes Romeo's perspective and explains how the character thinks and feels. Indeed, it is his feelings for Juliet, Tybalt, and the others in his now expanded family that the students emphasize. The preoccupation with the characters' feelings increases as the conversation continues:

MS: Jarvis.
JARVIS: Right away, Tybalt comes up with the fighting side and that kind of shows where his mind is set, where he is coming at. Then, Romeo comes back with the love side and kind of disperses this.
MS: Kevin.
KEVIN: Tybalt is denying Romeo's love for Juliet. He is saying, "No, I want to fight you. You cannot love Juliet." He is saying—
MS: Now remember, Tybalt doesn't know about Juliet.
KEVIN: Oh! You're right. But Romeo is saying that you can't stop my love for her because I love her and that's the way I feel.

The striking thing about the conversation thus far is that unlike yesterday's, the students seem to be getting "inside" the fictional characters and imagining their emotional responses, as opposed to standing outside the characters and speculating about their motives. This time, the discussants seem to be imagining what they themselves, or anyone, might feel in Romeo's and Tybalt's shoes, much as Rousseau urged that young readers imagine themselves in Robinson Crusoe's! Even Edna pursues the analysis of Romeo in like fashion:

MS: Edna.
EDNA: I was going to say it seems almost like Romeo is being more mature than them. Before we saw, not right before, not actually in the play, but when Shakespeare was describing Romeo, Mercutio, and Benvolio, it was like these playful guys who go around and take part in things. It seems like Romeo maybe was overdoing it. He realizes he is married now and has to be mature about this. You can't avoid the relationship between the families, so maybe Romeo is trying to fix it.
MS: Beautiful. In some way, this is an outgrowth of the difference

between love and marriage. One of the things you have to think
about when you are married is family.
EDNA: And Mercutio is their responsibility because he has joined
them.
MS: OK.

Edna, like the previous speakers, "gets inside" the character: imagining
Romeo's thoughts and feelings, she explains his actions accordingly. She says
that Romeo responds to Tybalt as he does because he is trying to "fix" the
relationship between the families. Marriage, asserts Edna, makes Romeo realize that he must be mature and act responsibly toward Mercutio.

Let us pause to emphasize the dramatic contrast between Edna's contributions of yesterday and today. Whereas now she is explaining Romeo's actions
with reference to his thoughts and feelings, yesterday she did not account for
Benvolio's moves by speculating about his perspective. Instead, she attributed
motives to Benvolio—that he was cowardly, power-hungry, aggressive, and
seeking attention—and used these attributions to account for his comments
and actions. For example, she argued that Benvolio was cowardly, which is
why he said "by my head," a line that she interpreted to mean: by the danger
of losing my head. Likewise, the reason Benvolio volunteered to describe the
fight to the prince, said Edna, was that he was power-hungry and seeking attention. By contrast, today Edna says that Romeo resists Tybalt's challenge
because he realizes he must act more maturely than he has in the past and must
try to fix the relations between the families. She is, then, imagining how
Romeo thinks and feels, given his marriage to Juliet, and using these imagined
thoughts and feelings to explain the character's actions.

As the discussion continues, the students' preoccupation with Romeo's perspective takes an argumentative turn:

MS: Very nice. Now, here is one question which is implied in all
that you have been saying: Does it take strength or weakness to
respond—and my question is a neutral one— as Romeo is
responding to Tybalt? Is it hard or easy to do this? Reed.
REED: I think it is easy. It depends on Romeo's mood. I think the
guy has no depth. Whatever his mood, that is how it goes. Right
now he is in a really happy mood; he finds out he is going to
marry Juliet—
MS: In fact they are already married!
REED: Are they? All right. So they are married and he is in a real
happy mood. No matter what is said he is not going to notice.
What he says is, "Well, I love you, too, Tybalt." And he is just on

his way out before he finishes saying it. I don't think he is paying
much attention.
MS: OK, Brian.
BRIAN: Well, I disagree. I think that the reason he doesn't choose
to fight Tybalt right away is that he really does believe that this
whole fighting thing is stupid. This is why he also tries to break
up the fight between Mercutio and Tybalt. It is not just like he is
in a happy mood to jump in front of two swords.
MS: Nice.

Reed and Brian have contrary ideas about Romeo's feelings. Reed says that
it is easy for Romeo to resist Tybalt's challenge to fight since "the guy has no
depth," is just in a happy mood, and can easily ignore the challenge. Brian
disagrees, saying that Romeo resists Tybalt because he believes fighting is
wrong, not because he is in a happy mood. Like the previous speakers, Reed
and Brian both explain Romeo's actions with reference to feelings and beliefs
that they imagine him to have. There is a difference between these two speakers, however, in that Reed envisions Romeo's feelings by attributing a
character trait to him—that he has no depth—rather than imagining his perspective. Mrs. Spring and I discuss this difference later on.
    Now, on what grounds do the students infer the thoughts and feelings that
they attribute to Romeo? Brian, Edna, Sarah and Abe—that is, all but Reed—
seem to have been imagining what anyone in Romeo's situation might think
and do. Furthermore, the source of these speculations is their own experience,
experience that has generated beliefs about human motivation. Indeed, the
role of past personal experience is even more vividly displayed in the following
exchange:

ABBY: I want to say something!
MS: Yes, Abby?
ABBY: Up until then, everyone was upset with Romeo. And
Benvolio, even. Fighting is what their life really revolves around.
This rivalry. So it is hard for Romeo not to fight.
MS: Edna.
EDNA: Was Romeo's mother a strong part of his life at all?
MS: I think that is an interesting question. Say why you asked
that.
EDNA: Because he seems more psychological. A lot of times,
strong mothership makes men need women in their life. Just the
way he jumps from Rosaline to being so loving to Juliet. He may
just be looking for a mother figure.

MS: Interesting. Janeen.

JANEEN: I think that, before, Romeo just didn't want to fight because he was involved with Juliet. He didn't want to fight anyone. It's like a negative emotion. After Mercutio is dead, he gets angry because forces are guiding him into anger at his friend being killed.

Given these speakers' remarks, the source of the feelings they attribute to Romeo seems clear. To begin with, Abby maintains that it is hard for Romeo to ignore Tybalt, since life up to now has "revolved" around fighting. Abby's own experience, as a high school sophomore, may suggest to her that it can be difficult to resist the pull of tradition and peer pressure. Likewise, when Edna wonders whether Romeo is seeking a "mother figure," it appears that this question has been inspired by other reading, perhaps Freud, or some event in her personal experience she is now relating to the text. And when Janeen says that Romeo is driven first by his love for Juliet and then his anger over the loss of his friend, she too seems to draw on a prior understanding about the effects of these emotions, understanding that would seem to arise from personal experience.

Again, let us digress to note the dramatic change in these speakers from yesterday. We have already mentioned that Edna is approaching the analysis of Romeo very differently than she did that of Benvolio. Indeed, her drawing on a "Freudian" hypothesis—the role of the mother in one's life—suggests that to-day she is groping for some relevant experience that will yield insight into Romeo's situation. Abby, too, who yesterday worked so hard to substantiate her claim that Benvolio was seeking power and attention, today appears to draw upon her own sense of what someone whose life has revolved around fighting and friends might feel if challenged by the enemy before peers. And Janeen, who yesterday argued that Benvolio was cowardly, is now envisioning the effects that love and anger can have on a person, a move that allows her to "get inside" the character of Romeo and see things from his perspective.

The next speaker, Brian, likewise draws on his personal experience in ex-plaining Romeo's actions:

BRIAN: This is going way back. Someone said it was easy for Romeo not to fight. I think that's right. I think he said to Tybalt, "Don't do that; I like you more than you know," because Romeo is kind of dying to tell somebody what is going on with Juliet. He has just gotten married and it has got to stay a secret. But, you would think that he would want to tell somebody, so he's kind of

like giving him [Tybalt] this.
MS: OK, nice.

___

When Brian says that Romeo is "dying to tell" someone about his marriage to Juliet, he seems to draw on his experience of what it is like to be saddled with the task of keeping an exciting secret. This circumstance, says Brian, could motivate Romeo to "tell" Tybalt by resisting his challenge, thereby indicating that something had changed. Indeed, Romeo's words seem to suggest as much, says Brian. Here again, the discussant seems to "get inside" the character by using his own experience as a basis for imagining Romeo's thoughts and feelings and hence, the meaning of his words.

The discussion we have just seen between the Chalmers students and their teacher does seem to differ dramatically from the one that took place on the preceding day (Conversation 9). This time, the students seemed to give interpretations that did not strike the teacher as "crazy." Furthermore, many of their analyses seemed to result from imagining the characters' perspectives on the situations confronting them. The thoughts and feelings the discussants attributed to the characters appeared to arise from reflection on their own experiences of human motivation as well as study of the text.

Today's discussion, then, was also very different from the exchanges we observed among the Chalmers students in Conversations 1 and 3. In Conversation 3, Mrs. Spring worried that the students were neither listening carefully to each other nor making defensible interpretations of the play. In both Conversations 1 and 3, we noticed the discussants' tendency to talk at an abstract level rather than use personal, concrete experience as a basis for their comments. In the present instance, however, we have seen the discussants bring their own ideas about human action into their analysis of the text, ideas gleaned from their personal experience. The flow of their comments—the fact that, with one exception, they all work to interpret Romeo's character by envisioning his perspective and building upon each other's comments in some way—suggests that they are also becoming more attentive to the contributions of others.

Since today's discussion differs so drastically from yesterday's and those previous, one wonders why these differences have occurred. Mrs. Spring and I take up this question in what follows:

___

SHG: Well, how do you feel now?
MS: There is no question that I feel a lot better about this class than the one we had yesterday. By looking at Romeo and

thinking about why he did what he did, at least we got away from all the crazy stuff about Benvolio that Edna, Abby, and Janeen got into yesterday.

SHG: Yes, we didn't hear much about Benvolio today.

MS: Look, it's not that I minded talking about Benvolio. It's *the way* they were talking about him that distressed me, the fact that they weren't really trying to understand his character.

SHG: And do you think the students understood Romeo better?

MS: Well, today their ideas, their interpretations, could be justified by what we see in the play. Even the idea that Brian came up with in the end—that Romeo found it easy to respond to Tybalt because he was dying to tell someone about the marriage—was reasonable, and I thought, quite creative.

SHG: I would agree.

MS: But here's my question: Why, today, were students like Edna, Abby, and Janeen, so willing to imagine Romeo's feelings, to try to see things from his perspective, when yesterday they made little such effort with Benvolio?

SHG: Well, part of it may be that, last time, you did not ask them to explore Benvolio's feelings, whereas today, you asked several questions about how Romeo felt—what things he valued and whether it was hard or easy for him to ignore Tybalt's challenge, for example.

MS: OK, those questions might be addressed by thinking about Romeo's perspective. And I have to admit that I hoped students would do that when I posed them. But the questions themselves did not demand reflections on things from Romeo's point of view. Remember how Reed said that it was easy for Romeo to ignore Tybalt's challenge because "the guy had no depth" and acted according to his mood of the moment?

SHG: Yes, I do.

MS: Well, that remark, it seemed to me, made no attempt to explore Romeo's views, to see the situation with Tybalt from Romeo's perspective. Yet, Reed's comment did answer my question about whether it was hard or easy for Romeo to ignore Tybalt.

SHG: I see what you mean.

MS: So the question is: Why did many of the students today respond to the questions about Romeo much more empathetically—and much more accurately, I think—than Reed did?

———

At first it appeared that the discussants responded as they did today because Mrs. Spring asked them questions that called for empathetic assessments, something she had done little of yesterday. However, closer scrutiny indicates that the teacher's queries made no such demands. When the teacher asked what Romeo seemed to value, given his opening speech, the students might have merely listed the things he cared about. Likewise, when she asked whether it was hard or easy for Romeo to respond to Tybalt as he did, all could have responded as did Reed, that is, by attributing character traits rather than empathizing with the character. Most of the speakers, however, took the opportunity to explore Romeo's situation from his perspective. If their doing so cannot simply be attributed to Mrs. Spring's questions, then how would we explain it?

> SHG: I wonder if the change we have seen in the students'
> responses has something to do with yesterday's discussion.
> MS: What do you mean?
> SHG: Perhaps the whole experience of being allowed to engage
> themselves with the play in the way that they wanted to, even if it
> seemed crazy to you, brought the students an important message.
> It was as if you were saying to them, "You know the rules of this
> game, so here, take the text; it's yours; treat it as you see fit, so
> long as you follow the rules." Maybe when Edna, Abby, and
> Janeen saw that you were going to stick by them, that you were
> going to let them develop their interpretation of Benvolio even if
> you didn't agree with it, it meant that you were committed to the
> discussion above all else. And maybe getting that message gave
> them a new sense of commitment to the enterprise.
> MS: To the enterprise of discussion, you mean?
> SHG: Right. I mean that's the difference between yesterday and
> today, isn't it? Today, they were talking about Romeo as though
> understanding his character properly was something that they
> wanted to do and that was important. Like they really cared
> about getting it right, not just making an interpretation that they
> could defend, some way, somehow.

Is it that participation in yesterday's conversation brought the students to a new level of engagement with the text such that they now wanted to make interpretations that were sensible and appropriate, not merely defensible? And if so, is the desire for sound explanations a consequence of the "message" that Mrs. Spring has given them about her own commitment to discussion? Something seems to be missing. Certainly, the fact that Mrs. Spring was willing to put up with what seemed to her a "crazy" interpretation may have signified her commitment to the process of interpretive discussion. But why should the students become likewise committed just because they see that their teacher is? The answer is not yet clear.

> SHG: I still want to go back to Edna, Abby, and Janeen. I mean, have we really explained why they were so different today, why even they seemed eager to understand Romeo's feelings and perspective?
>
> MS: I'm not sure.
>
> SHG: Here's another idea. Maybe building that interpretation of Benvolio as cowardly, power-hungry, and aggressive showed them the enormous pleasure that comes from telling stories that make sense out of unexplained events. Leave aside that their interpretation made it difficult to explain a lot of things in the play that they were not paying attention to. They still seemed to have the experience of making an interpretation that satisfied them yesterday, at least for the moment. In fact, that happened to Larry, too, although he came to a quite different understanding of Benvolio. But remember how he elaborated the idea that Benvolio was thoughtful and not power-hungry and aggressive?
>
> MS: Yes, and his idea made a lot more sense, too.
>
> SHG: OK, but here's my point: It is fun to make sense out of things, out of events in books and other forms of art as well as out of yourself and your own actions. And that's what I think happened to Edna, Abby, and Larry and maybe Janeen. They had fun making their interpretations yesterday. They got a big bang out of it.

Our next hypothesis, then, is that the pleasure of making interpretations yesterday, rather than the observation of their teacher's commitment to interpretive discussion, has inspired the students to take today's discussion opportunity more seriously, to work hard to understand Romeo's character adequately. Actually, I considered this same possibility in Conversation 4 when trying to explain the preoccupation that the Belden students had with whether Juliet was a Capulet or not. I suggested then that despite my frustration with the conversation, the students may have learned the pleasure of text interpretation through the experience and thus were subsequently willing to pursue it with more attention and vigor. The same may be true for Edna, Abby, Larry, Janeen, and others. The satisfaction of interpreting Benvolio as they did, even if the satisfaction was momentary, may have encouraged them to deepen their involvement in subsequent discussions.

And yet, Mrs. Spring casts a shadow on our newest hypothesis as she raises a further question:

MS: OK, but if they had so much fun making interpretations yesterday, why didn't they just go on in the same way today? Why didn't they treat Romeo the way they did Benvolio, even as Reed did do?

SHG: Hmm. That's a good question. Well, maybe what they did today was just sort of the next "natural" step. I mean yesterday you let them "run wild," so to speak, let them say what they wanted to about Benvolio, so that, as I said before, they experienced the fun of building interpretations. As a consequence, maybe they were ready to settle down to more serious consideration of the text today. And once they started down the path you set for them, they found it compelling.

MS: That's it! Maybe what happened was that once they started answering my questions about Romeo and began drawing upon their own experiences and beliefs to do so, they found their interpretations of Romeo at least as satisfying as those they had made of Benvolio.

SHG: Yes, and why not even more so? After all, as they started answering your questions, we saw that these students began thinking about Romeo by drawing on what they know of human motivation. First one did it, then the next one did, and so on. So whether they were right or wrong about Romeo's motivation should have made a real difference to the students this time, for what was at stake was not just their grasp of Romeo but their ideas about why people do what they do.

MS: Say more.

SHG: Look, when one works to "get inside" the character, when one draws upon personal experience to imagine what someone in the character's situation might do, then one's understanding of human motivation is put to work. If the interpretation that results can justify the character's actions, then one's ideas about people's motives are confirmed. And that's one thing that we want to be right about isn't it, our ideas about why people do one thing rather than another?

MS: Why don't we take an example.

SHG: OK, think about Brian again. When he said it might be difficult for Romeo to keep his marriage to Juliet a secret, he seemed to be drawing on his own personal experience of what it feels like to remain silent under some conditions. Given his personal experience, Brain seemed to be imagining how Romeo

might feel when confronted by Tybalt, who was, after all, Juliet's cousin. Then Brian referred to the line in which Romeo says to Tybalt, "I do protest I never injured thee, / But love thee better than thou canst devise / Til thou shalt know the reason of my love." Doesn't the comment suggest Romeo's desire to tell all?
MS: You mean because he says, "But love thee better than thou canst devise / Til thou shalt know the reason of my love"?
SHG: Yes, that's right. Doesn't it suggest that Romeo wishes he could explain the whole situation to Tybalt, the marriage and all? That's what Brian seemed to think.
MS: And with justification.
SHG: So you see, Brian seems to be drawing on his experience and at the same time looking at the text. The fact that Romeo says what he says appears to have a particular meaning to Brian because of the experience he has had; at the same time, the text—Romeo's words—seems to confirm Brian's beliefs about the difficulty of keeping secrets under certain circumstances. It is almost as though Shakespeare is saying to Brian: "You are right—it is tough to keep such a secret, especially at a time like this."
MS: OK, this is beginning to make some sense. Brian is eager for his understanding of Romeo to be right because if it is, then his ideas about how people respond in circumstances like those facing Romeo are confirmed. And Brian, like everybody else, wants to confirm his ideas about human reactions, for only when we understand how people will respond to various situations can we control things as we wish to do.
SHG: Exactly. If we don't understand why people do things—the conditions under which they react in various ways—then we have no control over them or ourselves; for we have no basis for deciding how we should behave towards them. Perhaps the students came to realize that text interpretation is a powerful resource in helping us to comprehend the actions of others and ourselves.

What caused the Chalmers students to respond so differently in today's discussion? The idea that Mrs. Spring and I have now come to is that in pursuing the teacher's questions, discussants discovered how to use the text to explore and confirm their ideas about why people do what they do. In explaining whether it was hard or easy for Romeo to ignore Tybalt's challenge, for example, these students began to draw on their own ideas of how someone would feel in such a situation. At the same time, they were looking at the text, which provided them with grounds for judging whether their ideas, gleaned from past personal experience, were applicable in this case. Brian's idea about Romeo's feelings—that he was eager to divulge his secret to Tybalt—seems to be consistent with what Romeo actually says. As a consequence, Brian sees not only that his interpretation of Romeo is confirmed but that his idea about the pressure of secrecy is, given the evidence in this text, an appropriate one.

Having come, now, to the end of our journey into the Chalmers and Belden Schools, we are in a position to make an interesting observation. There is some evidence—by no means conclusive—that the two classes of students have achieved a turning of the soul and have done so through opposite means. On the one hand, the Belden students, who began with little interpretive discussion experience, brought with them a wealth of powerful personal views and a history that they had difficulty linking to a literary text. As a result, they had little to say about the play of *Romeo and Juliet* at first. Although they could describe specific, personal experiences, they had trouble using these to illuminate the drama and likewise, using the play to acquire a perspective on their personal feelings and beliefs.

On the other hand, the Chalmers students, who had had extensive discussion experience, had a tendency to generalize about the play with little reference to relevant personal views and experience. While they always had a great deal to say about the text, the comments were sometimes glib and empty, as if they were unwilling to plumb the sources of their ideas. One consequence of their use—minimal use—of personal experience was the tendency toward bizarre interpretations that could not stand up to comprehensive study of the textual evidence.

What we saw was that over time, the students in both classrooms seemed to become able to talk about the play in a meaningful way, to make sense of the events and the characters' actions by bringing their own experiences and ideas to bear upon them. For the Belden students, this involved learning to explore the text by relating its events to questions the leaders posed, raising questions themselves, analyzing passages, and bringing relevant personal views to bear upon the analysis. By Conversation 8, these students seemed eager to be understood and anxious to get the text right. Recall how Richard reiterated his view of Juliet's response to Romeo's banishment and how Colette struggled to reach what seemed to her a sound interpretation of Juliet's line.

The Chalmers students, however, who had much less difficulty making textual interpretations, showed signs of learning something quite different, namely, to play the game of interpretive discussion for genuine rather than academic gain. While this may not be the case—our evidence is suggestive rather than conclusive—it may also be that the students have begun to realize that text interpretation can help them confirm or disconfirm their ideas about why people behave as they do. Perhaps the students see that by pondering the circumstances that confronted Romeo and his responses to them, they can explore their ideas about human motivation. If this is the case, it would explain why the Chalmers discussants, like those at Belden, seemed to become more anxious to get Shakespeare right.

CONCLUSION
Problems and Possibilities

The aim of Conversations 1 through 10 has been to explore the practice of interpretive discussion, a practice that may have potential for improving the educational experience of students in some situations. We now address the following issues: (1) How might interpretive discussion help to make school experience more educative? (2) Is such discussion a practical approach to education? In considering the second question, I shall take up such matters as the relationship between the student and the teacher-discussion leader, the relation of discussion to other educational activities, the conditions under which interpretive discussion may succeed best, and the preparation of the discussion leaders.

1. How Might Interpretive Discussion Help to Make School Experience More Educative?

> To "learn by doing" [according to Dewey] was neither to learn only by doing nor to learn only how to do. Doing was to go hand in hand with reading, reflecting, and remembering. And these intelligent activities were to eventuate in something more than efficient coping with the bread-and-butter problems of existence. They were to yield the capacity for rewarding experience, a doing and undergoing not merely for the sake of the material outcome; often, not for that outcome at all, but for the satisfaction of the work itself. Here lies the region which involves enjoyment—of problems and of work, of art, and of our relations with our friends and neighbors.[1]

In the passage just cited, Schwab reiterates a point made in the Introduction: Dewey believed schooling should enable one, eventually, to earn a living but that this is only one of its aims. Schwab emphasizes that according to Dewey, schools should also foster the capacity for rewarding experience, experience that brings pleasure, not merely material reward. Schools, then, should help students to discover the enjoyment that comes from attending to and resolving problems in work, art, and human relations.

"Work," for Dewey, is not equivalent to "a job." Instead, "working," means "learning by doing," which is why he says that working brings with it pleasure. In the introduction, I quoted a passage from *Democracy and Education* in which Dewey defines learning by doing as making a "forward and backward" movement between the things we do and the consequences of those actions.[2] Schwab says that "doing was to go hand in hand with reading, reflecting, and remembering." Reading, reflecting and remembering allow one to look toward the consequences of actions and uncover the relations between what is done and what is undergone, that which arises as a consequence.

One might say, then, that according to Dewey and Schwab, the central aim of education, with respect to the individual students who are educated, is that they should become lifelong students of their own actions and the actions of others. They should learn how to determine the relations between that which they do and that which they and the objects they act upon undergo. The "objects" may be material items or they may be other persons or ideas. The point is that the student must become sensitive to and learn to care about the relation between actions and outcomes.

This is not to minimize the goals of making a living, getting along with others, achieving social, academic, and economic goals, or otherwise improving one's health and well-being. Quite the contrary. Dewey's position, with which Schwab concurs, is that these aims are achieved only insofar as one comes to understand the relations between action and outcomes, between doing and undergoing. The ability to write well, for example, requires a recognition of the various psychological effects that language can have on readers; it also requires one to understand the relations between linguistic rules and the creation of a desired effect. Schooling, then, must develop one's sensitivities to and ability to explore such relations.

Given Dewey's formulations, the things that individuals and society each need from educational institutions are related to one another. If people become able to "learn by doing" in Dewey's sense—become students of their actions and thereby discover the relations between what they do and what they undergo—then they may come to care deeply about their relationships to other people and other things. The knowledge that individuals gain about relationships may enable them to control certain situations and institutions and, perhaps, to bring about desired changes. That knowledge may thus allow people to work toward eliminating social injustices of the sorts they come to recognize. And the interests that lead them to explore some relations rather than others may allow the cultivation of particular talents, another aim of education, as indicated in the Introduction. When exercised, those talents may bring about social good as well as individual pleasure.

Perhaps our best hope for making schools effective, then, is to follow Dewey's mandate and try to discover the relations between our current practices and our educational aims so as to modify our actions with respect to the school appropriately. Change that is based on doing and undergoing—that arises from acting and reflecting upon outcomes—seems to stand the best chance of solving existing problems without creating new ones; for it is a consequence of carefully studying situations and allows one to pinpoint the sources of difficulty so that the cures may be effective.

The visits to the Belden and Chalmers classrooms have allowed us to see that interpretive discussion provides an opportunity for what Dewey calls "learning by doing." Furthermore, in interpreting texts, students study relations between actions that affect other people, ideas, and things, and their consequences. Indeed, many of the interpretive questions that the teachers asked focused on relations between persons: Why did Capulet become so angry with Tybalt at the party? Why did the nurse help Romeo and Juliet arrange the marriage? Why did Friar Lawrence agree to marry the couple? Why didn't Juliet tell Romeo to leave the garden when she knew he was in danger? Was it hard or easy for Romeo to ignore Tybalt's challenge? These questions put the discussants in position for reflecting on the reasons for and effect of people's actions.

It seems that as work with the play progressed, the Belden and Chalmers students came to care more about the relations among the characters and possibly among people outside the text. The discussants in both groups showed increasing willingness to draw on views derived from personal experience in explaining the characters' responses to one another. For example, Edna cited the fact that Romeo had moved quickly from loving Rosaline to loving Juliet, and she wondered whether the youth and his mother had a strong relationship. That the textual evidence seemed to support her conjecture may have deepened Edna's convictions about the effects of relations between sons and mothers. Perhaps Edna will draw on these ideas to make sense of situations she encounters in the future. Her use of a text to provoke and test ideas about people's actions and their relations suggests that interpretive discussion "gives individuals a personal interest in social relationships and control," as Dewey puts it.

Interpretive discussion may also help to teach "the habits of mind which secure social changes without introducing disorder."[3] We have seen moments when the discussion seemed to encourage students to think for themselves, to read with understanding, to evaluate their own ideas, to persevere with difficult problems and analyses, to listen to and learn from others, to explore options that did not occur to them initially, and so to move beyond their initial impressions. These habits and tendencies, when applied to problematic situations of all sorts, may help people to assess the circumstances well enough to determine appropriate measures of change without resorting to violence or revolution.

E. D. Hirsch makes the following statement: "Believing that a few direct experiences would suffice to develop the skills that children require, Dewey assumed that early education need not be tied to specific content. . . . Only by piling up specific, communally shared information can children learn to participate in complex cooperative activities with other members of their community."[4] We have seen that Hirsch is mistaken when he asserts that Dewey denied the importance of "specific content," communally shared information (facts). Learning by doing, especially as it is exemplified by interpretive discussion, cannot occur in the absence of a concern for such information. Indeed, we have seen how the discussion fosters scrupulous attention to the facts in the text. Discussants come to realize that what appear to be minute details can make all the difference when one interprets a passage. The discussion, then, glorifies rather than minimizes the importance of information that a community takes to be factual. Furthermore, it teaches that facts are meaningful only insofar as they have a place in a given context, a message that drill and memorization can obscure for students. That very message is one that Hirsch would do well to contemplate, given his propensity for listing in decontextualized form, the "facts" that everyone should know.[5]

Finally, it appears that interpretive discussion may help to draw out and deepen student interests. Recall how Colette raised the question of why Juliet was in such a rush to marry Romeo (Conversation 6), which led to questions about a father's response to his daughter's elopement. On another occasion, Marcy and others wondered about the sexual relation between Romeo and Juliet, and between the friar, Romeo, and Juliet, which eventually led the group to discuss the sexual habits of priests and nuns and their own views of premarital sex. Even when questions remain strictly focused on the text, they arise because they seek to explore the personal interests that inspired them. And in addressing the questions, one often discovers interests that theretofore lay hidden.

Consequently, one can imagine how the experience that interpretive discussion allows may foster what Dewey calls "unique talents." It is impossible to say how the discussants we watched will manage the interests they have begun to uncover. But once the interests have been identified—once the students begin to understand what they care about—they are bound to deepen some of their concerns through further investigation.

For example, one can envision Edna, Abby, or Janeen writing an essay for Mrs. Spring trying to defend the claim that Benvolio is cowardly, power-hungry, and aggressive by reflecting on all of his actions in the play. Success or failure with such an effort might bring the student to new questions, perhaps even to reflect on Benvolio's feelings by imagining his perspective on situations. The questions about Benvolio may, at length, draw the student into analyses of certain sorts, both in other texts and elsewhere in her personal life. As their queries flower into full-blown interests, knowledge of a particular domain may deepen to the point where one functions as an expert there—as does someone with a "talent" in the field.

Dewey maintains that the cultivation of talents forms the basis for social contributions and lifelong pleasures of particular sorts. Again, one can imagine how the interpretive discussion experience might interest students in some author, some area of literature or art, or an entire field of study for a lifetime. The interests they cultivate may be even broader as well.

This is perhaps the moment for an anecdote. Fifteen months after leading the *Romeo and Juliet* discussions in the Belden classroom, I met Mrs. Prince for lunch, and we spent more than two hours reflecting on the experience, talking about the effects it seemed to have had on each of us and on the students. Because several in the group had remained in her special education class the following year, the teacher was in a position to comment upon what might have been some long-term effects on the discussants. More than once she said that the conversations seemed to have made the students more willing to persevere with difficult tasks. They seemed to "give up" much less easily, she said, and often took on challenges that she feared might present them with failure. Mrs. Prince spoke of how James had worked hard to master typing skills and how Mason, having just graduated, was now managing three jobs, one of which included a training program. Rightly or wrongly, she seemed to think that the conversations about *Romeo and Juliet* had helped the students to persevere. If she is right, there may be many endeavors that have been opened to them.

Perhaps, then, interpretive discussion can play a role in helping schools to meet the aims of education that Dewey identified, both individual and societal. But if it is to be of some help, then it must be practical for use in our schools today. So the question arises: Is interpretive discussion practical? It is to this matter that we now turn our attention.

2. Is Interpretive Discussion a Practical Approach to Education?

To address this complex question, let us briefly consider four topics that bear on its resolution.

A. The Relation Between the Student and the Discussion Leader

In reflecting on the practicality of interpretive discussion, the relation between the students and the teacher-leader is of central concern. Can one person be both a teacher and a discussion leader? Otherwise put, can one be both a "directive" teacher and facilitative discussion leader?

This question presses us when we recall Willard Waller's comment that "the teacher-pupil relationship is a form of institutionalized dominance and subordination."[6] If the teacher is, by definition, the superordinate, then how can she relinquish that position so as to bring a genuine question to the group in an interpretive discussion? If the teacher opens the discussion with an interpretive question, as often happens, then by definition, that question has no one answer. While she may prefer one resolution to another, she can bring the question to the group precisely because she is in genuine doubt about the answer and does not take an authoritative stand. Here, the teacher relinquishes authority; for everyone—students and teachers alike—is subject to the rules of the discussion.

Yet, it is not as though there is no authority. On the contrary, since the text serves as the basis against which ideas and interpretations are judged, and since the rules for participation constrain the remarks that people make, an interpretive discussion is a highly regulated activity. One might say, then, that the teacher as discussion leader becomes the guardian of yet another authority. As a result, the teacher remains "in charge" in the sense that she puts the constraints of interpretive discussion in charge and safeguards their authority.

Given that the teacher as discussion leader both is and is not the locus of control, another question arises: Is it possible for the students to believe that such a teacher does not have a "right" answer in mind when she poses questions for students to ponder? Surprisingly enough, it seems that this can happen. While the Belden students did not believe I was asking genuine questions at first, I had the impression that they came to believe it in time. Indeed, their readiness to address such questions as why the friar decided to marry Romeo and Juliet and why Juliet did not tell Romeo to leave the garden suggests that they eventually became unconcerned with my ideas about the issues I posed. In addition, Mrs. Spring, Mrs. Prince, and I all experienced moments when the students resolutely disregarded our ideas about questions on the floor.

Another question that arises is: Do the students come to believe that their ideas are the teacher-discussion leader's main concern? Again, there was evidence that this was happening, at least at moments, in both classrooms. Remember how much the Belden students were willing to say to Mrs. Prince about their views on premarital and marital sex. And recall how eager some of Mrs. Spring's students were to expound upon Benvolio's character, even when their interpretations clearly troubled their teacher. My experience has been that over time, many students come to expect that the interpretive discussion leader can and must be concerned with their ideas above all else. Indeed, her authority would be compromised were this not the case.

Finally, one might ask: Will students become unruly in the discussion? There is no doubt that this can happen, especially if classes are too large, students have not read the text, or the teacher is poorly prepared or inexperienced in leading discussion. If class size is appropriate (more on this topic below), each student will have a chance to speak several times and can remain involved. If the students have done the reading, they will share a common basis on which to participate with others and can therefore contribute to the conversation. We have seen no instances of disruption in either the Belden or Chalmers classrooms, in part because the groups were of appropriate size and the students had read (or read in class) the material. Of course, the experience and preparation of the teacher-leaders were also key to the success of these discussions. (Again, the topic of teacher preparation will be considered below.)[7]

The evidence presented in the preceding pages is insufficient to permit generalizations in response to these questions. Each topic needs to be carefully reconsidered in light of long-term observations of groups engaged in interpretive discussion. Nevertheless, Waller makes a comment that suggests a perspective on the evidence before us:

> Subordinates do not always hate their masters, and inferiors do not always rebel, and this is because the flow of self-feeling in the subordinate is away from the relationship. Subordination is bearable because it is meaningless. The self expands in a pleasant situation, and contracts in an unpleasant one. The self grows into a pleasant relationship, and moves away from a relationship in which one feels inferior or thwarted. Subordination in the institution is possible because institutional and noninstitutional selves are split off from each other. . . . Every man must have some pride, and he must have some relationship in which he really lives.[8]

Following Waller, one might speculate that the selves of discussants have the opportunity to "expand" in the face of a situation in which they stand as equals with the teacher. Since both are seeking understanding that neither possesses, and since both are subject to the constraints of the discussion, the selves of the discussants need not recede, and their stance need not be docile, for they are not in the position of "receiving" the truth from the teacher. Perhaps, then, it may be possible for the teacher as discussion leader to permit the students to emerge as selves and experience a turning of the soul without at the same time allowing the classroom to dissolve into chaos.

B. The Relation of Interpretive Discussion to Other Educational Activities

Clearly, we should expect no simple answer to the question of how interpretive discussion is to be used in relation to other educational activities. The place that it can have will depend not only upon the subject but the particular features of a given school—the numbers as well as the backgrounds, experiences, and values of the students and teachers, the commitment of the principal and other school administrators to interpretive discussion, and the fiscal resources of the school and school system. But Bloom states an hypothesis we need to bear in mind: "Where the environment is relatively constant over long periods of time we have hypothesized that a relevant human characteristic will be far more stable than when the environment is more changeable. . . . On the other hand, when the environment shifts markedly from one point in time to another, stability is likely to be lower."[9] The implication of Bloom's hypothesis is that if certain behaviors and habits are drawn out and developed through interpretive discussion, these will remain more stable if the supporting environment is stable. If, however, the environment that supports them is variable, then we are likely to see instability in these tendencies.

To be more specific: If the interpretive discussion experience encourages people to express their beliefs about the meaning of a text, to support their beliefs with evidence from the text, to question the texts' and others' ideas, including those of the teacher, to draw on personal experiences in making interpretations, to listen carefully to the ideas of others, then these behaviors are likely to be repeated if the situations are not too drastically altered and conditions call for them. It stands to reason, then, that if we wish the habits and tendencies developed by interpretive discussion to endure, the other school activities should not be antithetical to them and perhaps should require their repetition.[10]

Does this mean that teachers will no longer give lectures or require students to display knowledge of "facts" at some moments? Not at all. Indeed, it is hard to imagine any current educational practice automatically ruled out of order with the introduction of interpretive discussion into the curriculum. The changes made will depend on the particular circumstances. But one thing seems certain: The teacher who wishes to nourish the behaviors and tendencies that interpretive discussion cultivates will think carefully about the relation between this and other school experiences that the students have. She will ask: Is the environment consistently supportive of the habits and tendencies we wish to endure?

So, for example, Mrs. Spring adopted a number of practices with her students that seemed to sustain the habits and values fostered by interpretive discussion: She asked them to write personal essays in which the students were to relate the text they had discussed to their own lives in some personal way; she gave them "pop" quizzes "just to see if they had done the reading"; she asked them to record questions that they had in diaries that they kept on an ongoing basis; she asked them to form small (three to five students), leaderless groups to discuss particular issues so that each person could speak more often; she asked them to submit written resolutions to questions that had been posed in discussion and to rewrite these as necessary. Now, some of these activities would not be appropriate in some classrooms. But an argument can be made that they were suitable in this instance and that they encouraged the students to repeat practices that were cultivated by interpretive discussion.

I wish to mention one more relevant point. In recent years, scholars have argued against the practice of grouping students by ability in the schools. In a seminal study of twenty-five high schools, Oakes presented evidence to the effect that "bright" students were not "held back" by slower students, nor were the deficiencies of slower students remediated by grouping them together and isolating them from the stronger students. She argued lower-track placements tended to develop negative mental attitudes in students.[11] Oakes agrees with Bowles and Gintis when they argue that tracking "legitimates inequality"—makes the students feel that their low status is due to their own inferiority.[12] *Barriers to Excellence: Our Children at Risk,* and *Becoming a Nation of Readers* have urged that rigid tracking practices be eliminated.[13]

The elimination of tracking practices is a complex matter over which there is great controversy.[14] But the preceding analysis of interpretive discussion indicates that these discussions groups need not be formed on the basis of ability. Indeed, the labels "slow" and "smart" cease to have meaning very rapidly in the discussion setting. What one soon discovers is that everyone is "brilliant" some of the time, and no one is that way all of the time.

Consider but one example. When I first began meeting with the Belden students, I found myself thinking that Colette was "very bright" and James "rather slow." True, James was reluctant to participate at first, and since he refused to read, I assumed he was a poor reader. As time went on, Colette began to display confusion and "denseness" about the text at moments, while James seemed to become more and more insightful. As he volunteered to read more often, I gradually found myself thinking that his reading was really "not so bad." My point is that in time, the "smartness" labels that I had at first attached to these students ceased to have meaning.

Perhaps other teachers would find that experience in interpretive discussion groups widens their views of student abilities—at least, the reading, thinking, and speaking abilities. Such experience, then, might help them to think more flexibly about the complex issue of grouping students.

C. The Conditions under Which Interpretive Discussion Best Succeeds

There are a number of conditions that need to be fulfilled if interpretive discussion is to be effective. If the group is discussing a written text, then each discussant needs to have a copy that may be written upon so as to keep track of ideas. In most instances, it works best if each student has a copy of the same edition of the text so as to facilitate the location of passages. All discussants need to have read the work before the conversation begins (unless the reading is being done by the group in class). The leader, too, must have read the text carefully and perhaps prepared interpretive questions with which to open the conversation.[15]

So much is virtually obvious. What is less obvious but no less critical is the issue of size of the discussion group. The pupil-teacher ratio in the Chicago Public Schools, to take one example, is 23.3 to 1.[16] However, I was told that there are "lots of classes over thirty." This is not surprising, since the maximum class size in the middle elementary grades (four to six) is thirty-two. While maximums in the high school classes for many subjects is twenty-eight, I myself have led discussions in (high school) classes of more than thirty students in these schools. The question is: Can interpretive discussion with a group of thirty be effective?

The answer to this question is simply and unequivocally no. The problem is that no one, except perhaps the leader, has sufficient opportunity to speak when the group is that large. If the class is period is forty minutes, then each in a group of thirty will have less than one minute of talking time, given time needed for regulating the activities of the class. Even if the class is eighty minutes, each student will have less than two minutes—hardly enough time to make one substantial point. In such circumstances, the leader may struggle to involve everyone for a while but often gives in to the demanding few who wish to speak frequently. In many instances, the others lose connection with the conversation, and disruptive, inattentive behavior results.[17] Even if the group of thirty is experienced and well behaved, the leader must expend large amounts of energy and attention managing the conversation instead of thinking about the question on the floor.

In my view, the ideal size of the group varies from five or six up to fifteen, depending upon the age of the students and their acquaintance with interpretive discussion. Mrs. Spring, an experienced discussion leader with experienced discussants, managed a class of twenty-two very well. By that I mean that on most days when I observed the class, at least sixteen of the students spoke. Often it was eighteen or twenty. But even Mrs. Spring did not engage everyone in the class on any given day; and a number spoke only once or for short periods of time, so that certain students did a large portion of the talking.

Consequently, even in this instance, a group of fifteen would have been ideal. Still, no one would have had too much speaking time. If the class period is eighty minutes long—a good length for many high school discussions— then each person in the group can speak for four minutes and still leave twenty minutes for teacher questioning and regulating activities. Here, then, is an opportunity for a good discussion with everyone participating at some length. If the period is only forty minutes—as is generally the case in high schools— then each student will probably speak less than two minutes, given the talking that the teacher is likely to do. With fifteen, a discussion of forty minutes can still be good, however, as the conversation of a smaller group is often more coherent. The leader, too, can devote less attention to managing the speaking order and focus upon the topic.

In my view, fifteen would have been too large a group at Belden. Because the students in Mrs. Prince's special education class also worked with other teachers as well, there were often times when only six or eight were in the room. With eight students present, each student could speak for more than four minutes during a class period of forty minutes, leaving the teacher some eight minutes. During the first discussions at Belden, the teachers were speaking more and the students less than the allotted time. As the group became more experienced, the situation began to reverse and the students spoke much more of the time. Since students new to interpretive discussion need a lot of guidance and encouragement at first, and since it frequently takes them more speaking time to work out their ideas, it seems these groups should be smaller than more experienced groups.[18]

There are many, many advantages to small discussion groups. When there are fewer students, each has greater opportunity to explore his or her own ideas and respond to others. There is less tendency to sit back and let one speaker dominate the discussion, since it is easier to draw ideas out of all the participants. With fewer in the group, the teacher can keep track of discussants' ideas better and can question each speaker at length so as to help develop the thoughts. And such questioning is crucial for teaching students how to participate effectively in the conversations. It is also the basis upon which affective bonds between members of the group are built.[19]

Now, the question which arises is: How can the schools afford to support such a costly idea—one or more teachers with groups of eight to fifteen students? Such a suggestion seems patently unfeasible, especially in our overcrowded urban schools. I believe that the answer to this question is complex but that there are possible resolutions that deserve serious consideration. It is to this matter that we now turn.

D. The Preparation of the Discussion Leaders

The fact is that in order to have interpretive discussions of eight to fifteen students, we are going to need many more teacher-leaders. Just how many is impossible to calculate until we know how the students are distributed and what the particular situations are—the nature of the teachers' responsibilities, the background and experiences of the students, and so forth. But with the average teacher's salary (1987–88) in the Chicago public schools at $33,379 and the proposed (September 1989) beginning teacher's salary at $20,000, the addition of even fifty teachers means a minimum cost of $1 million.

Consequently, if more teachers wish to incorporate interpretive discussion into the curriculum, it could well mean that we will need to commit more resources to education. Particularly in schools of the "less advantaged" students, there would need to be small discussion groups so that each person would have the opportunity to speak often. While the addition of persons to the teaching force costs money, the sum is not as great as it might be; for not all interpretive discussion leaders need to be teachers, which means that we will not need as many new teachers as might seem to be the case at first. How might things work?

One possibility is that the teachers would both lead the interpretive discussions *and* engage in other activities that would support the discussions, such as selecting the materials for discussion, sequencing the readings, offering background on the texts that may be useful (such as information on the work's historical context or literary genre), working with its vocabulary, and assigning and evaluating essays on the texts already discussed. The discussion leaders, on the other hand, would leave to the teachers all activities except that of leading the discussions. As a result, their backgrounds and skills could be more narrowly focused than those of the teachers. What qualifications would the leaders then need?

First, the leaders need not have a college degree. But they must have read the text that the group is discussing, and have read it with care. In some instances, but not all, additional background in the subject matter the text addresses might help to deepen a leader's perspective. Second, leaders should have "prepared" for the discussion, perhaps by writing down and reflecting on questions that occurred while reading. Such preparation forces the leaders to study the text carefully. It also allows them to respond to student questions and comments with greater ease, since they have become very familiar with the work. Third, the leaders must understand the rules and goals of interpretive discussion so that they can lead the group.

Now, in order to lead effectively, the leaders need training, and they need the experience of participating in as well as leading interpretive discussions. Some training opportunities are already available,[20] but more are needed. Furthermore, to gain as much as possible from the study of the text, and hence, prepare adequately for discussions, the leaders need ongoing support. This means they must have opportunities to discuss the texts and their leading experiences with other adults as well as the students. Additional opportunities for leaders may also be advisable.[21] In short, teachers and other leaders will need strong support from school administrators and colleagues, such as I have seen in Sullivan High School in Chicago.[22] While the guidelines for getting started are simple enough, the complexities and difficulties can quickly accumulate once discussions begin.

But one may ask: If the leaders are not the teachers, then who are they? Where do they come from? There seems to be a natural answer to this question: leaders can come from the school community itself, parents and friends of the schools who wish to make a contribution to its operations. Indeed, current reform efforts are drawing parents into school functions with more and more frequency,[23] as has been recommended by national commissions.[24] Many fear parent involvement, as they worry that parents do not have enough background and experience to contribute wisely.[25] Here, however, is an opportunity for parents to provide a much-needed service to the schools. Indeed, many parents are already involved throughout the country.[26]

There are, of course, many other issues to consider as one contemplates the role that interpretive discussion might have in the schools. These include questions about its use in the lower and middle elementary grades, its effects on students who have participated over many weeks and even years, and its use in nonliterature classes such as science, mathematics, and social studies. All of these matters deserve continued research. Why? Because reflection on discussable texts in all fields—in literature, science, art, mathematics, music, and others—has the power to turn the soul; that is, it has the power to draw out a vision of life that can transform one's understanding oneself and the world.

NOTES

Introduction

1. D. Tyack, R. Lowe, and E. Hansot, *Public Schools in Hard Times: The Great Depression and Recent Years* (Cambridge: Harvard University Press, 1984), 221, argue that many feel reforms directed toward minorities and the underprivileged have failed. The response to that perceived failure, the authors say, is to turn away from those most in need and direct efforts toward more effective programs for mainstream and gifted students. Such a reaction only perpetuates our failing with respect to the poor, of course.

2. P. E. Peterson, *The Politics of School Reform, 1870–1940* (Chicago: University of Chicago Press, 1985), 136.

3. J. Dewey, *Democracy and Education: An Introduction to the Philosophy of Education* (New York: Macmillan, 1916), 99.

4. Ibid., 121.

5. See, for example, S. Bowles and H. Gintis, *Schooling in Capitalist America: Educational Reform and the Contradictions of Economic Life* (New York: Basic Books, Inc., 1976); I. Shor, *Critical Teaching and Everyday Life* (Chicago: University of Chicago Press, 1987); I. Illich, *Deschooling Society* (New York: Harper and Row, 1970).

6. E.g., S. W. Rothstein, "Schooling in Mass Society," *Urban Education* 22, no. 3 (1987): 277–283; Shor, *Critical Teaching and Everyday Life*, passim.

7. See, e.g., L. M. McNeil, *Contradictions of Control: School Structures and School Knowledge* (New York: Routledge & Kegan Paul, 1986), 168., and Shor, *Critical Teaching and Everyday Life*, 33–37.

8. L. McNeil, *Contradictions of Control*, 186, for example, describes the "deskilling" of teachers that occurs through the use of prepackaged teaching materials.

9. See Shor, Illich, and Bowles and Gintis, works cited n. 5 above.

10. For example, the Junior Great Books Program has prepared curricular materials, trained leaders, and in various ways fostered interpretive discussion in classrooms since the 1960s. Mortimer Adler's Paideia Project, which features opportunities for interpretive discussion, has been carried out in schools across the country since the early 1980s. Some of the teachers in the Paideia Project have been trained at St. Johns College in Santa Fe, New Mexico. The North Carolina Center for the Advancement of Teaching, at Western Carolina University in Cullowhee, North Carolina, provides opportunities for teachers to develop their interests in various disciplines. The program features seminars for teachers that emphasize interpretive discussion. See A. G. Rud, Jr., "Rewarding the Exemplary Teacher at the North Carolina Center for the Advancement of Teaching," *Journal of Staff Development* 10, no. 1 (Winter, 1989).

11. One exception, is Sullivan High School in Chicago, which has been administering Mortimer Adler's Paideia Program since 1984. Some four hundred students from around the city participate in a four-year program featuring weekly seminars in English and history, which are interpretive discussions lasting one hour and twenty minutes that focus upon some discussable text. Indeed, the seminars have been so successful that all students in the school of twelve hundred participate in the "All School Seminar" once a month. On these occasions, everyone in the school reads the same text, and the teachers lead discussions of small groups of students. See R. D. Brazil, *The Engineering of the Paideia Proposal: The First Year* (Champaign, IL: School Design Group, 1988). Some science classes at Sullivan have held seminars.

12. For example, in *Becoming a Nation of Readers: Report of the Commission on Reading,* R. C. Anderson, et al. (Washington, D.C.: National Institute of Education, Department of Education, 1984), 118, the Commission urges that teachers devote more time to helping students to comprehend what they read, not merely to decode the words. As the reader will see from the excerpts of classroom discussions presented herein, interpretive discussion fosters comprehension by asking students to explore the ambiguities in the texts.

13. The number might be as large as twenty, but already we begin to push the limits. If there are more students, then no one gets enough time to speak—an essential part of the experience. In order to make interpretive discussion a central part of public schooling, teachers and administrators need to make possible these small groups. The challenge is great, but not too great. This topic is considered in the conclusion.

14. Interpretive discussion differs somewhat from the Philosophy for Children Program found in schools across the country and abroad. The materials for the Philosophy for Children Program—the students' books and the teachers' guides—were prepared specifically for it rather than selected from existing sources. In addition, the program emphasizes not so much interpreting the text as helping students to explore their own ideas about great philosophical questions that have long fascinated people. Focus on the text varies with age and the book in use. Students' materials and the extensive teachers' guides are available for grades kindergarten through twelve.

15. The place of interpretive discussion in the study of these other subjects is a large and complex matter. It can be determined only after careful scrutiny of the aims and features of the subjects in question. Further research will enable me, in subsequent writings, to reflect upon the opportunities and difficulties that may arise as text interpretation is introduced into classes other than English literature.

16. Furthermore, it may be preferable to other instructional approaches because it involves students more fully, as it requires high-level cognitive thinking: analyzing, synthesizing, and evaluating. S. S. Stodolsky, *The Subject Matters: Classroom Activity in Math and Social Studies* (Chicago: University of Chicago Press, 1988), 94–95, reports that the highest levels of involvement in classrooms occur when students are collaborating with others on cognitively complex tasks. Interpretive discussion provides the students with just this sort of opportunity.

17. One of the most important features of interpretive discussion is that it fosters affective bonds between the participants. A. S. Bryk, V. Lee, and J. B. Smith "High School Organization and Its effects on Teachers and Students: An Interpretive Summary of the Research" (presented at the Robert M. La Follette Institute of Public Affairs,

University of Wisconsin at Madison, 18 May 1989), 37, stress the significance of these bonds for student learning.

18. See Plato *Meno* 81b–e for a discussion of the immortal soul; see Plato *Phaedo*, e.g., 65a–67b and other of his "middle period" dialogues, for discussion of the "Forms" of knowledge.

19. In *Becoming a Nation of Readers*, 55, the Commission on Reading argues that students do not readily see the relation between what they already know and what they read. The teacher, then, needs to help the students to discover the connections, much as Plato urges in the passage quoted from the *Republic*.

20. Augustine, who was influenced by Plato, shared his view on this matter. See St. Aurelius Augustine, *Concerning the Teacher*, trans. G. G. Leckie (New York: D. Appleton-Century Company, Inc., 1938), 56. Here, Augustine argues that through the study of signs, e.g., words, we are brought to turn inward, i.e., to draw out of ourselves our understanding of things.

21. There are great works in these fields that are accessible to people of all ages. I have observed outstanding discussions by ninth grade science students of works by Ptolemy and Copernicus, for example. For lists of discussable texts that have been used in nonliterature high school and elementary classrooms, the reader should contact the Great Books Foundation and the Institute for Philosophical Research, both in Chicago, Illinois, as well as the National Center for the Paideia Program, University of North Carolina, Chapel Hill, North Carolina.

22. In some respects, interpretive discussion is unlike both the "Socratic method" and the traditional "great books" program pioneered by Robert M. Hutchins and Mortimer Adler at the University of Chicago in the 1940s. For one thing, while both Socrates and the interpretive discussion leader elicit and scrutinize participants' views, the leader uses a text of some sort and asks discussants to relate their ideas to it. Socrates followed no such practice. For another, the "texts" read for interpretive discussions may be contemporary as well as ancient, oriental as well as occidental. Indeed, the works need only be "discussable," i.e., presenting the reader with ambiguity and evidence to explore the ambiguity. Criteria for text selection are, then, broader than those advocated by Hutchins and Adler, although Adler's views on this matter have changed in recent years. For further discussion of the early and contemporary Hutchins-Adler program, see M. J. Adler, *Reforming Education: The Opening of the American Mind*, ed. A. Van Doren (New York: Macmillan, 1988), xix–xxxiii. However, Socrates, Hutchins and Adler, and interpretive discussion share a commitment to exploring the beliefs of the discussants. This practice unites all three in a fundamental way.

23. My claim is not that these authors were Platonists. Indeed, many of them took issue with aspects of Plato's views.

24. D. K. Cohen, "Teaching Practice: Plus Que Ça Change," in *Contributing to Educational Change: Perspectives on Research and Practice*, ed. P. W. Jackson (Berkeley: McCutchan Publishing Corporation, 1988), 39, makes the following comment: "Contemporary instructional practices embody an ancient instructional inheritance. In this inheritance, teachers are active; they are tellers of truth who inculcate knowledge in students. Learners are relatively passive; students are accumulators of material who listen, read, and perform prescribed exercises.

25. Aristotle *Nicomachean Ethics* 6.3.

26. Ibid.

27. Ibid. 6, especially 6.1, 6.2, 6.3, and 6.7.

28. Ibid. 6.4 (art); also books 2, 3, and 4 (moral virtues).

29. Ibid. 6.5.

30. Ibid. 6.7.

31. Ibid. 6.7.

32. Or, as P. Friere, *Pedagogy of the Oppressed,* trans. M. B. Ramos (New York: Herder and Herder, 1970), 27, puts it, the bank depository into which money is deposited.

33. L. A. Cremin, *American Education: The Metropolitan Experience, 1876–1980* (New York: Harper and Row, 1988), 87.

34. Ibid., 88–89.

35. One might wonder why the Union Sunday School Institute had such a powerful influence. Perhaps the educational practices to which it subscribed offered a practical approach to the complex task of teaching. See J. Hoekter, and W. P. Ahlbrand, "The Persistence of the Recitation," *American Educational Research Journal* 6 (1961): 145–67, and W. Doyle, and G. Ponder, "The Practicality Ethic in Teacher Decision Making," *Interchange* 8 (1977): 1–12.

36. The two traditions of teaching discussed in this chapter, the teacher as demonstrator and the teacher as inquirer, correspond roughly to what P. W. Jackson has called the "mimetic" and the "transformative" traditions. As he argues, the two traditions espouse very different goals and outcomes for the learners. (See his last chapter in *The Practice of Teaching,* [New York: Teachers College Press, 1986]. Those who raised objections included Colonel Francis W. Parker and others who might be said to be of the transformative tradition.

37. Dewey refers to Plato and Rousseau explicitly in *Democracy and Education* and compares his views to theirs. He makes perfectly clear that he sees points of commonality between their positions and his own. See e.g., pp. 88–93, 112–18.

38. J. J. Rousseau, *Emile or: On Education,* trans. Allan Bloom (New York: Basic Books, 1979), 145.

39. Dewey, *Democracy and Education,* 107–8, 126, 130–31.

40. F. Nietzsche, *Schopenhauer as Educator,* trans. J. W. Hillesheim, and M. R. Simpson (Chicago: Henry Regnery Company, 1965), 5, writes: "Let the young soul, ask itself, looking back on life 'What have you really loved up to now, what has drawn on your soul, what has dominated it and made it joyful at the same time?' Consider these venerated objects in order, and perhaps they will show you, through their being and their sequence, a law, the fundamental law of your true Self." Nietzsche's comment seems to express Dewey's fundamental conviction quite nicely.

41. J. J. Schwab, "The 'Impossible' Role of the Teacher in Progressive Education," *Science, Curriculum, and Liberal Education: Selected Essays,* ed. I. Westbury and N. J. Wilkof (Chicago: University of Chicago Press, 1978), 173, nicely summarizes Dewey's vision of learning in the following passage: "Learning, for Dewey, is active participation in the pragmatic rhetoric—the recovery and test of meaning. Hence, the effective 'learning situation' is not the one which leads by the quickest, most comfortable route

to mastered habit and attitude, used precept and applied knowledge, but the one which is provocative of reflection, experiment, and revision."

42. Dewey, *Democracy and Education,* 131.

43. Ibid., 140.

44. Rousseau, *Emile,* 184.

45. Ibid., 185.

46. Nor do I urge that all interpretive discussions be led by teachers. D. Barnes, *From Communication to Curriculum* (London: Penguin Books, 1976), G. Hillocks, "Knowledge, Student-led Small Group Discussion, and Writing" (presented at the American Educational Research Association Meeting, 1988), and Stodolsky, *The Subject Matters,* have studied small group discussions led by students, some of which aim at exploring a text. All found that such groups can function at a high level of effectiveness. There is no reason why students should not be given the opportunity to lead interpretive discussions, especially as they become experienced discussants.

47. A recent vocal critic is E. D. Hirsch, *Cultural Literacy: What Every American Needs to Know* (Boston: Houghton Mifflin Company, 1987). Hirsch accuses Dewey of denying that education should be tied to specific content (p. xv), among other things. As I argue in the conclusion, Hirsch's charge signals serious misinterpretation of Dewey's position. How can learning occur by doing, by treating things in various ways and reflecting upon the consequences, if there is nothing—no specific content—to treat?

48. E.g., see H. W. Stevenson, "Making the Grade: School Achievement in Japan, Taiwan, and the United States," *Annual Report for the Center for Advanced Study in Behavioral Sciences* (Stanford, CA: 1984), 41–51, and H. W. Stevenson, S. Y. Lee, and J. W. Stigler, "Mathematics Achievement in Chinese, Japanese, and American Children," *Science* 231 (14 February 1986): 693–99.

49. Kozol, *Illiterate America* (Doubleday & Co., 1985), indicates that 74 to 78 million American adults are illiterate (p. 9). Furthermore, 44 percent black and 56 percent Hispanic people are illiterate in English (p. 115).

50. D. K. Cohen, "Origins," in *The Shopping Mall High School: Winners and Losers in the Educational Marketplace,* ed. A. G. Powell, E. Farrar, and D. K. Cohen (Boston: Houghton Mifflin Company, 1985), 302, presents data that support the claim that teachers respond to poor student performance by teaching "more facts."

51. I continued to observe this teacher as she taught *Romeo and Juliet* to a group of sophomores. The reader will come to know her as Mrs. Spring.

52. The students at Chalmers did read the text outside of class and also wrote analyses of it.

53. In preparing these excerpts, I sometimes modified the transcription of the students' comments to make them more readable. Insofar as was practical, I left the speakers' words as they were recorded. However, in Conversation 2, where I show the students reading from the text, I present unedited excerpts so that the reader may see the difficulty that the students had reading Shakespeare at first.

54. These aftermath "teacher dialogues" may remind the reader of a line of research practiced and described by C. M. Clark and P. L. Peterson, "Teachers' Thought Processes," in *Handbook of Research on Teaching,* ed. Merlin C. Wittrock, 3d ed. (New York: Macmillan, 1986). The researchers ask teachers to reflect upon their teaching

and explain why they acted as they did in specific classroom situations. As indicated, the "teacher dialogues" presented here are not transcriptions of actual conversations; hence they pursue the teachers' reflections and the issues that arise therefrom in greater depth than empirical research generally allows.

CONVERSATION 1

1. Where the teacher recognizes a volunteer to speak, I follow the student's name with a period. If the teacher asks a student who has not volunteered to speak, I follow that student's name with a question mark.

2. The analysis here in both the text and notes issues from a perspective inspired by Ludwig Wittgenstein and Hans-Georg Gadamer. In terms of literary critics, the perspective lies in close proximity to that of M. H. Abrams (see "What's the Use of Theorizing about the Arts?" and "A Note on Wittgenstein and Literary Criticism," in *Doing Things with Texts: Essays in Criticism and Critical Theory,* ed. M. Fischer [New York: W. W. Norton & Company, 1989]). I do not assume that the meaning of a text is radically indeterminate because of the reader's preconceptions (as H. Bloom, *The Anxiety of Influence: A Theory of Poetry* [New York: Oxford University Press, 1973], and S. Fish, *Is there a Text in This Class? The Authority of Interpretive Communities* [Cambridge, MA: Harvard University Press, 1980], seem to do). Instead, I take it that the reader's preconceptions need to be explored, as they affect the interpretation—a Gadamerian point—but that the nature of the interpretation is also constrained by both the contents of the work and the rules that govern the practice of interpreting a text.

Ludwig Wittgenstein, in *Philosophical Investigations,* 3d ed., trans. G. E. M. Anscombe (New York: Basil, Blackwell, & Mott, 1958), part 1, section 7, speaks of using language as playing "language games." Language games are not games with words but rather patterns of words and actions. These patterns are governed by rules: one cannot say and do just anything and still be playing a given language game. In part 1, section 23, Wittgenstein gives examples of language games: giving orders and obeying them; describing the appearance of an object, or giving its measurements; constructing an object from a description; reporting an event; speculating about an event; making a joke; telling it; solving a problem in practical arithmetic. To play the game, one must learn the constraints that govern the use of words and the ways one may treat a given object under particular circumstances. We may think of interpretive discussion as a language game. Here, too, participants "play" by using words and actions with reference to texts in certain rule-governed ways. The interpretation that arises—what readers understand a given work to mean at a given point in time—depends in part upon the constraints that govern the treatment of it.

3. Hans-Georg Gadamer, *Truth and Method,* 2d ed., trans. Sheed and Ward, Ltd. (New York: The Crossroad Publishing Company, 1985), unlike Wittgenstein, comes from the hermaneutic tradition in philosophy. Yet, Gadamer's discussion of language is compatible with and complements Wittgenstein's at some points. Gadamer treats the metaphor of "play," chapter 2, section 1 (a–d), much the way Wittgenstein describes the notion of a "game." On pp. 93–94 Gadamer writes: "If we examine how the word "play" is used . . . we find talk of the play of light, the play of waves . . . the play of gnats, even a play on words. In each case what is intended is the to-and-fro movement which is not tied to any goal which would bring it to an end. . . . The movement back-

wards and forwards is obviously so central for the definition of a game that it is not important who or what performs this movement. . . . The play is the performance of the movement as such. . . . The structure of play absorbs the player into itself."

The to-and-fro movement Gadamer speaks of is the consequence of following rules of the game. In the case of interpretive discussion, the "rules" are rules about the conditions under which participants may say things. As people follow the rules and contribute, the conditions change, for topics emerge, that is, the discussion assumes a focus. One might say that the focus absorbs the individual participants into itself.

4. One might wonder how the rules of the discussion get established. This is a complex question we will continue to explore. For now, it is interesting to note that many of Mrs. Spring's questions and responses allow students the option of giving "safe" answers. Why? Because they may respond at a general, abstract level instead of revealing personal feelings or thoughts. On the one hand, this option may encourage students to participate. But the possibility that the comments will be glib or empty remains.

5. In other words, the Chalmers students know the conditions under which they may enter the "language game" of interpretive discussion. As Wittgenstein puts it in part 1, section 154 of *Philosophical Investigations,* the students can "go on"—can enter the conversation by following the rules—when given circumstances arise.

6. Note that class size in Chalmers is twenty-two, while that in Belden is about twelve.

7. Gadamer, *Truth and Method,* 100, distinguishes between "change" and "transformation." In the case of change, he says, something in that which changes remains the same. If the sky changes color, then only some aspects of its color are different, while others remain what they were so that the differences stand out against them. In the case of "transformation," nothing of the previous object remains the same. One who has been transformed, says Gadamer, "has become, as it were, another person." When I claim that discussants have been "transformed," I mean that their responses to the discussion—to the text, or perhaps, to the discussion opportunity as a whole—are not what they were. Sometimes this involves a radical change in perspective of which they are aware, so that they see a situation completely differently. Sometimes, however, they are unaware that their response has altered completely. In the latter instance, the transformation may occur slowly, through a series of gradual changes. Gradual as the changes may be, there is "transformation" if nothing in the response remains what it was. I return to the topic of "transformation" periodically throughout the book.

8. How do students learn the rules of interpretive discussion? Wittgenstein, in *Philosophical Investigations,* part 1, sections 5, 143–45, 244, suggests that people can be "trained" to follow the rules. He discusses the example of a child who hurts himself: "A child has hurt himself and he cries; and then adults talk to him and teach him exclamations and, later, sentences. They teach the child new pain-behavior" (section 244). Wittgenstein's idea is that to teach someone the rules of a game, one responds to the student's actions by following those rules. One responds to the crying child by telling him words that he may use under the condition when he feels pain, words like "ow!" The child learns the words or responses appropriate under given conditions, and he or she comes to use the words when the appropriate conditions arise. In asking Marcy to compare her response to Colette's, for example, I was following a rule that Marcy herself could follow in order to enter the discussion at that point.

CONVERSATION 2

1. The quotations from Shakespeare's *Romeo and Juliet* are taken from the Signet Classic edition (New York: New American Library, 1986). The material in brackets in quoted passages is taken from notes provided by that edition.

2. Gadamer, *Truth and Method,* 237, comments on the role that "fore-meanings"— unexamined assumptions, preconceptions—play in our thinking about situations. In general, he argues that what we understand of particular occurrences is greatly influenced by such fore-meanings. He is speaking to historians in this passage, and he urges that they examine the "origin and validity of the fore-meanings present within [them]." Gadamer's injunction is appropriaqte for teachers as well, I think.

3. D. C. Lortie, *Schoolteacher: A Sociological Study* (Chicago: University of Chicago Press, 1975), 106, helps us understand why the pain at such moments is so great for teachers. The following comment is made after questioning 5,818 teachers: "It is of great importance for teachers to feel they have 'reached' their students—their core rewards are tied to that perception. Other sources of satisfaction (e.g., private scholarly activities, relationships with adults) pale in comparison with teachers' exchanges with students and the feeling that students have learned."

4. Gadamer, *Truth and Method,* 405, argues that only human beings can have the sense of a "world," for such a sense is based on the use of language. A picture of the world and its features is a linguistic conception. My aim in the discussion with the students is to help them see the world that Shakespeare is presenting in the nurse's speech. Once they grasp its features—the events the nurse tells of—they will grasp other events or ideas that these imply, e.g., the meaning of the word "wean." For such is the nature of language; it links the events it portrays together.

5. Wittgenstein (*Philosophical Investigations,* part 1, sections 7–9) might argue that the students in this situation were being asked to play a new "language game," one that followed rules with which they were unfamiliar. Having had little experience with the game, they may also have had little experience with its goals and outcomes. From this perspective, one might say that the students were reluctant participants because they were used neither to the procedures nor the benefits of participating.

CONVERSATION 3

1. I do not mean to suggest that all the "good" conversations occur in the Chalmers school. Indeed, the discussions in both schools have strengths and weaknesses, as the reader will see.

2. Gadamer, *Truth and Method,* 95–96, points out an important feature of any language game, including that of interpretive discussion: "All playing is being-played. The attraction of the game, the fascination it exerts, consists precisely in the fact that the game tends to master the players. . . . The game is what holds the player in its spell, draws him into play, and keeps him there." Participants in interpretive discussion are following its rules. They are aware of and respond appropriately to the various conditions arising in the course of the conversation. So, if a question is posed, it will be addressed, unless a speaker invokes a rule—also part of game—that permits an alternative response. By observing the rules or constraints of interpretive discussion,

participants are drawn into the activity and experience the effects that follow these actions.

3. Some argue that it is better for teachers to make no positive or negative judgments, that the students should derive reinforcement from one source only, namely, the text itself. If the text provides evidence for the idea, then the idea is a good one, as speakers will discover for themselves.

4. M. Weitz, *Hamlet and the Philosophy of Literary Criticism* (Chicago: University of Chicago Press, 1964), chapter 15, discusses the grounds on which interpretations are made and would seem to concur with this conclusion, as would other literary critics.

5. Recall how Colette responded to the question: What do we do to babies? Her answer—"spank, slap"—was a consequence of free association.

6. Certainly, there are moments in interpretive discussions when it is most appropriate to ask a "fact" question. One such moment occurs when the interpretations on the floor seem to fly in the face of the facts in the text.

7. The distinction between actually listening to others so as to grasp what they say and merely using their remarks as a vehicle for entering the conversation is an important one. Only when the first occurs do discussants have a real conversation. Gadamer, *Truth and Method*, 341, explains why: "Every conversation presupposes a common language, or, it creates a common language. Something is placed in the centre, as the Greeks said, which the partners to the dialogue . . . share, and concerning which they can exchange ideas with one another. Hence agreement concerning the object, which it is the purpose of the conversation to bring about, necessarily means that a common language must first be worked out in the conversation. This is not an external matter of simply adjusting our tools, nor is it even right to say that the partners adapt themselves to one another but, rather, in the successful conversation they both come under the influence of the truth of the object and are thus bound to one another in a new community. To reach an understanding with one's partner in a dialogue is not merely a matter of total self-expression and the successful assertion of one's own point of view, but a transformation into a communion, in which we do not remain what we were."

By listening to others, the participants work out their "common language," their shared assumptions and positions. As they do so, they focus the question that concerns them; and their ideas about its resolution—the "object" of the conversation—begin to emerge. Each idea guides subsequent contribution until agreement about the resolution occurs. As members contribute, they begin responding in new ways, drawn as they are by the movement toward the resolution. Hence, as Gadamer says, they do not remain what they were. Mrs. Spring is eager for the students to have a "real" conversation in Gadamer's sense.

8. The fact that Kevin's point seems to arise out of remarks made by others earlier in the discussion is consistent with the comment that Gadamer, *Truth and Method*, 96, makes: "Every game presents the man who plays it with a task. He cannot enjoy the freedom of playing himself out except by transforming the aims of his behavior into mere tasks of the game." Kevin's comment, seeming to draw upon the remarks of others as it does, comes as a consequence of following the rules of interpretive discussion. And by following those rules—playing the game—he has transformed his intentions into

the goal of reaching his conclusion. (Note: His intentions are "transformed," rather than "changed," because they are not what they were before he started having the discussion.) Kevin's conclusion, I will argue, begins to express the "object" of the conversation. Jarvis, the next speaker, then elaborates the "object."

9. That rule is: You may enter the discussion by building upon someone else's comment in some appropriate, rule-governed way. In notes 7 and 8 above, I explain how listening to others and entering the conversation by following the rules allows discussants to have a "real" conversation.

10. See notes 7 and 8. Gadamer, *Truth and Method*, 330–31 says more about the "object" of a conversation: "To conduct a conversation means to allow oneself to be conducted by the object to which the partners in the conversation are directed. It requires that one does not try to out-argue the other person, but that one really considers the weight of the other's opinion. . . . Dialectic consists not in trying to discover the weakness of what is said, but in bringing out its real strength. . . . [It is being] able to strengthen what is said by referring to the object." The "object," of a conversation, then, is the idea that emerges as the conversation proceeds, the idea that addresses the question that participants wish to resolve. It is also the idea that follows from what is said, the necessary implication or "truth" that emerges from the conversation. As such, it constitutes the "strength" in the discussion, the point participants are seeking to uncover.

11. Here, a "genuine concern or issue" is distinguished from a question posed by the teacher. While the teacher's question may become the group's concern, it need not. The "object" of the conversation, however, addresses the issue that the discussants wish to resolve.

CONVERSATION 4

1. D. A. Schön, *The Reflective Practitioner: How Professionals Think in Action* (New York: Basic Books, 1983); and *Educating the Reflective Practitioner* (San Francisco: Jossey-Bass, 1987). Schön's work has received much attention of late. He presented two invited addresses at the Annual Meeting of the American Educational Research Association in 1988. In "A Critique of Schön's Views on Teacher Education and Issues," presented at the same meeting, I. B. Harris identified both the utility and some shortcomings in Schön's position.

2. On this point, Schön's position is much like Gadamer's on "fore-meanings" (see note 2, Conversation 2, above).

3. Gadamer, *Truth and Method*, 326–27, describes the process by which questions arise: "To ask a question means to bring into the open. The openness of what is in question consists in the fact that the answer is not settled. It must still be undetermined, in order that a decisive answer can be given. . . . The object has to be brought into this state of indeterminacy, so that there is an equilibrium between pro and contra. The sense of every question is realized in passing through this state of indeterminacy, in which it becomes an open question. Every true question achieves this openness." It seemed to me that the question of whether Juliet was a Capulet was not an indeterminate matter, given the text.

4. Gadamer, *Truth and Method*, 327, distinguishes between true and false questions: "The asking of [a question] implies openness, but also limitation. It implies the explicit establishing of presuppositions, in terms of which can be seen what still re-

mains open. Hence a question can be right or wrong, according as it reaches into the sphere of the truly open or fails to do so. We call a question false that does not reach the state of openness, but inhibits it by holding on to false presuppositions." Again, the issue for me as the teacher was whether the question "Is Juliet a Capulet?" pointed to a state of genuine openness or not.

5. See Conversation 2, note 2. From my perspective as teacher, Gadamer's injunction might have served the students well in this instance. Perhaps their fore-conceptions—their assumptions about the origins of family relationships—had created a problematic interpretation.

6. Gadamer, *Truth and Method*, 236, discusses what happens when one interprets a text. He writes: "A person who is trying to understand a text is always performing an act of projecting. He projects before himself a meaning for the text as a whole as soon as some initial meaning emerges in the text. Again, the latter emerges only because he is reading the text with particular expectations in regard to a certain meaning. The working out of this fore-project, which is constantly revised in terms of what emerges as he penetrates into the meaning, is understanding what is there." Gadamer's comment reminds us that interpreting the present situation, the text before us, changes our preconceptions as we come to understand what is *there* in the text. For what is there is not the same as what we ourselves believed and "project" onto the text as we begin reading. All of us, like the Belden students, "overlook" textual evidence until we examine and modify the "fore-meanings" or preconceptions we bring to the text, Gadamer would say. To carry out such examination allows the text to illuminate us.

7. S. E. Toulmin, *Human Understanding: General Introduction and Part I* (Princeton, NJ: Princeton University Press, 1972), advocates the use of metaphors from population genetics to explain how change occurs. One of the central ideas in the model he discusses is that of random change "spreading" through the population over a series of generations. The idea is that while the change may be the result of some chance mutation in one member in a given generation, it will be seen in more and more members of the species in succeeding generations, provided it is adaptive (increases the survival rate of the species). This metaphor, if applied to the formation of discussion habits or patterns, focuses upon the rate and nature of these habits as they spread over a sequence of discussions. In the conversations that follow, we will from time to time observe the "spreading" of such habits.

8. See Gadamer, *Truth and Method*, 266.

CONVERSATION 5

1. That is, she is playing the language game of interpretive discussion.

2. I have deleted the decoding errors that Colette made in reading this passage so that the reader may focus on the text rather than upon the student's ability to read it. I will continue this practice henceforth. In general, the text became easier for the Belden students to decipher as time went on, although they continued to have difficulty at times.

3. In my view, Mrs. Prince's question is crucial. At this point, the discussion becomes powerful because in responding to her question the students link views that come out of their personal experience to the text.

4. The reader may have the sense that when Mrs. Prince asks, "Is it possible that

young love may be a little selfish?" she is urging the students toward a particular resolution of the question about why Juliet does not ask Romeo to leave the garden. The role of the discussion leader is to draw out the students' ideas, not to urge interpretations upon them. Yet, even if Mrs. Prince is advocating a particular view here, the students are by no means agreed to it. We will return to the topic of interpreting the text for the students in Conversations 6 and 7.

5. Wittgenstein, *Philosophical Investigations,* e.g., part 1, sections 1–16, might agree with Mrs. Prince here, I think. He would seem to argue that what "pops into one's head" depends on the particular circumstances in which one is located. Why? Because when we think, act, or speak, we are always participating in some language game or another. The particular game we play depends upon the circumstances we find ourselves in. As we play the game and follow its rules, thoughts spring to mind, or we say and do certain things—thoughts that might be said to be "consequences" of the rule-following.

6. Of course, not every comment that students make can be so scrutinized. A teacher must make choices. Yet, the inclination is to pursue those remarks which seem compatible with one's own interpretation, thereby bypassing contributions that may have great potential for enlivening the conversation.

CONVERSATION 6

1. As the reader will see, there is a kind of coming together that occurs between students and teacher. As it occurs some old rules are broken and the "object," the resolution we are pursuing, draws us together. We are seeing what Gadamer, *Truth and Method,* 330, describes when he says, "To conduct a conversation means to allow oneself to be conducted by the object to which the partners in the conversation are directed." As the object draws us on, some of the rules we have followed up to now begin to give way.

2. In note 8 to Conversation 1, I describe Wittgenstein's account of training (which he gives in *Philosophical Investigations,* Part 1, section 244). In beginning the discussion with a question, Colette seems to exemplify Wittgenstein's point; she is repeating behavior that she has seen me perform under similar circumstances.

3. See Gadamer's comment, quoted Conversation 4, note 3. In questioning the students, I hoped to become clearer about "the sense" of Colette's question, that is, exactly where the doubt lies.

4. I have spoken before about Gadamer's notion of "fore-meanings" (Conversation 2, note 2). In *Truth and Method,* 262, he makes the following related comment: "The first of all hermaneutic requirements remains one's own fore-understanding, which proceeds from being concerned with the same subject [as the text]. It is this that determines what unified meaning can be realized." The "fore-understanding" is the understanding that the reader brings to the subject of the text, understanding of which "fore-meanings" are a part, it seems. The reader and the work, then, are struggling to grasp the same "truth" or idea. The reader's beliefs about that idea puts those of the text in a particular perspective. As Colette draws upon her ideas about a father's response to a daughter's elopement, her vision of Romeo's and Juliet's dilemma changes. Her engagement with the play deepens as she ponders their situation from her own perspective.

5. One might argue that by telling the other students to pay attention to Michael, Mrs. Prince indicated that he was correct. My sense, however, was that the text, rather than Mrs. Prince's remark, provided the reinforcement.

6. Sometimes, when the leader directs the discussion toward passages participants have not identified, the discussion is illuminated. Sometimes the practice can force the direction of the discussion unnaturally, especially if the discussants are looking at other passages. I was hoping for the former outcome in directing the students toward the friar's "herb" speech. But it is not clear that I succeeded.

7. See Conversation 3, note 7, for Gadamer's wonderful description of the point at which a group of people becomes a real conversational group. His claim is that when this happens, the power of the object—the resolution of the issue the group is pursuing—along with the rules of conversation controls the course of the discussion. Many things start to happen then, including the abandoning of some of the rules.

Conversation 7

1. Can we say that the students are posing more and more questions about the meaning of the text as time goes on? It seems so. Hence, we have another example analogous to the phenomenon Toulmin points to in his account of change spreading across populations. See Conversation 4, note 7.

2. In other words, I am accusing Mrs. Prince of trying to "teach values" to the students. Much of the current literature on the teaching of values, which stems largely from the work of Lawrence Kohlberg, advocates the "clarification" of values rather than indoctrination. My position is that such clarification is more appropriate than "teaching values" in the school setting. Mrs. Prince has a somewhat different view of the issue, as the reader will see.

Conversation 8

1. See Conversation 1, note 7, for Gadamer's distinction between "change" and "transformation."

2. Gadamer, *Truth and Method*, 102.

3. In the following analysis, I am concurring with A. A. Kass in her conclusions about the advantages of teacher autobiography. See A. A. Kass, "Autobiographers as Teachers: Toward Solving the Problem of Civic Education," in *From Socrates to Software: The Teacher as Text and the Text as Teacher,* Eighty-ninth Yearbook of the National Society for the Study of Education, eds. P. W. Jackson and S. Haroutunian-Gordon (Chicago: University of Chicago Press, 1989).

4. I realize that it sounds a little strong to say that people are "transformed" by discussion. My point is that when participating in discussions people give themselves up to the conversation: its purposes become theirs, its rules govern their actions. Discussants are not, then, what they are outside of the discussion; and over time, their participation in conversations does not remain what it was, either. As we have seen, students and teachers alike are now participating very differently than they were before—as though their sense of what they are doing in the conversation has been transformed, not merely changed.

5. We, are not, then, talking about what Aristotle identified as "efficient" causes. See Aristotle *Physics* 2.3. An efficient cause is, as he puts it, "the primary source of the

change or coming to rest." So, for example, pulling the trigger of a loaded pistol is the efficient cause of the bullet's departure from it. My claim is that neither the teachers nor the students were effecting change in the way that firing a pistol changes the location of the bullet that was in the gun.

6. One might argue, with Schön, that the conversations between the teachers (or teacher and observer) had effects on subsequent interactions with students. While such may seem to be the case, my analyses provide little basis for drawing that inference; for as I indicated, the "teacher dialogues" are not reported exactly as they occurred. Therefore, it is difficult to conjecture about the impact that they had.

Conversation 9

1. The claim here is not that there is a "correct" interpretation but that the teacher often has the sense that one interpretation is "correct" and others are not. The issue is: What is the teacher to do when she feels the students are missing what she takes to be the "correct" interpretation?

2. Plato might have been sympathetic to Mrs. Spring's argument here. When she says that all she can do is "point them to passages that I think raise questions about their interpretation," she is echoing Socrates' sentiments when he says in the *Republic* 518d that the teacher must help the students to direct their vision and "look where they should."

3. Gadamer, *Truth and Method*, 95, describes the dilemma well: "The game itself is a risk for the player. One can only play with serious possibilities. This means obviously that one may become so engrossed in them that they, as it were, outplay one and prevail over one. . . . All playing is a being played. The attraction of a game, the fascination it exerts, consists precisely in the fact that the game tends to master the players."

Edna and Abby, then, seem to have become so engrossed in following certain rules of interpretive discussion—seeking evidence in the text to support their claims—that they lose perspective on what they are doing and on the play itself.

4. See the previous note for a quotation from Gadamer that explains what the students were doing.

5. Gadamer, *Truth and Method*, 319, writes: "The truth of experience always contains an orientation towards new experience. That is why a person who is called 'experienced' has become such not only through experiences but is also open to new experiences." Here, Gadamer points to the idea that experience orients one to new experiences in certain ways. However, while extensive experience can make one more open, more able to understand the place of a new episode that occurs, it provides a powerful perspective that may not accommodate a new event. Such seems to have been the effect of Edna's and Abby's claims on Mrs. Spring. In this instance, her experience seems to have made it more difficult for her to accept their proposals.

6. Proust argues this point repeatedly in his *Remembrance of Things Past*. See, for example, *Swann's Way*, trans. C. K. Scott Moncrieff and T. Kilmartin (New York: Random House 1981), vol. 1, 404, where "the cruel name of Maison Dorée" brings to Swann's mind "a misfortune of which he had just become aware." Having connected the Maison Dorée to the event, thought of the former brings with it recollection of the latter.

7. Plato argues a similar point in the *Meno* 97–98, where he speaks of the statues of

Daedalus that "if no one ties them down, run away and escape. If tied, they stay where they are put." Likewise, Socrates urges, if opinions are not tied to reasons, they are forgotten. Reasons, then, function as the stakes to which opinions may be fastened.

8. The argument here is not that Edna's perspective caused her to notice Benvolio's action in act III but that it opened the possibility for her to do so. Her perspective provides her with what Gadamer, *Truth and Method*, 269, calls a "horizon": "The horizon is the range of vision that includes everything that can be seen from a particular vantage point." Given her perspective on Benvolio, Edna's horizon allowed her to see a fact in act III that others had not noticed.

Conclusion

1. In J. J. Schwab, "The 'Impossible' Role of the Teacher in Progressive Education," 182.

2. See Introduction above, p. 12; also Dewey, *Democracy and Education*, 140.

3. Dewey, *Democracy and Education*, 99.

4. Hirsch, *Cultural Literacy*, xv.

5. Ibid., 152–215.

6. W. W. Waller, "Teaching as Institutionalized Leadership," *On the Family, Education and War: Selected Writings*, ed. W. J. Goode, F. F. Furstenberg, Jr., L. R. Mitchell (Chicago: University of Chicago Press, 1970), 278.

7. I should add that C. B. Cazden, *Classroom Discourse: The Language of Teaching and Learning* (Portsmouth, NH: Heinemann Educational Books, 1988), 198, argues that speakers in classrooms learn to accommodate to the linguistic rules in effect, so that the adjustment we have seen the Belden students make to interpretive discussion might be expected to occur in other classrooms as well. Furthermore, W. Labov, who has done extensive research on the subject, argues in "The Logic of Nonstandard English," in *Language and Poverty: Perspectives on a Theme*, ed. F. Williams (Chicago: Markham Publishing Company, 1970), 153–54: "In fact, Negro children in the urban ghettos receive a great deal of verbal stimulation, hear more well-formed sentences than middle-class children, and participate fully in a highly verbal culture. They have the same basic vocabulary, possess the same capacity for conceptual learning, and use the same logic as anyone else who learns to speak and understand English." Labov's conclusion is consistent with what we have seen of the students in the Belden classroom.

8. Waller, "Teaching as Institutionalized Leadership," 276–77.

9. B. Bloom, *Stability and Change in Human Characteristics* (New York: John Wiley & Sons, Inc., 1964), 199.

10. In *The Paideia Program: Equity and Quality in Education* a 1987 evaluation of the Paideia program, Dr. Trudy Wallace of the Department of Research, Evaluation, and Planning, Chicago Public Schools, reports on a comparison of 79 Paideia students in grades five and nine, who had participated in interpretive discussions ("Socratic Seminars"), with 117 non-Paideia students. The students in the two groups were matched on grade level, reading scores, and school characteristics, and were given the Student Writing Assessment, an instrument that requires students to take positions and defend these with textual evidence in writing. The students in the Paideia group scored significantly higher than those in the non-Paideia group (see pp. 11–14 of the

report). A 1988 follow-up study of sixth, tenth, and twelfth graders confirmed these results (see pp. 19–25 of *The Paideia Program: Equity and Quality in Education,* Evaluation Report of Year Four—1988). This evidence suggests that practices encouraged by interpretive discussion may be repeated in other contexts if conditions call for them.

11. Oakes, J. *Keeping Track: How Schools Structure Inequality* (New Haven: Yale University Press, 1985), 7–14 and passim.

12. Ibid., 144–45.

13. *Barriers to Excellence: Our Children at Risk,* 114; *Becoming a Nation of Readers,* 92.

14. For example, P. A. Cusick, *The Egalitarian Ideal and the American High School: Studies of Three Schools* (New York: Longman, Inc. 1983), argues that in the three high schools he observed where tracking had been eliminated, there was a visible lack of community.

15. The kind and amount of leader preparation is somewhat controversial. The Great Books Foundation urges that teachers prepare "clusters" of questions for use in discussion: a basic interpretive question plus eight other interpretive questions that, if resolved, would have implication for resolving the basic problem. The Paideia Program, on the other hand, emphasizes the formation of questions somewhat less.

16. I am grateful to Dr. William Rice, Director of Technical Services, Chicago Public Schools, for providing me with this and the following statistics.

17. In the 1987 evaluation of the Paideia program cited in n. 10, Dr. Wallace reports an inverse relation between class size and participation in the discussion. Hence, with an average class size of 16.1, the mean rate of students participating was 95 percent (250 elementary and secondary students observed). With a class size of 23, the mean rate of student participation was 60 percent (see pp. 5–6 of the report). These results were confirmed in the 1988 evaluation (see note 10 above; pp. 15–16 of the report). I was told that when the size of the class rose to 28, the number of students participating in the discussion dropped precipitously (figures unavailable). While conclusions cannot be drawn from such small sample sizes where controls on other variables were missing, these statistics suggest that group size may significantly affect the number of students contributing to an interpretive discussion. If all are expected to participate, then a group of fifteen may be ideal. More research is needed on the matter.

18. These conclusions are consistent with those presented in the 1988 evaluation of the Paideia Project in Chicago, Illinois (n. 10 above).

19. C. E. Bidwell and J. D. Kasarda, "School District Organization and Student Achievement," *American Sociological Review* 40 (1975): 62–63, have argued that student achievement is "some positive function" of the rates of student-teacher interaction. While "student achievement" here refers to progress on standard measures of academic achievement, there is every reason to think that progress in ability to discuss ideas in interpretive discussion groups is also related to the amount of time that the teacher spends interacting with the students about their ideas. Also, Bidwell, "The School as a Formal Organization," *Handbook of Organizations,* ed. J. G. March, (Chicago: Rand McNally, 1965), 979, 988, stresses, with Waller, that effective teaching demands strong affective bonds between student and teacher. Interpretive discussion fosters such bonds, as we have seen in our study of the Belden and Chalmers classrooms.

20. As mentioned in the Introduction, interested readers may contact the Great Books Foundation of Chicago, 40 East Huron Street, Chicago, Illinois, and Institute for Philosophical Studies, 101 East Ontario Street, Chicago, Illinois 60611 (the Paideia Project) for information on leader training sessions and texts to use in the classrooms.

21. Interested readers may contact, for example, the National Center for the Paideia Program, Chapel Hill, North Carolina, or the North Carolina Center for the Advancement of Teaching, at Western Carolina University, Cullowhee, North Carolina.

22. For further information about the role that a supportive administrator plays, see Brazil, *The Engineering of the Paideia Proposal: The First Year, 1984–85* (Champaign, IL: School Design Group, 1988).

23. For example, the reform legislation in Chicago (Illinois Senate Bill 1840) gives parents and community members additional control over principals and teachers.

24. See, for example, *Barriers to Excellence: Our Children at Risk*, p. 119–20.

25. Indeed, some might argue that training parents is a poor resolution. For parents, especially of students in the inner-city schools, are likely to be working or may be too poorly educated to be effective leaders. And how could a parent untrained in the disciplines lead discussions in high schools? Even if they were able, how many would volunteer for such a time consuming activity? These issues might seem difficult to resolve in some communities. And yet, the fact is that leading interpretive discussion is enormously satisfying, even if one knows little about the field to which the text belongs (as I am far from an expert in Shakespeare). Many people who have no children in the schools will find leading discussions a worthwhile use of time for this reason alone. The main task is to invite those interested to participate, and to provide them with training and support. Financial remuneration for leaders should also be considered.

26. The Great Books Foundation trains about twenty thousand leaders per year in seven hundred to seven hundred fifty two-day leader training courses. More than eight hundred thousand students participate in the discussions that are run by trained leaders each year. These statistics are courtesy of Teri Ozawa, Regional Coordinator, Great Books Foundation.

INDEX